Professional Perspectives in Marketing

Edited by Colin McIver

To Sue

David
Bernstein:

Creative Advertising
For *this*
you went to Oxford?

A personal textbook of advertising

Longman

Longman
1724-1974

LONGMAN GROUP LIMITED
London
Associated companies, branches and representatives
throughout the world

© Longman Group Limited 1974

First published 1974

ISBN 0 582 45036 5

Library of Congress Catalog
Card Number: 73–86102

Set in Baskerville 169 and
Printed in Great Britain by
Bell and Bain, Ltd. Glasgow

Contents

Acknowledgements

I want to thank James O'Connor and John Foster of the IPA who thought I might care to write a book; Colin McIver who convinced me I *should* write a book; my partner, Laurence Isaacson, and my other colleagues at The Creative Business who let me sit down and do it; Mel Calman who did the drawings; John Ashcroft who designed the cover; Linda Nuthall who deciphered my scrawl and kept her cool; and Jerome Robert and John Wheeler who checked detail with insight and imagination.

Ann Burdus, Alan Hedges and Francis Harmar-Brown have graciously let me quote them at length. I have been helped by Maurice Smelt who put together 'What Advertising Is' from which I have drawn heavily (particularly the interesting chapter by David Bernstein).

The Advertising Creative Circle, Marketing Society, Market Research Society, Advertising Association, IAA, AAAA, IPA and various other societies assisted indirectly by asking me to speak, thereby forcing me to examine topics I might otherwise have left alone.

My thanks also to all the kind and co-operative advertisers and agencies whose ads I have quoted or shown.

I've been inspired by the good sense of the late Leo Burnett, the wit of Jeremy Bullmore and the practical teaching of the man who first hired me, Robert Caplin. But everyone I've worked with has had a hand in this book.

There are echoes from all over—and some I don't even recognise. The errors, responsibility, blame, not to mention the italics are, however, all mine.

DAVID BERNSTEIN
Croydon and Florence

We are grateful to the following for permission to reproduce copyright material: George Allen & Unwin Ltd for an extract from *Principles of Mathematics* by Bertrand Russell; Association of National Advertisers, Inc. for extracts from *Defining Advertising Goals for Measured Advertising Results* by Russell Colley; The Bodley Head and Harper & Row Publishers Inc. for extracts from *Madison Avenue U.S.A.* by Martin Mayer; The author and The Market Research Society for an extract from a Lecture by Ann Burdus; W. & R. Chambers Ltd for extracts from *Chambers Twentieth Century Dictionary* 1972 Edition; The Clarendon Press for an extract from 'Upon Julia's Clothes' from *The Poetical Works of Robert Herrick* edited by L. C. Martin 1956 and an extract from *The Shorter Oxford Dictionary*; Crain Communications Inc. for extracts from an article 'The Positioning Era Cometh' by Jack Trout and Al Ries in *Advertising Age* (1972); Crown Publishers, Inc. for extracts from *Scientific Advertising* by Claude Hopkins. (c) 1966 by Crown Publishers, Inc. used by permission of Crown Publishers, Inc.; the Estate of Robert Frost, the editor, Jonathan Cape Ltd and Holt, Rinehart and Winston, Inc. for an extract from 'Once by the Pacific' from *The Poetry of Robert Frost* edited by Edward Connery Lathem; Faber and Faber Ltd and Harcourt Brace Jovanovich, Inc. for an extract from 'The Love Song of J. Alfred Prufrock' by T. S. Eliot from *Collected Poems 1909-1963*; Hamish Hamilton Ltd for 'Armistice' from *The Fern on the Rock* copyright © 1965 by Paul Dehn (Hamish Hamilton, London); the author for an extract from 'How Advertising Works' by Francis Harmar-Brown from *S. H. Benson Report*; the author for extracts from 'Analysis of Market Segmentation' by Alan M. Hedges from *S. H. Benson Report*; author's agents for an extract from 'D Day

Minus' by Edwin Brock from *Penguin Modern Poets 8* (1966); Incentive Marketing and Sales Promotion for an extract from *Incentive Marketing Magazine*; New English Library for an extract from 'Elegie XIX' from *The Selected Poetry of John Donne* (1966) and Pelham Books Ltd and the editor for an extract from 'What Media Are' (1972) by Simon Broadbent from *What Advertising Is*, an extract from 'What Research Is' by Gerald de Groot from *What Advertising Is*, an extract from 'What Art Direction Is' by Douglas Haines from *What Advertising Is* and extracts from 'What Copy Is' by Maurice Smelt from *What Advertising Is* edited by Maurice Smelt.

We are grateful to the following for permission to reproduce extracts from Advertising Copy:

Allen, Brady & Marsh Ltd on behalf of the Proprietors of 'Badedas'; Allied Breweries Ltd; Armour-Dial, Inc; Atkinson, Baldwin & Company Ltd; Avis International; Barclays Bank Ltd; Birds Eye Foods Ltd, England; B.O.A.C; Bovril Ltd; Bristol Myers Ltd; British Gas Corporation; British Leyland Motor Corporation; British Railways Board; Brook Street Bureau of Mayfair Ltd; Brooke Bond Ltd; Brown & Polson Ltd; Cadbury Schweppes Ltd; Central Office of Information; Charnos Ltd; Christian Aid and Doyle Dane Bernbach Ltd; Cinzano U.K. Ltd; Colgate-Palmolive Ltd; Coty England Ltd; Dancer Fitzgerald Sample, Inc; Del Monte Foods Ltd and the Advertising Agents McCann-Erickson; The Department of the Environment; The Department for National Savings; The Economist; Esso Petroleum Company Ltd; Fabergé, Inc; General Wine and Spirits Company; *The Guardian*; Arthur Guinness Son and Company (Park Royal) Ltd; Hector Powe; H. J. Heinz & Company Ltd; The House of Piccadilly, London; International Distillers and Vintners Home Trade Ltd; Jantzen, Inc; Johnson & Johnson Ltd; The Joint Credit Card Company Ltd; Lever Bros. & Associates Ltd; Life Savers, Inc; London Transport; Long John International Ltd; The Metal Box Company Ltd; Mobil Oil Corporation; Morton Salt Company, division of Morton-Norwich Products, Inc; Nabisco Ltd; National Dairy Council; *The New Statesman*; Parfums Givenchy Ltd; Pedigree Petfoods Ltd; Pimm's Ltd; John Player and Sons;

Acknowledgements

Post Office Telecommunications; Pretty Polly Ltd; Procter & Gamble Ltd; 'Quake-Up', U.K. registered trade mark of Quaker Oats Ltd; Rank Radio International; Rank Xerox Ltd; Reckitt & Colman; RHM Foods Ltd; James Robertson & Sons Preserve Manufacturers Ltd; Rover Triumph, British Leyland UK Ltd; Rowntree Mackintosh Ltd; Sancella Ltd; Brand Communications Shell Marketing Ltd; Thorn Lighting; *The Times*; *The Sunday Times*; Wasey Campbell-Ewald Ltd on behalf of the Proprietors of Truman Beer; Underberg; United Rum Merchants Ltd; Volkswagen/GB/Ltd; *Die Welt*; Whitbread & White Horse Distillers Ltd.

We regret we have been unable to trace the owners of the following Advertising Copy and would appreciate receiving any information that would enable us to do so:

'Climb upon my knee Sony boy'; 'When they run out of Löwenbrau order Champagne'; 'What you feel in a Warners isn't the girdle'; and 'The girl you love is 70.2 % water . . . for telling her'.

We are grateful to the following for permission to reproduce advertisements:

Brook Street Bureau of Mayfair Ltd and Garland-Compton Ltd; Canada Dry (UK) Ltd and Foote, Cone & Belding Ltd; Central Office of Information and Masius, Wynne-Williams Ltd; Coty (England) Ltd; Evening Standard Co. Ltd; Garden Pride; Imperial Chemical Industries Limited; Ind Coope and Young & Rubicam Ltd; Procter & Gamble Ltd and Young & Rubicam Ltd; Save & Prosper Group of Unit Trusts and Sharp MacManus Ltd; The Scandinavian Room; Time-Life International Ltd; Thos. W. Ward Ltd and Morgan Grampian Ltd.

For this you went to Oxford?

went to see my Uncle Joe one evening after work. I hadn't been in advertising long. He asked me how I had spent the day.

It had been a day like any other in advertising – atypical. There had been a recording session. Fifteen takes before all of us thought the announcer had got it right. I had also written a leaflet for a garage, checked numerous proofs and done some lasting damage to a jingle.

I explained all this in considerable detail. I waited. My uncle, a tailor long left Poland, looked at me. After a pause he said:

'For *this* you went to Oxford?'

He wasn't so much asking a question as telling me something. And what could I tell him? It is difficult to convey the satisfaction one gets out of advertising, the stimulus, the intellectual and emotional involvement with other people's products and yet other people's behaviour and response to those products. This book, hopefully, will convey some of it.

'For *this* you went to Oxford?'

To spend three years at Oxford and end up writing leaflets when I could have been in a profession. . . . But when I came into advertising, more or less by accident, my mentors were telling me that I actually *was* in a profession. By the time of my uncle's question I knew I wasn't. But I had learned to respect the professional. The announcer in the recording studio. Fifteen takes changing his delivery. Each take timed to thirteen and a half seconds, even when we added text. That was professionalism. It is something to aspire to, but it has nothing to do with *being in a profession*. We are in a trade, a business, an industry, a quandary but not, definitely *not*, a profession.

However, you can get letters after your name even today simply by sitting tight in the business for a certain number of years in the right type of agency, progressing sufficiently high up the hierarchy and surviving. Mind you, anybody who survives in advertising deserves some letters after his name, other than merely RIP. The fallout is heavy: some five thousand people have left agencies in the past five years. Advertising's loss has been . . . whose gain? Manufacturing, marketing, public relations, hotel-keeping?

Twenty years ago the business was getting its house in order. It was trying – too hard as it happened – to become respectable. 'Trade' in this country, even yet, is no occupation for a gentleman. To make things is respectable: to sell them, somehow unclean and underhand. And advertising is the most visible part of selling. The most obtrusive and, since it comes into your newspaper, roadside, carriage, drawing room, the most *intrusive* part of selling is advertising.

To the intellectual, the 'opinion leaders', pontificators, leader writers, letter writers, tub-thumpers, pedagogues, pedants and priests, trade is at best a necessary evil, the working of which they don't understand. But if trade is a closed book, advertising is its lurid cover. Many of the attacks on advertising are actually attacks on selling, materialism, the profit motive, capitalism. But they are very rarely put like that. What is attacked is the cover not the book.

Little wonder therefore that agency men needed to band together. The Institute of Practitioners in Advertising is a very active and worthwhile corporate body. It represents the interests of its members – the advertising agencies and their staffs – and by initiating industry action has raised standards of conduct within the industry, thereby benefiting the consumer. Though it could have done more in this respect, and sooner, it has certainly protected the consumer from the worst excesses of advertising as practised before the IPA came into being.

After the war advertising was consciously trying to make itself 'respectable'. It was busily changing its terminology. This is a constant obsession. The only advances in advertising are, seemingly, semantic. What used to be called contact man, for the simple and commonsense reason that he made contact with both the agency's creative people (the copywriter and the artist) and the client, became an *account executive*. The term 'contact man' was 'prewar' : when I joined the business the term was already on the way out as were those who used it. 'Ideas man' was another. It described someone who lived on his wits, a person of nimble mind who thought quickly and to the point: the perfect description of the man or woman in the creative department whose job is to write or draw but, above all, to *have ideas*. Advertising is a business of ideas or it is nothing.

Yet twenty short years ago the term 'ideas man' had fallen into disfavour. A layout man had become a visualiser or, more importantly, an art director. The term copywriter, as old as advertising itself and borrowed from journalism, stuck. Though there are other more elevated forms, such as creative supervisor, creative content manager, conceptualist. The person who looks after, nourishes, cajoles, inspires and leads all these artists and writers is called creative director. It's a very pretentious title. At a cocktail party the bird in the black dress asks you, over her Martini, what you do. *You* say 'I'm a creative director'. *She* chokes on her olive. The man who occupies the global creative supervisory role for a multinational agency is called Creative Director of the World. Which is not only pretentious but blasphemous.

Advertising is preoccupied with titles. I started my training in the despatch department of a small agency which consisted of two charming old messengers and the man who ran it. He, since he supervised the checking of the voucher copies (i.e. copies of newspapers containing the agency's advertisements) was called Voucher Manager. On my second day in advertising, manning the empty lunchtime office, the phone rang. I answered it: 'Deputy Voucher Manager–good afternoon.' I never looked back.

Agencies of course had long since begun to dislike the word 'agency'. It was *infra dig* to think of oneself as an agent, as someone existing upon commission : hence the term 'practitioner'. One was, according to one's letter-heading, a 'practitioner in advertising', or a 'registered practitioner', or, if you had gained election to the IIPA as it was then called, 'incorporated practitioner'.

But the term 'practitioner in advertising' was clumsy and high-minded. 'Advertising man' had the twin merits of simplicity and exactitude, and was therefore ruled out. The *Advertisers' Weekly* ran an exchange of correspondence on the subject, with contributors suggesting alternative titles such as 'advertor'. And while all this was going on layout men were laying out, copywriters were writing copy, contact men were contacting, ads were appearing and goods were moving off shelves. The workers were getting on with the work probably unaware that their masters were endeavouring to raise their status in the eyes of their fellow citizens. At that time I was told, in confidence, by someone very high up in the IPA that it was virtually certain to be granted a royal charter. Respectability could go no further. This period in which the trade deluded itself into thinking it was a profession has had a lasting effect on advertising, much of it beneficial (in terms of standards, trade representation, etc.) but much of it unfortunate. If only the energies expended then in the drive towards respectability had been spent on explaining the function and contribution of advertising to the community! By which I mean not only the community at large but also the business community.

Instead of explaining the essential role of advertising in the economy to the public which benefited from it and used it, we were busy kidding ourselves and trying to kid others that we were just like doctors or lawyers. Indeed so anxious was the agency business to forget its *raison d'être* that it aped the manners of the larger client organisations, breeding, during the fat 'fifties, supplementary services and departments and hierarchical infrastructures, with the result that its management, instead of concerning itself with the business of ads was concerning itself with the *business of business*.

The last thing at that time which a chairman of this sort of agency chose to discuss was an advertisement. He would meet the client on seemingly equal terms, and the golf course, and discuss the economy or commerce or the government. The account would thus be safe for another year, the appropriation increased and the campaign (which he ought really to get round to seeing) eventually approved.

Things were easier then during those 'thirteen years of Tory misrule'. In a sellers' market sellers don't have to sell. At least they don't have to sell hard. Consequently, at two levels the idea of advertising was being undersold. Neither the Advertising Association nor the IPA was making much of a case for it, and though a few individual agencies were, they were naturally also making a case for themselves rather than the industry. And the successful managers of successful agencies, though they might work very hard at their jobs, were, on the whole, content to assume that advertising worked rather than proving it to themselves, to the public, or more especially to the clients they serviced. They would point to a statistical link between advertising expenditure and sales. But very little work was done to discover a *causal* link or to examine the mechanics of the advertising process.

These same agency managements were shocked to discover in the early 1960s that their companions at the club house or the club, their fellow members of committees and boards of good causes were viewing their activities with a great deal of disfavour. Research conducted by the IPA into attitudes towards advertising revealed that the chairmen of manufacturing companies didn't really like advertising. Most of them liked their own advertising (some clearly didn't even like that) but practically all didn't like the advertising of other manufacturers.

Here then were people in key positions, using and presumably benefiting from advertising, admitting a dislike of advertising and, more to the point, seemingly doubting its economic benefit to themselves, let alone the country! Compared with this the celebrated comment of Lord Leverhulme ('Half the money I spend on advertising is wasted: the trouble is I don't know which half') sounds like a positive hymn of praise.

Advertising's problem is that it neither defined nor projected its role. But the advertising industry errs in good company. For just as advertising has not explained itself to business, neither has business explained itself to the community. The result is a polarisation between manufacturers at one end and consumerists at the other, the inevitable consequence of which is that business is forced to adopt only one posture – *defensive*.

Advertising could not have defined its role without reference to the larger context of marketing and the economy and therefore the prosperity of this country. Had it done so and projected it, I believe the country would be less divided on the subject of Europe. This book tries among other things to define advertising. Unfortunately it won't tell you how advertising works, though it will tell you something about certain advertisements which worked. It is a personal view of the business of making advertisements. It is a subjective and therefore selective textbook. It tells you how ads are made but not how advertisements are physically manufactured. It touches on *marketing* since marketing forms the context of one's activities. It touches on *media* as media provide the context for the end product of one's activities, i.e. ads. It touches upon *research* since research throws some light upon what one is doing. Its purpose is to help you, whether you're a manufacturer or a consumer, to look at advertising, and more particularly advertisements, with greater understanding. If it helps you create an advertisement I shall be pleased and somewhat surprised: if it helps you judge an advertisement I shall have succeeded.

Whether or not ultimately I answer Uncle Joe's question I leave to you.

2

Towards a definition – with a bit of history thrown in

'Come, Jack, now produce your explanation and pray make it improbable.'

Any attempt to define advertising is doomed to failure because it will be too comprehensive or too restricted or subjective. Rather than examine several existing definitions and adopt or modify any of them, we shall proceed towards a definition by examining instances, by induction.

The first few chapters of this book may lay me open to the criticism that I am taking a selection of large hammers to crack one small nut. I offer, not an apology, but an explanation. By looking at advertising in an historical perspective, at advertisements *per se* and advertisements in the context of marketing, at advertising's claims to be called a science, at advertising's claims to be called an art, we may in fact learn more about what advertising is than by starting with an acceptable premise and building upon it. To get things into perspective here is a one minute history of modern advertising.

Modern advertising dates from the middle of the last century. It was a result of mass production. Mass communication channels for the advertiser's message were provided by the popular press: compulsory universal education had meant that the majority of the public were literate enough to read copy. In the beginning was the word. Images (pictorial, brand, or moving) came later. The words initially were written by the advertiser himself. He also booked his own space. The newspaper or poster site owner then employed intermediaries or brokers to sell the space.

A broker would represent several papers. He would contact several advertisers. The broker or, as he became known, the agent, would receive a commission of 10 per cent of the cost of the space from the newspaper or medium to recompense him for his effort in selling that space. The advertiser of course paid the full rate for the space. He could still go direct to the medium and pay full rate there. The agent, however, provided the copy; he would not only book your holes for you, he would fill them – first with persuasive words then with attractive pictures.

That basically was it from the middle of the last century until today. New media arrived, new techniques of reproduction, new styles of art and new forms of copy; the rate of commission slowly edged up, but the principle of operation and the method of agency remuneration, remain the same. Though clients pay fees if their appropriations are not sufficient or the work they require does not involve commissionable media booking (e.g. new product development) and though many agencies are on a mixed fee structure, the commission system has survived virtually unscathed for over a century.

But the service offered for that commission has undergone considerable change.

In the late 1920s agencies began to provide research. Research into the structure of the market – who buys what, where, when and how much – is known as market research. In the 1950s came research into the more difficult area of 'why?' What made consumers buy? This was known originally as motivation research but – and here is another example of advertising, chameleonlike, changing words to protect its skin – this is now referred to as 'attitude' or 'behaviour' research. In addition agencies provided marketing services and a very good job some of them made of it. The leading marketing men in the country were in those days to be found in the agency world. Agencies also provided merchandising services, help with the business of getting the product in and out of the store, package design and occasionally public relations.

And all this was at little or no extra cost. These were the agency equivalent of the supermarket's 'loss leaders'.

But these were boom years. Despite heavy expenditure on ancillary services there was a sizeable profit at the end of the year. But though profits generally went up in actual terms, in percentage terms they often declined. Nevertheless, the boom continued, aided at the end of the decade by the national development of commercial television, a medium which, having proved itself, not only provided the agencies with bigger budgets (and healthy mark-ups on production) but also actually increased the size of total advertising expenditure. Other media were to suffer but the size of the cake increased.

Then two things happened more or less simultaneously.

There was a pressure on profits. Agencies had overreached themselves. Clients who had accepted these services given for nothing (though naturally without too much enthusiasm) were questioning their worth when required to pay for them.

More important, the tutors found themselves overtaken by their pupils. Whereas in the 1950s the standard of marketing was far higher in American-owned agencies than in the general run of British manufacturing companies, by the time the 1960s had got into their stride there was little to choose between them, and the future clearly had to lie with the client rather than the advertiser. The far-sighted agencies saw this in time to do something about it: the rest, having caught the bandwagon somewhat late and not having read the destination board, were stuck in stationary and expensive postures.

Slowly it began to dawn on the agency world that most of the services they provided could in fact be performed by the advertiser himself, or could be obtained by him directly without reference to the agency. If, for example, he wanted merchandising help why not go to a merchandising specialist? It would not necessarily follow that the agency one chose for its *advertising* would provide the best *merchandising*, particularly since a merchandising specialist would be more likely to attract the best talents in that field. Similarly agencies who equipped themselves with research departments with large field forces found that they were in conflict with outside organisations who could afford a degree of specialisation which the agency in its endeavours to satisfy all types of client could not. Consequently the agencies' specialist services disappeared about as quickly – though with less publicity and more hurt – than they had arrived.

The realisation came towards the end of the decade that the essential services a client demanded of an agency were media buying and, above all, creativity. So we were back to the task of buying holes and filling them. The wheel had come full circle. And that, dear reader, is the only revolution there has ever been in the advertising business.

Media buying incidentally is not all that secure within the agency world either. Independent media buyers acting directly for clients, after a shaky start, are beginning to establish themselves.

This brief history will have served to put the creative man centre stage. The whole agency is built upon his talent. Advertising is a business of ideas. He provides them. It is as simple – and as difficult – as that.

Take two matched samples of account executives. Feed each of them a marketing problem and the chances are considerable that they will come up with identical solutions in the form of advertising strategies. Take two matched samples of agency media men, feed them identical advertising strategies and it is almost certain that their media schedules will resemble each other. But take two matched samples of creative people, feed *them* identical advertising strategies and it is 100–1 against them coming up with identical ideas.

What differentiates one agency from another is essentially the style and calibre of the creative work. And what differentiates the agency from the client is precisely this ability – to create ideas.

You will often hear agencies speak of themselves as extensions of their clients' organisations. This may be what the client wants: it surely cannot be what he needs. He does not need more of himself: he needs something totally unlike himself. Assessing an agency is difficult. Clearly it is important to find 'people one can work with'. But this desire for harmony must not lead you to seek replicas of yourself. Since you are asking an agency to provide skills your company does not possess, your criteria for choosing an agency must by definition be different from those for hiring an employee. Too often this appears not to be the case. Witness the close identification with the client's attitudes and opinions of certain account men. If the account executive is a carbon copy of the brand manager one of them is redundant.

No, the agency is a maverick, left of centre, the grit in the oyster, a catalyst . . . and other sundry clichés. If this description seems to you to fit not an agency but a creative department all well and good. For that sound you can hear in the background is the grinding of an axe. With it I hope to hack some sort of path through the jungle to a clearing of misconceptions.

3

Nobody knows how advertising works

Try this test. Walk into your neighbourhood advertising agency, into the creative department, find a room where a writer and art director are working together on a problem and ask each of them separately, out of earshot of the other, to define advertising. The resulting silence, embarrassment, hilarity, bodily assault, whatever, will convince you of one thing: advertising is a haphazard undertaking.

Now ask each of them to describe exactly what he is doing, to construct a model of the advertising process against which they are jointly working. The fact that *nobody knows* how advertising works must never be allowed to prevent us from constructing some sort of working premise against which to plan. If you are fortunate enough to be given two models the fact that they don't correspond will by that time hardly surprise you. But think about it.

Suppose you went into a factory and asked two mechanics at a bench to describe what they were mutually trying to achieve? Suppose you asked two surgeons at an operating table to do the same thing? (You would of course hope that the same thing was precisely what they *were* doing.) Each writer and creative director will have his own vague theory of how advertising works. They are unlikely to coincide. They will change from time to time, from job to job, from agency to agency,

Since there is no agreed model of the advertising process, the people at the receiving end of the creative men's work, the clients, are similarly naked when it comes to criteria, though they may be somewhat less dogmatic in their assertions to the contrary, more likely to admit that their criteria are inadequate, that their yardsticks are subjective and shifting.

Thus, to complete the bizarre picture, the making of advertisements is an activity conducted by people who cannot agree upon a definition of what they are doing, *the result of whose labours is submitted for approval to others who are ill-equipped to judge it.*

Obviously since advertisements actually appear they must have been created and, presumably, approved. And therefore one would assume that the creators and the approvers would, even if not subscribing to any external 'law' of advertising, at least share some set of common beliefs about its mechanism. It would be rash, however, to make such an assumption.

In my experience very few client and agency associations begin by defining a mutually agreed set of principles on how advertising works. They will initiate a *modus operandi*, establish a pecking order, even define terms (mostly admittedly on the client side), but I cannot recall one client–agency association which began by trying to agree a model of the advertising process. Nor, for that matter, in a dozen years of presentation to potential new clients has one of them ever asked the agency how advertising works. That many of these subsequent associations have been happy would seem to prove that ignorance is bliss. That most of these associations have been mutually profitable would seem to prove that a model is irrelevant to their needs.

Both these attitudes are perfectly understandable. Certain agencies have associated themselves with particular philosophies which are briefly examined later but, by and large, business has got along without much analysis of its mechanism. However, it would seem axiomatic that some attempt should be made by the two sides – client and agency – to compile an agreed language, inadequate though it must be, in order that their dialogue is mutually comprehensible.

The basic fact about advertising – from which everything else stems – is this: *Nobody knows how it works.*

The trade reacts to this fact in one of three ways. It denies it by pointing to examples of the successful use of a 'house' formula. This is almost certainly specious since the formula will work on a very narrow band of products. *Or* it enters into a conspiracy of silence: by not discussing the subject it hopes it may go away. *Or* it reacts pragmatically: adopting a different formula for each job in hand. The last reaction is of course the most realistic and practical. Undoubtedly most of the successful agencies have, through trial and error and patient observation, compiled a set of principles for tackling specific advertising problems. Although in their more candid moments, they would subscribe to the general proposition that nobody knows how advertising works, they would vehemently deny that nobody knows how it works *in certain product types*, and/or certain media categories. (We shall examine a few of these in later chapters. Though if you are anticipating revelations you are in for a disappointment. Although some of us know some of it, those who do aren't telling.)

Advertising does not work universally. What works one day may not the next. What works in one place may not in another. What is successful for one type of product is unlikely to be successful for another. No amount of painstaking research prior to the appearance of an advertisement is any guarantee of sales. Nevertheless it does work. One would assume that all of its practitioners agree on this. After all, modern advertising has survived since the nineteenth century and expenditure has increased steadily throughout the twentieth. However, many people engaged in advertising frequently doubt its efficacy. Many of those people who claim not to be influenced by advertisements actually work in the business!

Others who take a less cynical view, the more realistic advertising men, frequently doubt if advertising is the most efficient way of tackling certain marketing problems which advertising has been asked to solve. Advertising, they feel, is not necessarily the best (certainly not the only) way to move products. But since they are employed in a business financed by the commission system, they must perforce be advocates of advertising in 'billable' media. Sometimes the response is purely automatic. They are conditioned by their environment. They would argue that if a manufacturer comes to an advertising agency then what he needs is advertising. The better agencies (big or small) will tell him when advertising is not the best solution. The reputable agency does *not* believe in advertising as a universal panacea. But it takes an enormous effort of will to turn away a large appropriation, deflecting it to public relations, say, or repackaging or merchandising or re-organisation of the sales staff or simply reinvestment. And then even if advertising is correctly assessed to be the best solution it takes the further effort of will not to recommend the media schedule which represents the best profit margin to the agency. Once again the more respectable agency will advocate what is best for the client. The less scrupulous, however, will be tempted to take the soft option of television, say, instead of a series of two-inch doubles in every national newspaper with copy changes each week supported by blanket coverage of the trade and technical press.

The majority of agencies *are* reputable and the majority of advertising and marketing men are convinced that advertising does work. Even advertising's critics agree. What they question is not its efficacy but something else. The purist bemoans its defiling of the English language. The intellectual questions its scale of values. The moralist questions its exploitation of human weaknesses, its appeal to man's basic instincts and its adoption of the nobler instincts for purely commercial ends. Consumerists criticise it for its reliance on emotion rather than information. Advertising is criticised for its intrusiveness, insidious nature, frivolity, mendacity, childishness, cunning, blatant misrepresentation, insensitivity, deliberate confusion, pseudo-science, overstatement, over-simplification and over-kill. But it is rarely if ever criticised for not achieving what it set out to achieve. Economists, though they may look askance at the mechanical efficiency of the machine, nevertheless concede that the machine delivers. But they, too, are at a loss to explain how it works.

Now it may strike you as curious that this industry is responsible for the expenditure of over £700 million a year on an activity it doesn't quite understand. (Though even more peculiar, to my mind, is the fact that a large proportion of those engaged in advertising are not even *aware* of this ignorance!) I am sometimes tempted to believe that the majority of people in the business actually do not want to know how it works. Once the secret is out maybe the fun will stop. 'To travel hopefully,' said Stevenson, 'is better than to arrive.' Advertising is staffed by hopeful travellers admittedly in different directions.

Undoubtedly much of the attraction which advertising holds for those who engage in it is its uncertainty. Not just the possibility that tomorrow an account may leave the agency closely followed by those working on it but the inner mystery of the mechanism. This uncertainty attracts artist and scientist alike. The artist is reassured by it, the scientist baffled. One regards it as an opportunity which he seeks to exploit: the other regards it as an enigma which he seeks to explain. When the artist (e.g. the creative man) and the scientist (e.g. the research executive) talk of the challenge of working in advertising they refer to different things. But the root cause is the same.

● *Nobody knows how it works.*

4

A definition at last

If you are panting for a definition try this:

● *That science in which we neither know what we are talking about nor whether what we say is true.*

That would appear to sum up the situation at the end of the previous chapter, if not describe the condition of our business as I write. The quotation, however, comes from Bertrand Russell, the subject – mathematics. If a science can be so described what hope is there of pinning down as wayward a subject as advertising? But we shall try.

We begin with the dictionary: *Advertise: to inform, to make known*. From now on we are on our own.

On the fold-out at the end of the book, you will see several examples of advertising. For the sake of the discussion in this and the subsequent chapter we shall regard this as source material. The advertisements are a representative sample. Though they differ widely in media, style, product category, cost, target audience, technique and presumably effectiveness, they nevertheless share enough characteristics from which we may, through inductive reasoning, arrive at a working definition. The exercise will be as important and beneficial as the definition.

The exhibits are in no particular order as follows:

(a) A classified advertisement in the *Evening Standard* for a second-hand car.
(b) A poster for Double Diamond beer.
(c) A prestige advertisement in *The Times* on behalf of ICI.
(d) A direct mail shot for *Time* magazine.
(e) A television commercial for Fairy Liquid.
(f) A 'bargain' space in the *Daily Express* for a gardening implement.
(g) A technical press advertisement in *Construction and Plant Equipment* for Atlas excavators.
(h) A trade press advertisement in *The Grocer* for Canada Dry.
(i) A cinema commercial for seat belts prepared by the Central Office of Information.
(j) A financial advertisement in the *Daily Telegraph* offering an investment bond.
(k) A tube card in the London underground for Brook Street (secretarial employment) Bureau.
(l) A sandwich board for a furniture store.
(m) A woman's magazine advertisement for a cosmetic.

Look at those thirteen advertisements and list characteristics (no matter how obvious) common to all of them. These should then provide you with a list of ingredients from which you can make up your own definition of advertising.

Irrespective of their many differences all these advertisements offer *information*. The amount of information varies. The relevance of that information to the recipient varies according to personal needs and desires. Some of the information may be extraneous for another reason – namely the recipient is already aware of it. Nevertheless, these thirteen examples bear out the dictionary definition: advertising *informs*. (It is obviously not an all embracing definition. Ask a consumerist!)

Since we are concerned with the *transmission of information* we may expect that an eventual definition will incorporate the word:

COMMUNICATION

This word underwent a metamorphosis in the 1950s and 1960s. It became a trendy, comprehensive and virtually meaningless term. It became fashionable to talk about 'lack of communication'. Should a factory or company have a problem the consultant would diagnose severe communication deficiency quite irrespective of the *content* of that communication. As long as your communications were good it didn't seem to matter what it was you communicated. As one cynical victim of such a diagnosis mutters: 'Whenever somebody tells me we've got a communication problem he, almost certainly, *is it*.'

Elaborate books were written. Companies were formed. Communications counsellors set up shop. Middle-aged executives went on expensive seminars to learn new words for old things and returned home to find their teenage sons telling them 'Dad, we don't seem able to communicate.' So it is with some trepidation that I use the word, let alone expatiate . . .

What sort of communication is going on in these thirteen advertisements? What information is being transmitted? Before reading further, look again at each advertisement.

Right. No doubt you will have found it easier to say what some of those advertisements were communicating than others. The financial advertisement is communicating details of the investment. Long copy, much of it difficult to read and understand at one sitting. Nevertheless, there is no doubt about the message. Nor obviously with the sandwich board announcement for furniture. (It may surprise you to see that example included in this company. But, as we shall see it is just as much an advertisement as the rest of them.) Similarly the classified advertisement for the secondhand car is not what most people think of when the subject of advertising is discussed. It is too basic, too practical, too ordinary and unassuming. Advertising's intellectual critics generally ignore classified advertisements when they attack advertising. Yet classified represents a considerable portion (20 per cent) of the total annual expenditure. Many agencies specialise in it to the exclusion of every other form. (Writing classifieds is an excellent preparation for a copy-writing career. The discipline is tough. The results – success or humiliation – are immediate. Fine writing, self-indulgence, wasted words are revealed for what they are.) The example illustrated is terse and to the point. Having read it you could tell a third person what it was about, as you can with the technical advertisement for the excavator.

But what information is being transmitted in the cosmetic advertisement? That the product makes you beautiful? Perhaps. And how about the poster for the beer? This is part of a widespread campaign. Everybody knows it, yet having looked at it can you immediately yourself transmit the information which the poster transmits to you? This surely is the test. If an advertisement is transmitting information successfully then the recipient should be able to *retransmit* that information. Take the prestige advertisement for ICI. Can you retransmit the information from that? The information here is not so simple to transmit as that in, say, the classified advertisement.

We shall examine the nature of advertising information in a later chapter. Obviously other elements enter into it. Suffice it to say that some sort of sea-change happens in some of these advertisements to the message between the time it leaves one mind (the advertiser's) and the time it reaches another mind (the recipient's). All we need conclude at this stage is that communication has happened.

Communication about what? Products? It is a portmanteau word. It certainly embraces most of the subjects of the thirteen advertisements. Beer, an excavator, a gardening implement, a washing-up liquid . . . these are all products. But seat belts? The COI film is not promoting a specific model (i.e. a make of seat belt) but the *general use* of seat belts, which could be termed a *service*. (The government, incidentally, is the largest single advertiser in the country.) Similarly the secretarial bureau is not a product in the conventional sense. It too is offering a service. Thus, provided we understand that the term 'product' may also comprise 'service', it should qualify for inclusion in our definition. All the examples and, by extension, all advertising is communication *about products*.

Prestige advertisements (e.g. ICI), though they feature large, complex organisations rather than specific items, do in fact say, by extension, 'We make things.' Thus overtly or covertly all advertisements, even this one, are about 'products'.

● *Advertising is communication about products.*

If this is all advertising is, then – provided the communication is honest – advertising would not incur the wrath of its critics. Some would say that they could get along without any communication (some even that they could maybe without products) but the majority would not object to straightforward communication – i.e. information about products. The difference between straightforward product information and modern advertising is the central concern not only of this book but of the consumer movement. It is the *casus belli*. The battleground like most battlegrounds is rich in confusion. But you can begin to determine which side you are on merely by asking yourself 'What is the purpose of an advertisement?' If it is 'The straightforward presentation of facts about products' [period] you align yourself with advertising's severest critics. If on the other hand you find this a jejune and inadequate definition, it means not that you countenance everything done in the name of advertising, but that you believe advertising has an active rather than a passive role to play in the economy. The point is crucial: the test acid.

What is the purpose of these thirteen advertisements? More, obviously, than the mere presentation of product information. The information about the product is presented in such a manner as to attempt to move the recipient towards purchase. Advertising is part of the selling process but it is too glib merely to assert that advertising is selling or 'salesmanship in print' (John Kennedy, 1905). This popular quotation certainly gets its priorities right and serves as a constant reminder to advertising people concerning the ultimate objective of their activities. It is a corrective to the self-indulgent. But as a definition it is too facile.

An advertisement's job is to persuade. Vance Packard calls advertising people 'hidden persuaders' though whether he is attacking the covert nature of the persuasion or persuasion itself is a moot point. And, as I said, the ultimate objective of such persuasion is a sale. There are many steps between the drawing up of a marketing plan and the expression of that plan in the form of an advertisement: and there are many more between the appearance of the advertisement and the sale of the product. The number of steps will depend on the nature of the product. In two of the thirteen examples illustrated the number of steps is few, the distance between consumer *reaction* to the advertisement and consumer *action* (i.e. purchase) is short. But they are exceptions. Hence the caveat expressed above: 'Move the recipient *towards* purchase.'

I should explain that the distinction between this and the common assumption that 'advertising is selling' is something more than hair-splitting. This is a better definition, first because it actually describes what is meant to happen, whereas the other form of words is too often only a pious hope. Secondly, it describes the function of *each and every advertisement*. Thirdly, and most significant of all, it is a practical aid to the creation of more effective advertising. If you accept the words 'move towards purchase' you commit yourself to creating or being responsible for advertisements irrespective of type or product category, which are meant to *do* something – and probably something which can be *measured*. On the other hand, simply to assert that the job of every advertisement is to sell a product is blatantly inadequate. It may give you a warm feeling to utter it, it may deceive others to whom you report, but it is a bland generalisation which, since it does not apply universally, once made, relinquishes you from all responsibility.

To recapitulate thus far:

● *Advertising is communication about products which moves consumers towards purchase.*

(I have used the word 'consumers' though I could equally as well have said 'people'.)

Is this sufficient? Not in my book (which this is). Two amendments and we are through.

First, although the word move is adequate (move vt: *to impel . . . persuade*), I prefer the word 'motivate'. Here is another word, as 'communication', which has fallen into disfavour through wrong and abundant use. Nevertheless it suits our context better. Motivate means 'to provide with a motive'. Every advertisement must provide a consumer with a motive.

Second, the communication is not simply about products. This again is too general. It suggests that any item of information about a product could qualify as a motivator of people towards purchase.

The missing word we have met already. IDEAS. Each of those thirteen advertisements contains an idea. (List what you believe are the ideas being communicated.) What advertising creative people communicate is ideas. Ideas which they have themselves – most of the time – originated. Most of the time. Because quite often the idea was originated prior to the creative man's entry on the scene and his job is merely to communicate a given idea. It is important to draw attention to both these aspects of the job: origination and communication. And to distinguish between them.

Thus, to conclude, here is our definition:

● *Advertising is the origination and/or communication of ideas about products in order to motivate consumers towards purchase.*

This definition is as comprehensive as one can make it. If it embraces all our thirteen examples it will do for any advertisement you are likely to see (or create). Moreover, it is practical. For example, should you be called on to judge an advertisement, all the important questions you need to ask of that advertisement are contained within the definition.

1. What is the product?
2. What is the idea being communicated?
3. Who is the consumer?
4. What is the consumer asked to do?
5. Why should he (or she) do it?

Cumbersome the definition may be, but it is businesslike. And if you regard advertising as a business that's no bad thing.

5

Towards purchase ... the continuum
from the corporate end

We have taken a considerable time to arrive at a definition. We are now about to put this definition to work. This chapter will attempt to establish certain 'laws'.

1. All advertisements are calls to action.
2. Advertisements differ from each other not in kind but in degree. All advertisements may therefore be said to exist on a continuum.
3. Any advertisement can be made more effective by 'moving it along the continuum'. (You may now begin to see why so much emphasis has been placed upon the words 'towards purchase'.)

Our thirteen advertisements differ by media type, by size or length within the same medium, by product category, by audience, by the job each advertisement is called upon to do. Nevertheless, we have in fact discovered common characteristics which have enabled us to construct a general definition of advertising. Each advertisement is a *call to action*. For the moment let us equate action with purchase of product. Imagine a continuum at one end of which is the word action.

———————————————————— action.

We'll call this the sharp end. It mixes metaphors but no matter.

Examine the thirteen advertisements and decide which of them is closest to the sharp end. In other words which advertisement demands an *immediate response* which if taken will result in a purchase. Then decide which of the thirteen advertisements is furthest away from the sharp end. Having positioned the two end advertisements then put the remaining eleven in order.

Another way of looking at the same problem is to imagine that an advertisement is a single communication between a manufacturer and a consumer and that between them is a piece of string. The string is at its shortest when the manufacturer and consumer are closest together. The further away they are from each other the slacker the string.

The exercise of assessing the order should prove the validity of the proposition – namely that all advertisements can in fact be positioned along this continuum. I shall refer to it as the *proximity* continuum. Proximity – since the advertisements are assessed not against any criterion of size or the more subjective criterion of impact, but against the objective criterion of distance.

In an activity which nobody properly understands it is reassuring to have something to measure. Many research companies have realised this of course, and have marketed techniques – I almost said nostrums – with lists of figures, scores, percentiles, quartiles, in an impressive display of numerology to satisfy any numerate stranger lost in the world of subjective criteria known as advertising. The age of the numbers game has passed its zenith but infinite measurements can be made in the belief that if a thing can be measured it must be worth measuring. In adding to the list with a proximity continuum I offer the one excuse – it helps.

As we saw in the last chapter it is inadequate and misleading simply to say that an advertisement's job is to sell. An advertisement's job is to move a consumer towards purchase. Let us look first at the remote end of the proximity continuum represented in our examples by the advertisement for ICI.

This is an example of a 'corporate' advertisement. Rosser Reeves, quoted in Martin Mayer's book *Madison Avenue, U.S.A.*, differentiates between corporate and packaged goods advertising by comparing a campaign for U.S. Steel with a campaign for Viceroy cigarettes. 'If U.S. Steel stopped advertising for a year they wouldn't sell one ton less steel. If Viceroy stopped advertising for a year you'd feel pain all over your body.' Another name for corporate advertising less in vogue is 'prestige' advertising. (Prestige probably fell into disfavour because it sounded too pompous – which most of the advertisements were and still are.) Corporate advertisements are put out by a large organisation with several separate divisions who normally also advertise independently. In a corporate advertisement they are 'united in a body so as to act as an individual' (*Chambers' Dictionary*). Unfortunately the individual they project often seems to be a rather dull fellow with very little to say which is either original or meaningful. He is prone to pompous utterance or platitudes indistinguishable from those uttered by his fellow big organisations. An individual he may be: individual he isn't. Look through the pages of the *Financial Times, The Economist, Director, Fortune, Time* etc., tear out the corporate advertisements, pin them on a wall, blank out the names of the companies and ask a colleague to name the advertisers. Unless he has made a study of the subject he is unlikely to get above a quarter correct. Indeed he will find it difficult not merely to name the advertiser but the type of service – bank, chemical company, engineering company, financial house, institution, conglomerate whatever – which is paying for that important and expensive space!

Corporate advertisements so grey and lifeless and oblique in their approach seem so far removed from the purpose of advertising as we have defined it that we may be forgiven for questioning whether they merit a place on the continuum at all.

And yet presumably they have been produced for a purpose. And since the organization itself is presumably in business also for a purpose, namely the making of a profit, everything which that organisation does must be undertaken with that ultimate objective in mind. It could be argued that a corporate campaign is another way of using up money which otherwise might go to the Exchequer in the form of tax. Nevertheless, that is no reason why the advertisement should deliberately not attempt to say something connected eventually with the sale of its product.

Furthermore, should these 'discretionary monies' be used in another fashion (e.g. the sponsoring of croquet at Hurlingham) then here again 'enlightened self-interest' rears its well groomed head! The ultimate objective must be sales. The links in the chain, the steps along the way from the advertiser to the action, are many and not immediately obvious.

It is difficult, for example, to answer the five questions raised at the end of the last chapter by our definition.

Take a typical corporate advertisement for gas. It shows a wheatfield, trees in the distance and a caption beneath: 'Cobbs Corner Field, Heath Farm, Breachwood Green, Herts'. Not a person in sight. Nor, as the copy points out, the product.

A YEAR AGO THE GAS UNDERGROUND GRID WAS LAID THROUGH HERE

There's nothing to see. And yet, just over a year ago, under this placid English field near Hitchin, the great new gas underground grid went on its way, ready to carry natural gas right through the centre of England.

As Britain's economy expands, the gas industry is alert to its responsibilities as a vital provider of heat for industry, warmth for the home. Every technological aid to better distribution of gas, even better service to manufacturer and consumer, is given its chance to help. Natural gas from under the Sahara will be refrigerated and brought in tankers to Canvey Island at the mouth of the Thames. There it will be turned back into methane gas, and pumped through the grid, under this field, to gas stations as far away as Coventry, Sheffield, Leeds. If the vast natural gas resources now being sought under the North Sea are discovered and tapped, they, too, will be pumped into the grid. Under this field. *In today's high speed world . . . the gas industry thinks of tomorrow.*

Taking our five questions in turn.

1. *What is the product?*
Obviously that tomorrow-thinking product – GAS.

2. *What is the idea being communicated?*
The idea which originates in the product rather than in the mind of the creative man is the 'invisible evidence' of gas. Pylons are unsightly. Gas leaves no mark. The mood of the advertisement . . . the use of actual homely names and the tone of the copy . . . is an attempt to reinforce the idea.

3. *Who is the consumer?*

4. *What is he expected to do about it?*
The advertisements appeared in *The Daily Telegraph Magazine* and other AB publications. Presumably there are two possible types of 'consumer'.

  (i) The upper middle class houseowner who is in a position to install gas instead of electricity (or oil maybe in the case of central heating):
  (ii) the so-called opinion-leader who can influence a decision at board or local council level concerning an installation; or who can, less tangibly, effect what is known as a 'climate of opinion'.

It will be seen that the number of steps is shorter in (i) than in (ii) but that nevertheless the ultimate objective is the same. The gas industry is not spending this money (£2,000 for a full page), *our* money incidentally, for the sake of its health.

5. *Why should he do it?*
Why indeed? What's in it for him? The benefit when he is a landowner is not particularly tangible. There is no mention of cost. The benefit is, allegedly, a benefit to the community. The 'consumer' therefore is helping to protect England's green and pleasant land by putting the gas industry into the black.

This exercise has, I trust, proved that even a corporate advertisement can, albeit not effortlessly, be subjected to the five question dialectic of our definition. The further one goes along the continuum the easier the questioning becomes.

Corporate advertisements may be at the farthest, remotest part of the continuum but they must *face the same way* as all other advertisements ... TOWARDS PURCHASE. All advertisements are calls to action. The ultimate action is purchase. The *immediate* action need not and often cannot be. Nevertheless action must result and that action must be *relevant to purchase*. It must move the consumer towards purchase.

If an advertisement does not at first sight appear to be inciting anyone to action relevant to purchase there are two reasons:

1. It is not an advertisement.

2. The action may, like the gas beneath the English field, be hidden from view.

Let us briefly examine both.

You may look at an advertisement and be left in a state of total bewilderment. This may be due to the advertiser's incompetence or your own ignorance. We need not waste time with the former, though there are too many so-called advertisements which serve merely to keep agencies and their suppliers busy, and to decorate (and subsidise) the media. You may stare at a certain advertisement for an hour and not know what it means or what you are supposed to do! In the second case it is important to know above all whom the advertisement is addressing. An apparently bland 'message' in a distinguished journal may be a subtle means of convincing a mere handful of important people (possibly just one person) that the advertiser is respectable, honest, community-minded, patriotic, a good employer, a supporter of the government, an opponent of the government or simply solvent. The object of a corporate advertisement is to influence the influential. It may be aimed at the *investor* (large or small) so that the company becomes a candidate for the investor's share portfolio. It may be aimed at the *trade*. A new company – or, more likely, an existing company operating in a new field – may decide upon a background corporate campaign in order to influence the stockist, wholesaler, regional buyer, individual retailer so that the next time the company's representative calls upon the stockist he has at least *heard* of it.

It may be aimed at a wider audience. For example, acquisitions and mergers are rapidly altering the scenery. Old established names are disappearing or assuming totally different identities. Names of companies are changing. In this situation the corporate advertisement serves to *identify* the organisation. The main purpose of the advertisement is to tell the particular audience who in fact is advertising and what in fact he makes!

The growth of acquisition and diversification leads to severe communication problems in this respect. The Metal Box Company for instance work also in plastic and are acutely embarrassed by their name. A few years ago their corporate slogan became: 'There's more to Metal Box than metal boxes'. However with environmentalists up in arms they may soon change that to 'Metal Box make *only* metal boxes'. That's one solution: retain your name but make sure, via corporate advertising, that your consumers know what else you do.

Another solution is to ignore the problem and rely on your normal trading communication with your customers, not to mention your customers' good sense. (The clients of the 'Scottish Widows' Fund and Life Assurance Society' are presumably neither exclusively Scottish nor exclusively widows.)

Yet another solution is to adopt initials. This seems to create more problems than it solves. Either consumers know what the initials mean or they don't. If they do, you are no further forward. If, alternatively, they do *not* know what the initials mean can this qualify as a solution? You have voluntarily embraced anonymity. An article in *Advertising Age* by Jack Trout and Al Ries points out that of the five hundred largest industrial companies listed in *Fortune* no fewer than sixteen 'have legally changed their names to meaningless initials'. They list them:

ACF	CPC	NVF	SCM
AMF	ESB	NL	TRW
AMP	FMC	PPG	USM
ATO	GAF	RCA	VF

There is, of course, yet another option open to the corporate advertiser. He can attempt to change the words for which the initials originally stood. This demands, in equal parts, legerdemain and gall. For example, Fifty Shilling Tailors, unable either to reverse the inexorable tide of inflation or to make a waistcoat let alone a suit for fifty bob, changed their name to FST which they would have you believe represented Fit and Style Tailors. The smartest move in this direction was taken by the research company AGB. Originally set up by three gentlemen Messrs Audley, Gapper and Brown, it now boasts a stock exchange quotation and the proud name of Audits of Great Britain. My own attempt to make OBM signify Only Bernstein Matters was thwarted only by the resilience of Ogilvy, Benson and Mather.

Occasionally one initial may change in significance. The P in NPA, from Newspaper *Proprietors* Association (recalling the autocratic influence of Northcliffe or Kemsley) to the more democratic Newspaper *Publishers* Association or the C in BBC, from British Broadcasting *Company* to British Broadcasting *Corporation*.

But initials lead a life of their own only when they themselves form a word. For example, I wrote advertisements for Esso for four years before I realised it stood for Standard Oil (ess-o, get it?).

But I digress. To repeat:

● *The object of a corporate advertisement is to influence the influential.*

This is not to deny that the ordinary consumer may also simultaneously be influenced (or to assert that he or she is not for that matter also influential). For example, a corporate campaign may attempt to create a generally favourable aura for a company at two levels. It may speak to opinion leaders at the topmost level – ministers, government officials, senior civil servants, etc. – and, at the same time, seek by means of the aura it creates, to convince the ordinary consumer that its products are reliable, economical or, for one of many other reasons, worth buying. It may adopt a posture such as that taken by Ampol in Australia, an indigenous oil company which, with one eye on the government, made use of patriotism as the theme of its advertising, motivating consumers towards purchase by telling them that filling up with Ampol would also fill the nation's coffers.

Corporate advertising thus stands at the extreme end of the continuum. So much so that many companies regard it as a totally different animal, preferring to call it 'public relations' and allocate resources from a separate budget. Be that as it may, a corporate advertisement belongs on the continuum – the same continuum as the tin of soup, the packet of cereal and the classified ad for a secondhand car. Our same definition applies, the same questions can be asked of it and, though its immediate goals may be different the ultimate purpose is identical.

6

The continuum . . . continued

Having shown that the corporate advertisement belongs on the continuum it should not prove too difficult to show that all other advertisements belong there too. What determines that position is, as I said, the distance between the advertiser and the action. At one end of the continuum (the sharp end) the advertiser is at the scene of the action. At the other he is remote. The corporate advertiser may have hold of the piece of string but it is slack and it may take constant draughts of reassurance to make sure he maintains his hold upon it particularly if there is a persuasive PR man around with other ideas about how and where the client should spend his money. Clearly the nearer the advertiser is to the scene of the action the more sensitive he is to the *re*action of the consumer, the more control he has of the situation. By the same token any claim advertising may have to be called a science must lie in this region.

The continuum is a useful visual aid. It enables you to position each advertisement you are called on to create – or judge. If for example you have to choose between two advertisements simply place each along the scale and, by assessing which is nearer the action, you can guess which is more likely to succeed. (Needless to say this is not an infallible rule but it is better than most of advertising's rules of thumb. Furthermore, the most useful measurements in advertising are *comparative*. Research rarely provides finite answers.) By positioning the advertisement on the continuum one is really assessing odds and saying just how remote are one's chances of persuading somebody to do something. The odds are less in your favour the remoter you are. The handicaps are greater. But it is in your power to reduce them!

Advertising is a form of communication. The more remote the transmitter (advertiser) is from the receiver (consumer) the more difficult is it to communicate successfully. Communication stands most chance of succeeding when the advertiser and the consumer are face to face. Eyeball to eyeball confrontation occurs in a market place, over a counter, or on a doorstep. Here the advertiser is both advertiser and salesman. This is not salesmanship in print but salesmanship. The line of communication is at its shortest. The salesman accosts the customer, he shows his wares, or rings a doorbell, or a sign attracts attention for him. The customer responds by stopping, answering the door, or coming closer.

Communication has been effected.

The salesman, having gained attention, proceeds to interest. Perhaps he makes a promise or perhaps he delays coming to the point, approaching his objective indirectly, even denying that a sale is in fact his purpose in communicating!

So far the communication is mostly one way.

The customer asks a question, maybe eliciting more information which the salesman gives; alternatively, the customer puts a counter argument which the salesman answers directly or obliquely.

Dialogue has begun. Objectives are either satisfied or not satisfied. And as a result a sale is made or lost.

The salesman adjusts his 'pitch' according to the response of the consumer. In computer language this is known as 'real time'. A missile, for instance, can be launched and the computer can feed back, during the flight, information which can be used to correct the direction of that flight. The response affects the order of the arguments, the content of the arguments and the tone of voice. The sale, in other words, is tailormade (whereas an advertisement is off-the-peg: it will fit a lot of people but by no means all). The salesman will adjust his pitch according to the consumer's age, sex, social class or the presence or absence of a pram in the front garden. The promise which clinches one sale may be ineffective at another encounter where success may depend upon a relatively subsidiary point. Similarly, whereas one sale may be due to reasoned argument logically presented, another (of the identical product) may depend upon an appeal to the emotions. This is the most direct of direct responses. The line is at its shortest. The communicator is hypersensitive to each response. He can interpret accurately every bounce back of his own signal.

Reaction, or 'feedback', is an essential part of all communication, commercial or otherwise. The growth of studio audiences in television is due not to a cynical belief that if the viewing public hears laughter they will then know that the show is meant to be funny, but to the artist's need to get a response. The lack of an audience adversely affects the timing of a comedian's material not to mention the material itself (since he has no means of telling if the audience likes what he likes). What adjustments he may have to make to both the timing and the material. Tyrone Guthrie in a lecture at Oxford once described a theatre audience as a single entity pulling on a rope. The smaller the house the slighter the hold and the less sensitive the actor to its response. Each empty seat makes the actor's task more difficult. Very rare are the artists who can exist without a public. In the commercial world this attitude is suicidal. The advertising creative man who is not interested in consumer reaction to his advertisement is betraying an arrogance matched only by his ignorance. For without feedback he is unable to improve; without knowledge he has nothing to build on. Luckily, most creative people are vain enough to want to know what people think of their work and, more to the point, professional enough to want to know what they *do* as a result of it. A creative man who eschews research is writing his own death warrant.

Feedback has the shortest route to travel in the salesman/ market-place situation. Here the response is direct. And the closest parallel to it in advertising is therefore called 'direct response'. There are two main categories: direct mail and mail order.

Direct mail advertisements arrive by post. The householder receives a letter, apparently personalised, together with a colourful leaflet or two and a prepaid card or envelope. The *Time* magazine leaflet is one example. Many publishers adopt this method. They collate mailing lists, sometimes unaided, carefully building them up over years, often supplementing them from the existing lists offered by specialist direct mail houses. Such lists can be priceless since they represent not merely years of patient and persistent work (and constant updating) on the part of the advertiser but also a most important item of his stock-in-trade, as vital almost as the goods he has for sale.

Suppose, for example, that you wanted to sell a small item of domestic furniture, easily packaged and assembled. Suppose too that it represented good value for money but was definitely not cheap. You might therefore define your target market as AB.[1] But more specifically the house-proud upper middle class.

How could you reach them? The glossy Sunday supplements are the obvious answer. However, what if you could get hold of the Habitat mailing list? Wouldn't this give you exactly the sort of audience you want? Before we discover if it is available (and, if so, at what cost) note that what we have done in fining down our target audience and, more especially, in *defining our ideal medium,* is to move the position of our advertisement further along the continuum towards the sharp end.

Let me put you out of your misery: Terence Conran may let you have his mailing list for £50,000.

A further example. You manufacture gold replicas. You decide to reproduce in gold a special commemorative stamp, to limit your issue to two thousand numbered pieces, to make it available at the time of the stamp's publication and to destroy the master plate, thus ensuring the scarcity value of each replica. The quality press (e.g. *The Times, Sunday Times, Observer*) suggest themselves, as do certain specialist publications. For instance,

---

[1] 'Social groupings: A mishmash of how rich people are and how they lead their lives, commonly used in defining the target customer group for a product or service. Usually described in shorthand as A/B (the well-off and toffee-nosed), C-1 (the more prosperous working classes), C-2 (the less prosperous working classes), D/E (the poor and the very poor)' Colin McIver.

why not take space in a magazine read by art collectors or, better still, stamp collectors? Come to that, what if you could persuade the GPO to sell you the list of enthusiasts who receive their first day covers? One company did just this, and this only, and received three thousand applications for their two thousand issue in just ten days. The direct mail advertisement is the closest approximation to the market-place situation.

Our furniture manufacturer, denied an appropriate mailing list, will resort to the penultimate position on the continuum – the mail order advertisement. He will take the page in a glossy Sunday supplement. But he will make sure that it works for him.

We may have had difficulty answering our five basic questions at the remote end of the continuum but here – where the action is – there is no hesitation whatsoever. We know what the product is, what idea is being communicated, who the consumer is, what motive for action he (or she) is being offered and, above all, *what he is expected to do*. There is no doubt at all. The instructions are explicit and repeated. There is a coupon. You know it is a coupon because it looks like a coupon. It is positioned where a coupon is always positioned – at the corner and not in the middle of the page – and at the corner where access is easiest. Thus in making sure the advertisement is working for him our furniture manufacturer is trying his damndest to turn his advertisement into a mailing shot. He is moving it along the continuum. If he tries hard he may almost succeed. If he has the space (i.e. money) his mail order advertisement will include a prepaid 'postcard'. This demands a feat of newspaper carpentry on the part of the consumer. Nevertheless, it can be very effective, which proves that the lure of a bargain can overcome even the hazards of origami.

Mail order advertisements offer goods for sale *direct* from the manufacturer or vendor to the consumer by mail. They appear in virtually all newspapers and magazines. As yet they have not been offered on television though, as we shall see, there *are* means by which TV can elicit a direct response apart, that is, from switching off the set. And of course mail order advertisements also appear in mail order catalogues. Montgomery Ward, the American pioneer of mail order celebrated its centenary in 1972 and the US Mails issued a special commemorative stamp – as well they might!

The art of writing and designing direct response material is highly developed. So much so that some would say it has graduated from art to science. One reason above all others is that the ad is the only means of selling. So if the ad doesn't work – neither does the vendor! It just has to work. If not it is rewritten, redesigned. Maybe only a single word is changed. Or the emphasis is switched from, say, price to benefit (the 'selling point' is altered). Practitioners of direct response accumulate scores. They know how well each advertisement pulls. They 'key' each advertisement – put a distinctive mark or number in the coupon or the address (e.g. write to J. Bloggs, Dept 4) so that the effect of every advertisement and every appeal can be exactly measured and results compared.

Of all advertising's workers the master of direct response is the most scientific. He is something of a chemist. He combines elements and observes what happens. He changes one element and compares the results of two experiments. Advertisement A scores against advertisement B. Perhaps because he put the word 'Free' in the headline. Or chose to devote more of his limited space to illustration. Like the chemist he then experiments with the environment, the context of the original experiment, switching the position of the advertisements. For example if A beats B when A is run first what happens if the order is reversed? Or has the position in the newspaper or magazine a decisive effect on performance? Has geography any influence? Assuming that the media men have delivered identical types of reader in terms of income and social grouping is there more potential for his product north or south of a line drawn from Birmingham to the Wash or wherever? In which case it may be worth the advertiser's while to concentrate his expenditure on half the country. Or alternatively he could run different appeals in different regions. The media owners are becoming more cooperative in matters of this sort, printing 'split-runs' – i.e. half the country sees Advertisement A, half Advertisement B. Even more sophisticated tests can be arranged whereby the split is one of alternating copies so that half the circulation *throughout* the country reads advertisement A and the other half advertisement B – irrespective of area. Of course in all this the advertiser tries to limit his variables to one. It could be the audience, the ad or the key element in the ad. But whereas the scientist knows after repeated experiments that he has discovered a law true for all time, the advertiser is not so fortunate. Other factors enter into it. Wear-out or fatigue; competitive activity; fashion; saturation. Nevertheless, as I hope I have indicated, there is sufficient use of scientific method in direct response for this department of advertising to earn respect.

In direct response the advertiser receives a direct signal. As with the salesman, the success of his communication can be measured in the simplest of ways – by a sale made or lost. A mail order ad is in fact at the penultimate position on our continuum. The vendor and purchaser may be a hundred miles away but in advertising terms they are as near as it is possible to get. And the probability of the vendor's commands being obeyed is at its highest.

The classic advertising textbook teaches you to end your advertisement with an injunction. Leave the consumer in no doubt about what he or she has to do. In a mail order advertisement there is no confusion: 'Send a postal order for two pounds plus postage to J. Bloggs and Company . . .' And, as we have seen, to facilitate response a coupon is included. And to remove the last shred of doubt this is accompanied by an illustration of a pair of scissors. Now it's easy to scoff but you can be pretty certain that someone somewhere has actually measured the effect of those scissors and compared the response rates of two advertisements, one with and one without them!

All advertisements are calls to action. The direct mail shot with the enclosed prepaid post card stands the greatest chance of that call being answered. Hence its 'pole' position on the continuum. The mail order advertisement with a coupon comes next. Then the mail order advertisement without a coupon. And so forth.

In the next chapter we complete the proximity continuum, till we reach the corporate ad. But remembering as we do so that an advertisement's position on the continuum is not fixed, that the complaint of remoteness – if it can't be avoided – may at least be alleviated.

7

The continuum . . . concluded

The further backwards we proceed along the continuum the more other factors intervene.

The advertiser has matters taken out of his complete control. He cannot demand a direct response. He can merely direct the consumer to a place of purchase. He may own a chain of shops. In which case the sovereignty he loses is slight. He can say 'available only at Bloggs Stores' and list the addresses. Nevertheless he has to induce a reader to go to a store and not be swayed by what she sees in rival stores en route. Whether she buys what was advertised or something else is of no great consequence since all the goods are Bloggs goods.

The technical name for this is vertical integration. The manufacturer controls the means of distribution and selling. There is no intervening wholesaler or retailer. But this is still the exception. The more intervening factors there are – and the lessening control the vendor has upon them – the further along the continuum lies the advertisement.

The advertiser can still maintain some control by asking the reader to write 'for the name of your nearest stockist'. Once the reply is received the stockist is informed but whether the reader goes there is another matter. Suppose for example the ad ends with the line 'available everywhere' (and it is), the advertiser is still at the mercy of the independent sales assistant and increasingly the independent shopper. The assistant can recommend a rival product. The shopper can compare prices and packages and the special offers and choose the rival brand. The assistant can be vocal in praise – or probably the supermarket silently – of the store's 'own brand'. The shopper can decide not to buy any of them. The product may in fact be out of stock. The shopper may decide to spend her 'disposable income' in quite a different way in quite a different store. The opinion of a friend she trusts may dissuade her from purchase. Etcetera. Etcetera. The intervening factors are innumerable. No question here of a direct response.

Of course by no means all products are 'available everywhere'. Not every outlet stocks every commodity which it could reasonably be asked to stock. Space alone probably prevents this. Competition in some fields is too crowded. Some manufacturers arrange better deals with some stockists with the result that rival products are either not stocked or are given inadequate support at point of sale. A consumer asks for Q and is told 'there's no demand for it'. This may well be true: but there may be no demand because it isn't stocked and not the other way about.

The list of possible diversions from a sale may make depressing reading for an advertiser. It should certainly answer some of the criticism levelled against advertising for its 'manipulation of consumers'. The advertiser could understandably question the wisdom of advertising at all.

Today the advertiser is devoting more and more of his advertising appropriation to promotional activity. Putting it 'below the line' on such things as competitions, trial offers, price reductions, banded packs, special deals with retailers and the like. Yet he knows he must use advertising to make consumers *aware* of his products, to give them a status in the market place. Advertising is still the most economical method of doing this despite the large expenditure involved. What other method is open to him? Take the critics' favourite target 'soap powders' (by which is generally meant synthetic detergents). The total annual appropriation of one leading brand is scarcely more than the cost of sending one postcard a year to every household in the country. If you were the manufacturer faced with these two options which would you choose?

Furthermore you can do things in advertisements you can't do elsewhere. You can tell your story the way you want it told. You can include as much information as you want. You can talk to roughly the sort of people you think will be interested. You can exert pressure at the appropriate times of the year. You can launch a new brand, new size, new pack or make a special offer. You can inject news value into your product. The fact that you are rubbing shoulders with the world's news in the world's news media can add an immediacy, an urgency to your sale. You can control the image you wish to project. Sometimes the image is the only thing an advertiser can control. And then only if he is clever or lucky.

Take for instance cosmetic advertising. Here image is (almost) everything. The mood of the advertisement, the choice of illustration, the 'magic' of the name, the promise of the package . . . all these are potent. These elements are as much a part of the product as the product's actual ingredients. A cosmetic advertisement is in effect the product itself.

Another product category in which the advertiser loses control of the image at his peril is that of consumer durables.

So far we have concentrated upon advertising for products in general distribution, mass-market goods: the frequently purchased low-priced items. What Dr Timothy Joyce prefers to call 'cheap goods bought often'.

What about the dear goods bought seldom? Such merchandise – unless it is sold by means of direct response – is still further back along our proximity continuum.

Advertising's part in the sale of cars, refrigerators, washing machines, television sets, etc., is tenuous. Very few sales are made directly as a result of an advertisement. Certainly very few indeed are made *solely* as a result of an advertisement. The more expensive an item the more consideration goes into its purchase. However, though a consumer durable is in no sense of the term an 'impulse purchase' it would be wrong to infer that such a product should be advertised solely on its more worthy (durable) features. Provided the product is reliable and has a good name (and here again advertising, probably corporate, has helped), the trigger for a sale can be quite slight.

A new colour, a new name, a stylistic change . . . any of several non-functional innovations can provide the impulse for purchase. And it could be the job of the creative man to concentrate on this one aspect to the virtual exclusion of all others in an attempt to motivate the consumer to take action. That action will not, initially, be purchase. It may be a visit to a store. Perhaps the trigger, cocked by the advertisement, will only be released if and when the consumer passes the store window and is reminded of the feature he saw in the magazine. From then on the sale is in the hands of the sales assistant.

In this world of consumer durables the intervening factors may be no greater in number but they are stronger. The opinion of other people based upon experience is often crucial. 'They've got one and they know.' The best method of compensating for this remoteness in these circumstances is to print a leaflet or better still a comprehensive brochure and invite readers to write in, preferably incorporating a coupon in the advertisement.

The position of each advertisement on the proximity continuum is determined by the number and intensity of the 'remoteness factors' which it contains. Remoteness, as we have seen, has to do with the following conditions which obtain in the particular marketing and advertising environment in which the advertisement exists:

1. The actual distance between the vendor and the purchaser.

2. The amount of *effort* required by the purchaser.

3. The amount of direct or indirect *control* which the vendor can exert upon the purchasing situation.

4. The number and nature of the *intervening* people involved in the sale.

5. The nature and cost of the *merchandise* being sold.

6. The nature of the *medium* in which the advertisement appears.

The last point – the nature of the medium and the relationship of the medium to the *action* – is the most crucial, if not from the advertiser's point of view, then certainly from that of the advertising agency. And that of the creative man. Because of the six considerations listed, it is usually *the only one which he can influence.*

And more often than not he does damn-all about it.

8

The medium and the action . . . or
'Move along the continuum please'

This chapter will not introduce you to the mysteries of media (we've hardly been introduced ourselves). Neither will it attempt to define cost effectiveness, the media man's most potent weapon with which to beat the creative man.

If you're looking for an explanation of computer runs, target group index and response function you've bought the wrong book. Barely numerate enough to understand reading and noting, I dared to attend an international media conference last April in Amsterdam. Taking my courage (Dutch) in both hands, I delivered a paper to the assembled media researchers against an overall conference subject, 'Hard Thinking on Soft Data', the meaning of which, though I must confess I barely grasped when I arrived, had quite escaped me by the time I left.

I have every respect for the media man. Some of my best friends are Simon Broadbent. I part company with them when they talk medium to the virtual exclusion of message – and when their terminology races away from my comprehension.

I was presenting a television script for McCann-Erickson one afternoon, a decade ago, to the gentlemen of Philips, Scott and Turner. PST make 'Milk of Magnesia'. In the client's ranks, newly imported from Procter and Gamble, were some strange and serious faces with minds to match. Having done my turn (the commercial subsequently became world famous) there was the usual acknowledgement which gives away nothing and the discussion turned to the media policy. 'Mr Bernstein, what about OTS?' What about it? I thought. 'What is it?' I asked the McCann man on my right, this being the first time I had heard the term, never then having visited downtown Newcastle where such things were meat and drink. By the time he had whispered the answer ('opportunities to see – you know, frequency') the discussion had drifted to the other end of the table. The breathing space, however, was short. 'OK, Mr Bernstein, what about OTS?' 'Well,' I said, 'I think we ought to run this commercial PST.' There was a pause while they looked at each other. At last one of them admitted ignorance. 'PST?' he asked. 'Probably Several Times,' I replied.

These notes then are written by an amateur in media – someone to whom 'Guaranteed Home Impressions' sounds like an impersonation of the Foreign Secretary. Nevertheless – and here the story really starts – it is important for creative people to understand the media scene and, in the current jargon, to establish a dialogue with media men. No aspect of agency life has changed quite so much in the last fifteen years. Simon Broadbent is without doubt the most understandable and understanding of all commentators on the subject. When you read him you realise the force of good media decisions and the advantages of not adopting entrenched positions.

> The feel for media which you should cultivate and your intuitions about how messages are received should of course primarily be applied to writing advertisements. These faculties should also be exercised when it comes to the choice of medium. The creative man should have the flair and taste to suggest – or at least catch fire about – the right media choice. The planner is the straight man, the one with the checklists. He carries in his mind, or on paper, a range of more or less relevant facts which should be added to this intuition and used to correct or to stimulate it.[1]

----

[1] 'What media are' by Simon Broadbent from *What Advertising Is*, edited by Maurice Smelt, p. 106. Pelham Books, 1972.

For a comprehensive treatment of the subject read Simon Broadbent's *Spending Advertising Money* (Business Books 1971). All this chapter will touch on is the nature of the media choice – and the relationship of the media to the action. And, remember, we have widened our definition of action to action *relevant to purchase*.

One mistake commonly made by beginners in advertising – and, I have to admit, certain hard-core media men – is to think that there is a scale of unchanging values for different types of media. Or, to put it another way, rather than place *advertisements* on our continuum you could save a lot of bother by placing the various *media*. There is *some* truth in this, of course – but a good deal more dogma.

We begin by returning to our original market-place situation. How does the medium relate to the action? Obviously they are located together. The stall-holder has his wares in front of him. The action (purchase of product) takes place where the medium (the salesman's voice and gestures, if you like) is situated. There are, of course, subsidiary media: a sign and whatever messages may be contained on whatever packaging he has displayed in front of him.

The same media components exist in the shop though the performance of the sales assistant is less dramatic, less domineering and far less urgent. He has more than one product to sell in any product field and thus acts more in the capacity of an adviser, albeit a sales motivated one. However, the support media are greater in number and more professional. These include not only the range of packaging, counter cards, self-standing displays, window bills, but also the national media advertisements (e.g. television, press, poster) which have backed up the sale and even stimulated the customer to go into the shop. Nevertheless, the sale is made in the store and the most important medium at this juncture is that found within it.

Naturally, with the development of self-service, supermarket and hypermarket shopping, the role played by the assistant or manager in the active persuasion process is rapidly decreasing. The manager's contribution is the decision to stock the product at all – and the price at which he sells it. And maybe that decision has been made for him at head office.

The packaging designer is replacing the old-fashioned salesman – though not many companies or advertising agencies have yet appreciated the full implications of this. The pack designer used to be regarded as a supporting player. Today he is beginning to play the lead. The creative team who willingly offload the pack design of a new product or blithely accept whatever is offered them has its head in a sack. Equally at risk is the brand manager who lets creative advertising and pack design work run in parallel. The trouble with parallel lines is that they never meet.

The relationship of media to action in the case of a door-to-door salesman has already been described in the previous chapter. In some cases the purchase takes place then and there. In others a form is filled in – action *relevant to purchase* takes place. In both cases, thanks to welcome legislation, a cooling-off period is allowed and the purchaser can change his mind.

In the case of direct mail the action (returning the prepaid postcard or envelope containing a cheque or 'bill me later') is contained within the medium. Here again recent legislation has come to the aid of the consumer. Not only was the action contained within the medium, so too was the product. A book for example would be mailed to an address. The surprised recipient would then have to return it within a specified period. Otherwise it would be assumed that he had agreed to purchase the unsolicited article and an invoice would be sent him followed shortly by another and, eventually, a solicitor's letter. Inertia selling has been outlawed. *Caveat emptor* does not cover cases in which the *emptor* didn't want to be an *emptor* in the first place.

The relationship between medium and action is very close also in the case of mail order. The action is contained within the medium. In descending order of importance:

1. The prepaid do it yourself postcard.

2. A coupon.

3. An offer with the address of the vendor (pressure of space precluding the inclusion of a coupon).

Furthermore, ordinary newspaper and magazine advertisements may also, we have seen, contain the wherewithal for action: actual purchase (sending off for the goods advertised) or action relevant to purchase (sending off for more information about the merchandise).

However, I must utter a warning note about the enclosure of a coupon (or its equivalent). Once you decide to do it you have *altered the nature* of your advertisement. You may regard it is an afterthought. 'Why not add a coupon?' 'Let's ask them to write in ... maybe there's something we could send them?' 'How about a free sample?' 'Look – if enough people reply we'll get a mailing list.' Adding a coupon (or its equivalent) is not an optional extra. Once you add an offer you are – as the Americans say – in a different ball park. Your advertisement which set out to do one thing will be judged by its ability to do another. It will be judged solely as a direct response advertisement.

You can't be partly pregnant.

An interesting device is the buried offer, the primary purpose of which is not to communicate with your market (though this, of course, also happens) but to check the efficacy of the straight advertisement. There is a common belief among the unfaithful that people do not read long copy. (As a universal law it is patently absurd. People read every word on a topic which interests them.) There is a simple trick to help you discover if your page scanner has got beyond the headline and the lead-in. Some way towards the end of the text you insert – in ordinary, not bold type, in lower case not capitals – an offer which, if he's interested, he can hardly refuse to take up. The replies the advertiser receives are an indication of reader involvement with the advertisement. And though the purpose of the offer is not to get a mailing list, the names the advertiser compiles represent truly interested respondents as opposed to those inveterate 'coupon-clippers' who keep the Post Office in funds and scissor grinders in business.

Now in all the examples we have so far examined – with the exception of the market place and the shop – the action is not complete. The purchase has not taken place. Simply an action relevant to purchase. When money is sent the purchase is completed only when the goods are received by return. When more information is required or goods on free approval are asked for, or a representative is asked to call, actions have been taken *relevant to purchase.*

Now it would seem that certain media are better suited to achieve this proximity (of medium to action) than others. Obviously a television commercial cannot contain a coupon. Neither can a poster nor a hoarding. Each medium has its own limitations. But it would be wrong and shortsighted to accept a universal law which said a newspaper is always closer to the action than a television commercial or a poster. It depends on two factors. The nature of the product and the ingenuity of the advertiser and/or his agency. Let's take them in turn. A couple of examples will suffice to demonstrate how the nature of the product can affect the situation.

Imagine you are advertising a local store. Suppose there is a special offer available for a limited period. The obvious means of making this known would be a local newspaper. Rather than simply announce the offer you could incorporate a special voucher 'worth 5*p*' when the customer calls in at the store. Here the action is contained within the medium. Surely no other medium can get as close as that? Well how about this? A poster site is bought for the exact period of the offer adjacent to the store. The poster in suitably exciting language announces the offer and exhorts the passers-by to hurry in. Who is to say that the poster isn't as effective? The proximity in this case is proximity to the point of purchase. The line of communication is short. Furthermore, a large proportion of the passers-by are actually in a shopping frame-of-mind, whereas the newspaper reader will probably be reading the ad at leisure. Thus the proximity of medium to eventual action could be closer in the case of the poster. A similar instance is the use of small posters (single or double crown) for newspapers and publications which are strategically placed at railway stations adjacent to bookstalls.

Cinema would probably rank as one of the remotest media when assessed independently of product. Yet if a cinema sells ice cream in the intervals and gangways, then a cinema commercial for ice cream approximates to our ideal market place situation.

The action of the ad and the medium are located together.

Television too need be less remote than one might consider at first glance. It may be impossible to incorporate a coupon in the commercial but the commercial can draw the viewer's attention to a coupon in the press or, more appropriately, the *TV Times*. Response can be even more direct by screening an answering phone service number and inviting interested viewers to ring – immediately.

Much depends upon the ingenuity of the advertiser. Which brings us to our second factor: if a medium has limitations then it is up to the so-called creative man to exploit them. And here it is impossible to distinguish his contribution from that of the shrewd media man who chooses his medium not merely to minimise waste but also to minimise remoteness. Note for instance how local advertisers in the London area use bus advertisements on routes along or near their outlets. Another example of clever media buying – also on London Transport – is that for Mum Rollette Deodorant. They use tube cards, the small rectangular posters just above head height, an obvious media choice when you consider the conditions of travel, the crowded strap-hangers. Remoteness is further minimised when the creative man gets to work and pens a simple message:

● Hands Down Those Not Using Mum.

A direct and personal message which hits home when the respondent is at his most vulnerable. Now if Mum were available from slot machines on station platforms remoteness would have been annihilated!

In 1966 *The Times* newspaper was offered a special poster site near Trafalgar Square. Known as 'trivision', it revolved and allowed three separate facings to appear in turn at ten second intervals. The trouble with posters as a medium for advertising newspapers is that they can't be topical, certainly not as topical as a newspaper itself. However, *The Times* managed to change the three sets of facings completely each day – at midnight – covering each facing with the day's headlines. Instead of a printed poster the areas were covered with individual letters, white on black squares, which were hung on hooks in the manner of a cricket scoreboard. Thus a poster site was endowed with a rare immediacy. Remoteness was further reduced by incorporating adjacent to the site a self-standing, self-service newspaper dispenser.

You may think that action relevant to purchase has taken on a wider meaning than it was first given. Certainly there is a considerable difference between sending money as a response to an advertisement and reacting in a tube train to a deodorant message. Nevertheless, the difference is one of degree not kind. All advertisements must be calls to action. Television, for example, which is understandably regarded as the most dynamic of media (sight, sound, movement, immediacy, captive audience) is, nevertheless, very remote from the place of purchase. And if someone exhorts you from the box to 'buy some today' you may put on your shoes and overcoat only to discover that the store closed about three hours before. Nevertheless, as the examples of the *TV Times* coupon and answering phone have shown, the medium can elicit a direct response. But there are other responses too, admittedly not so direct, but still 'relevant to purchase'.

It is too easy and wasteful to regard television as a passive medium. This is an attitude which stems from a belief that television is primarily an entertainment medium. Probably no single misconception has done TV advertising as much disservice. Television is or can be a participatory medium (witness Sesame Street, schools programmes, the Open University, etc.). A commercial can invite you to do something. Not simply in the future. Right there and then. Even if it is only to compare your own performance and possessions with those of the people and of the product in the advertisement. It can ask you to do something more active. Shut your eyes. Get up from your chair. Examine the picture on your television screen (a very successful device used by Murphy many years ago to sell the clarity of their TV sets – 'Is *your* set up to the Murphy standard?'). It can make you less comfortable in the easy chair you are sitting in, aware of the inadequacy of your wallpaper, uneasy about the security arrangements for your house (watch out there's a thief about), get you to ring a distant relative, etc., etc.

To conclude:

● All advertisements are calls to action (purchase or action relevant to purchase).

● All advertisements belong on the proximity continuum.

● It is the job of the creative man not to regard an advertisement's position on that continuum as fixed by divine right (or by the media man) but to attempt to move it along the continuum towards the action end. TO SHORTEN THE STRING.

● And though I am wary of golden rules I would wager that one which went something like this would be true most of the time:

> The closer the Ad to the Action
> The Better the Chance of a Sale.

(If nothing else it scans!)

9

Is advertising a science?

The answer to the question which heads this chapter is known before we begin. Nevertheless as with the chapter which follows, it is worth pursuing the question for the light the working out of the answer sheds upon the nature of advertising.

The word 'science' is much abused. A strict definition of the word would not comprise many activities possibly more worthy of inclusion than advertising. Alternatively if one adopts the more general adjective 'scientific' then virtually anything may be described in comparative terms. Advertising it could be said is more 'scientific' than pools forecasting or entrail-reading and, against palmistry, it wins hands down.

Chambers, our constant companion, says: '*Science: n. Knowledge. Knowledge ascertained by observation and experiment, critically tested, systematised and brought under general principles.*'

Clearly advertising does not fulfil all these requirements. Clearly however it fulfils some. Advertising has amassed a corpus of knowledge. It's been going long enough. There are 'want' advertisements in Pompeii. Classified advertising, very much as we know it today, is as old as the newspaper. Display advertising, however, is barely a century old. But time enough to have assembled a body of facts from which to draw conclusions and material enough to afford innumerable opportunities for experiment. Indeed, observation and experiment are happening continuously. It would be ludicrous to suppose otherwise.

So far so good. What about: '*critically tested, systematised and brought under general principles?*'

Advertising is tested – and critically. But within limits. It is almost impossible to isolate an advertisement, to examine the working of an advertisement as if in a laboratory. Research has yet to come up with a valid method of testing advertising in either a market place or a simulated situation. Many research companies will provide commercial devices for testing but will not claim much above minor successes. The researcher says, with the humility of the scientist, that given A, then B, in circumstance C. It would be nice to repeat the experiment, exactly to replicate it at a later date in another place. But it's extremely difficult to set up, and the outcome is seldom the same : the researcher simply cannot eliminate the variables. It has been estimated that in a normal marketing situation as many as fifty factors can affect the sale of a product. Advertising is merely one. Even in a controlled simulated situation, an isolated test market for example, or a far stricter test such as those conducted in a theatre or a room off a shopping centre, the intrusive elements are numerous and distracting. Moreover, the more laboratory-like the environment, the more artificial the situation and the more suspect the results. Many pre-test findings have blown up when the real world has replaced that of the pre-test.

You can test everything and then find you've got it wrong. You can try to discover cause and effect and then, come the day, you don't know which is which, whether the attitude produced the sale or the sale produced the attitude ; which came first, the chicken or the egg on your face.

There was this actor . . . He was resting. He'd been out of a job for six months when one day he read in the local paper that a company was putting on a play about Abraham Lincoln. Since he was tall and thin he reckoned he stood a good chance of getting the part. So he read the play, learned the part, visited the library, mugged up all he could on Lincoln, grew a beard. He went to a costumier and got fitted out with a frock coat, narrow

c

black trousers and boots. The great day arrived. He went to the audition.

He didn't get the part but on the way home he got assassinated.

When even a small scale test is no guarantee of actual market place behaviour, to wish for a general universal law of how advertising works is to cry for the moon. As we have stated *ad nauseam*, the supreme fact of this business is that nobody knows how it works. Worse still we have no accepted model of the advertising process against which to plan our activities.

Advertising people have only recently begun to admit their ignorance. What sounded like heresy in the early 1960s has become received dogma, and scores of admen are standing up to proclaim it. But the fact that we have no general theory should not prevent us from discovering – but spur us to discover – all we can about particular instances, to use research pragmatically ... to help us make better advertisements. But with our current state of 'critical testing' we are far from a situation of 'systematised' knowledge. Isolated pieces we may have. But not a coordinated whole. There is no corpus of general principles. Or rather none that bears with it a universal truth.

Advertising will never be a science until it can predict – for prediction is the fundamental characteristic of a science. At the present moment no known method of research can guarantee that an advertisement will work – or that it won't. All it can do is isolate certain areas and indicate probable consequences of our action. It can with hindsight discern cause and effect – and then it often gets it wrong as subsequent attempts to replicate have shown. Nevertheless in its attempts to abstract – to perceive common qualities from different things and form from them a general idea ... in its attempts to seek proofs – to argue from premises to a conclusion, no matter how unsuccessful the outcome, it must qualify as a science of sorts, an inexact science. No more. But that's something.

After all 'sciences' more respectable are hardly more exact: social sciences – sociology and psychology for example – are notably inexact and I would guess for the same reason namely that, like advertising, they deal with human behaviour. And behaviour is not predictable. Not universally. Furthermore, advertising is essentially a changing business. Its keyword is new.

It creates its own malign environment. It stimulates a fashion-conscious society and itself suffers from the whims and irrationalities of that fickle god to which it is dedicated. The graveyards of manufacturers are littered with products which failed because they were behind the times – or too far ahead.

But if the central area of advertising – how it works – is no more than an inexact science, what of the outer area? Surely media, the planning of which medium to choose for your advertising message and with what frequency, has of recent years acquired the status of a science? After all much of this is now done by computer! And in a subsidiary way media is something of a science. Making the most of a given amount of money (or appropriation) so that it is spent against the optimum number of relevant respondents, potential consumers . . . all this can be done 'scientifically'.

But there are two factors – clear and incontrovertible – which serve to deny media its status as a science. The first is that media decisions can never be made without the exercise of judgment. To decide between impact and frequency, between the relative effect of, say, an advertisement measuring 11 inches across three columns and one taking a half page, between either of these and a fifteen second television commercial, to decide how often to repeat the same advertisement, when to change, whether to alternate a group of commercials or to run them consecutively, whether to carry the identical message in two different media or use one to complement or supplement the other . . . all these are judgmental decisions.

The second factor – as the preceding will have indicated – is the impossibility of detaching the medium from the message. It is patently absurd to talk of impact and frequency without reference to what is being transmitted, as if laws for duration of a campaign or superiority of one medium (or size) over another can be determined *in vacuo*. And since we have seen that the science of message-making is at best inexact, the related science of media must also be inexact, as must all the surrounding 'sciences' – marketing, campaign planning, merchandising.

Nevertheless, there is an area of advertising where the term 'science' can be used with less of one's tongue in one's cheek.

Where observation and experiment are part of the job and a systematised corpus of knowledge has resulted in some general principles. I refer, of course, to direct response advertising, to the 'sharp end' of the continuum. The closer the advertisement to the action, the greater the chance of the sale or, as one might put it, the more scientific the job.

Although today the advertising community as a whole admits its ignorance of advertising's mechanism, such reticence is not universal and many workers, card carrying members of a particular party, follow as rigid a set of operating procedures as those found in any factory. It must be stressed, though, that adherence to dogma varies according to the type of advertising the agency is primarily engaged in. It is obviously more likely to have a systematic approach to all its advertising if in fact a large proportion of its revenue comes from direct response advertising (e.g. recruitment). 'Systems' exist and models of the advertising process (though probably not graced with the name 'model') are as old as advertising itself.

Presumably the earliest advertisers saw no problem. They branded their goods and therefore their prime task was to make sure that people remembered their name (either their own or a 'brand' name). If the alternative to a branded product was simply an unbranded product sold loose, for example, their advertising task was not too difficult. When competition came about (i.e. between two branded products) then competitive advertising also came about. Nevertheless the importance of branding was still paramount. It was essential to make sure that it was your name and not your competitor's which was remembered. Particularly if you were making similar claims. Despite the fact that the earliest advertisers had things a lot easier than today (fewer competitors and fewer restrictions upon what they could say or where they could say it) it is, nevertheless, undeniable that the factors which they had to take into consideration, the criteria by which they judged their work, rough and ready rules of thumb though they were, are not much different from today. This proves either that progress in advertising simply doesn't exist or that there are some eternal verities which we ignore at our peril. Or both!

I was recently given a copy of a textbook issued by the International Correspondence School to accompany its course on advertising. Published in 1913 it makes as much sense (with less jargon) as the majority of textbooks which have appeared subsequently. One work published ten years later deservedly became a classic. It was written by Claude Hopkins then president of a US agency, Lord and Thomas, the most fertile seedbed in the history of advertising. He wrote it as an advertisement for his agency. It ran to 20,000 words, several editions, a major re-publication in 1952 and was called simply and assuredly *Scientific Advertising*. It began with the words: 'The time has come when advertising has in some hands reached the status of a science.'

Hopkins' theories were based on his life's work which was largely in mail order. As Martin Mayer wrote in *Madison Avenue U.S.A.*,

It was mail order which demonstrated to sceptical manu-facturers that it really paid to advertise; you could see the results. You put your ad in the paper, telling people to clip the coupon and send it with a dollar if they wanted the advertised product. Then you counted the arriving coupons and dollars, subtracted the costs of manufacturing, shipping and advertising, and banked your profit. Or put it into more advertising.

A similar procedure has been followed by Augustus Barnett in the past year. A two-man wine and spirits company, it has made tremendous inroads into the profits of its old established competitors by cutting costs and recouping them by the sheer volume of sales. The advertisements are small, crammed with prices, and frequent. Augustus Barnett's annual advertising appropriation is in the region of a quarter of a million pounds.

Augustus Barnett would unhesitatingly agree with the logical conclusion of Hopkins' credo: 'You cost advertisements as you cost salesmen – by results. A copywriter should write as a salesman speaks. Advertisements should not amuse, because salesmen do not. Advertisements equal salesmen.'[1] There have been several new teachers since Hopkins but, disagree as they may with some

---

[1] Quoted by Maurice Smelt in *What Advertising Is*, p. 43.

of his dogma, none to my knowledge has overthrown his basic tenets.

The seekers after, and imparters of, wisdom can be loosely divided into two categories: creative practitioners and researchers. In the first category are such luminaries as Rosser Reeves (the USP or Unique Selling Proposition), David Ogilvy (the Brand Image), John Caples ('Tested Advertising Methods'), Bill Bernbach (whose philosophy can be more easily recognised than defined and is something he himself has never codified into a technique let alone a dogma). In the second category are numerous research and marketing men (Ernest Dichter, Daniel Starch, Harry Henry among them) who have got within walking distance of the holy grail and have a few blurred snapshots to prove it.

Of the two categories of thinkers it is the former I believe which has made the more practical and lasting contribution. As a so-called creative man I may be accused of bias. However, if you were to question advertising men and watch them *in medias res*, you would undoubtedly detect methods of approach which owe more to the creative than the research influence.

Both parties are put under the microscope by Dr Timothy Joyce in an article published in the Esomar volume 'The Market Researcher looks at the Way in which Advertising Works.' 'What', asks Dr Joyce '*do* we know about the way in which advertising works?' Before he comes to his answer ('very little') he reviews all the various theories and attempts to discern what they have in common. And though we may feel that advertising has outgrown some of these simplistic theories and that subsequent research has questioned their relevance, nevertheless one thing they do have in common is an appeal to common sense. It is their very basic quality which has made them endure among those people in the industry who are concerned about such matters. Unfortunately, as I have pointed out elsewhere, they are in the minority. If a creative man knocks a model of the advertising process at least it signifies that he has heard of it (to some of them the concept of knocking models has other connotations) but I am more disposed to accept his iconoclasm if he has something to put in its place. Here then are some of the models which Dr Joyce reviews.

There is the theory of Dr Daniel Starch who instituted a celebrated technique of rating advertisements. He said that an advertisement must be

● Seen
● Read
● Remembered
● Acted upon

There is the Dagmar model. These are the initial letters of a book published by the Association of National Advertisers in the 1960s, *Defining Advertising Goals for Measuring Advertising Results*. The book was required reading. It endeavoured to make advertising 'accountable'. The central foundation of its philosophy was the assumption shared by all these models, that attitudes influence sales. If you could research the market and determine attitudes and subsequently alter those attitudes in a desired direction, sales would follow. You could moreover, measure both the shift in attitude and the shift in sales and draw some sort of conclusion. If one accepts that attitudes do influence sales (and I am inclined to, though it is by no means proved) one is still faced with these problems: identifying the attitude you believe is key; connecting its shift with that in sales; and finally paying for the whole exercise. Accountability was all the rage among the full-service agencies until somebody said 'Who pays?' and, with the advertiser saying understandably, 'Look, buster, you're the expert – why should we subsidise you to see if you know what you're doing?', the rage subsided as quickly as it had come. But the overreaction against Dagmar was as radical as the claims made for it. Looked at a decade later the book deserves commendation for its insistence on exact terminology and its lucid analyses of the *component parts* of a communication process which had until then in the main been regarded as an entity.

It was about this time that the phrase 'marketing mix' entered advertising's language, an advertisement being only one constituent of a complex mixture, the number of whose ingredients was many and their proportion infinitely varied.

The author of 'Dagmar', Russell Colley, was keen to distinguish objectives from goals. To demand of an advertisement that it sell the product was wishful thinking. Equally to demand of an advertising campaign that it capture a predetermined share of the market may seem like an advance in thinking (or semantics) but in reality takes us very little further. A specific increase in sales is a long-term marketing objective.

What then is an advertising goal? His definition:

● *An advertising goal is a specific communication task to be accomplished against a defined audience to a given degree in a given period of time.*

It is concerned *solely* with the small changes that occur in mental attitude and behaviour as a direct result of advertising.

The best way of explaining an advertising goal is to invent an example. Let's suppose you manufacture Bloggo. You conduct market research and discover that of people under thirty-five only 12 per cent are regular users of Bloggo. You decide to attempt to increase that to 22 per cent. That would be a marketing objective. Let's suppose also that you have conducted attitude research and have discovered that people under thirty-five regard Bloggo as an old-fashioned product. This you believe is responsible for its low volume of sales in this age group. You decide therefore to attempt to change the group's attitude. You decide to increase awareness of Bloggo as a young person's product from a present score of 18 to 40 per cent within six months. This would be a specific advertising goal.

Now the pseudo-science of this imaginary exercise begs two questions. First, the simple advertising one of what happens to your existing (middle-aged) consumers who represent your strength while you do a face lift or whatever? Second, and more to our immediate subject, *how do you know* that the shift in attitude regarding modernity is the key factor? How do you know that the statistical link between that particular factor and sales among the under thirty-fives is in fact also a causal link? The answer of course is that you don't – not until you try it. You have a good idea that it may be so, and while the majority of the people in the business are working in the dark you at least have the

benefit of twilight. Nevertheless, the decision to adopt the strategy
(of going after the under thirty-fives with a modern image) is a
judgmental one, as it was, you may remember when earlier in this
chapter we discussed media decisions.

Dagmar, despite its flaws and the problems it raised, was an
attempt to bring sanity and clarity to a confused area. Marketing
men, growing more and more appalled at the spiralling cost of
failure are still seeking, if not the philosopher's stone, then his
calipers. They want figures. The writer has his words, the artist,
pictures: the marketing man, scores. And in the 1960s there were
enough people to provide them. The Dagmar model on which
all its assumptions were based differs little from that of Starch.
The steps are

- Awareness
- Comprehension
- Conviction
- Action

From Dagmar to another set of initials: AIDA. It's not certain
who first coined this term (apart that is from Guiseppe Verdi).
This model assumes the following progression. A successful
advertisement must provide the following reaction from the
consumer

- Attention
- Interest
- Desire
- Action

(Incidentally I too have had a go. I believe that what we do is
as follows: We must: Gather Opinions; Test Theories; Eliminate;
Research; Diagnose; Analyse; Measure; Meditate; Evaluate;
Repeat Until Negatives Gone. Which spells GOTTERDAMMERUNG
– a far better opera!)

All these theories have two things in common. First, they all
incorporate the word ACTION. Second, they are all 'linear-
sequential'.

Dr Joyce's anthology is both useful and amusing but he is the first to admit that one can draw little comfort – and no mind-expanding conclusion – from his study. He concludes his review by constructing a model based on hypotheses common to all the other models he examined:

Advertising – Reaction   – Attitude – Purchasing – Sale
             to   to   of
             advertising product   product

These are what Dr Joyce calls 'minimum assumptions'.

His model makes sense but, as he goes on to show, it isn't that simple. For not only does attitude influence purchase but, as you will know from your own experience as consumers, purchase also influences attitude. For example, notice how much attention you pay to advertisements for the car you have already purchased and how, once having bought something, your attitude towards that item has become modified.

To return to *Chambers*'s definition of science. When you consider the list of variables and imponderables which even this cursory study of the subject has thrown up you may also throw up your hands. How can you hope to make sure that all your careful efforts will result in sales? How can all this be reduced to a straight-forward cause and effect situation? How can all this activity be systematised and brought under general principles? But to give up is a counsel of despair. To accept that advertising can never be a science is one thing: to deny that it shouldn't try is something quite other.

Creative people who attack research *en bloc* are fighting a past war. It is a meaningless exercise. The arrogance with which they assert that research cannot help them bespeaks a vanity which paradoxically research can help them enjoy! Thankfully this attitude is far less common than it was. Today the excesses on both sides have been eliminated. There is less polarisation of posture. The creative man and researcher work together. Here is Gerald de Groot, Director of Research at Lintas, commenting on the dilemma (and incidentally pointing up the paradox) in words which must surely elicit a favourable response from creative people everywhere:

> You could argue that research can offer no help in making decisions about advertising and that therefore you should not really try to assess the effectiveness of individual advertisements at all. This may be so but what is the logical conclusion? If you make no attempt to assess the effectiveness of advertisements, it follows from a business point of view that all you need do is fill the media space most efficiently at the lowest possible cost. In other words, ignore completely what is generally referred to as the 'quality' of advertising. Almost by definition creative people would not accept this. Their very *raison d'être* is based on the principle that quality does count. As soon as a concept of quality is introduced, this means that someone somewhere is making judgments which are, at least implicitly, about the effectiveness of individual advertisements.[1]

The central core of our activities is creative. The basic decisions are judgmental. The results of our work depend on human behaviour.

Thus advertising can never be a science.

But if you are in advertising and accept our working definition, if you believe in advertising's role in the economy, if at the end of the day you want to feel that you have helped the man who pays your salary (i.e. the client) by at least pointing him in the right direction ... then you'll have to try to make it a science.

---

[1] *What Advertising Is*, p. 161.

10

Is advertising an art?

We shall spend much less time on this since clearly while there is every reason for advertising to try to become a science there is no reason whatever for it to aspire to becoming an art.

Again, to start with *Chambers*: '*Art:* n. *Application of skill to production of beauty especially visible beauty and works of creative imagination, as the "Fine Arts"*.'

There are other meanings. I have chosen this definition in preference to others since it more closely corresponds to the sense which most people adopt when contrasting it with science. Art can simply mean 'cunning' or 'artifice' or 'knack', but though these undoubtedly play a part in creation, they are not the whole of it.

There are many reasons for calling advertising an art, all of them superficial. The first, I suppose, goes something like this: since advertising is demonstrably not a science it must be an art. But then the same could be said for stewed rhubarb. The second reason we have met already: art it must be since advertising is concerned with human behaviour and no science is capable of finite measurement in prediction of human behaviour. Advertising to people must forever be an art. But in this context the word 'art' is used in that other sense of 'knack' and though undoubtedly there is a knack in doing it well, as with playing cricket or 'Chopsticks', to call it such is really to beg the question. The use of the word 'art' in this sense is restrictive.

A third reason has more claim on our attention. The trade of advertising employs the skills and tools of artists. And it does them the honour or, possibly, disservice of retaining the terminology. Every agency has its artists, designers, writers. There are studios for the artists (though surprisingly the writers work not in studies but in offices). They use brush and paint, pen and paper, prepare their materials, produce or commission artwork, assemble words and images, create films, edit, direct . . . anything art can do, advertising does. Or rather, advertising *makes use of* and that, as we shall see, is rather different and the whole point.

A fourth reason for calling advertising an art is worthy of more attention. Advertising's works are often artistic. Victorian advertisers often used existing art, pop paintings of the period, such as Millais's *Bubbles* in Pears Soap.[1]

Even when advertising ceased to borrow (or, as some would have it, plunder) art, some indigenous pieces possessed a distinctive merit and both originals and prints find their way into serious collections today, as was proved at an exhibition of advertising art at Sotheby's a few years ago. Whether the value is intrinsic or curiosity, whether the collection of early advertising equates with that of genuine art or old picture postcards, it would be hard to say. Certainly much of it is no more than quaint and mildly amusing. As fashions go and come, interest grows and diminishes, prices rise and fall, what was just 'bad' becomes endearing, camp or even high camp.

But, is it art? In the 1930s, advertising art was regarded as a genuine blood relation to proper art. A term was coined which has lost currency, more's the pity: 'commercial art'. The great asset of this now discarded phrase is that it points up in no uncertain way what the job is all about, its commercial purpose. However, one of the dangers of this positioning of art and commercial art, unashamedly side by side, was the frequency of the no-passport excursions which took place across its border.

---

[1] It was the advertiser not the artist who added the tablet of soap.

Leading artists were working in both territories at the same time, for love in one, for money in the other, and it is my conviction that the distinguishing characters of the two activities were often blurred. There were artists who consciously adopted a more commercial technique and attitude when designing ads. They would admit to prostituting their art. But if this attitude is somewhat less than endearing it is certainly more honest than the opposing one which insisted that advertising was an art, that the border didn't in fact exist.

When art came to advertising between the wars, a significant part of the advertising fraternity, this ill-regarded sector of the community, saw salvation. Here was a chance to be respectable. They were artists like the real artists with whom they rubbed shoulders. They worked in studios and kept the same hours (often irregular). They wore the same clothes and sought inspiration. They joined the same clubs. There were patrons, too. Large companies who 'salved their conscience' by commissioning advertisements. These had little to do with the business of selling. They were illustrations of landscapes or cities, of flowers and trees. Occasionally there was some tenuous link with the advertiser but, more often than not, he was little more than a benefactor. Someone referred to the walls of the London Underground as a poor man's art gallery. How nice. How grateful we all were. Perhaps our gratitude would manifest itself in sales. And of course it would, always provided we could first remember the name of the product and devise from the advertisement a possible benefit which purchase of that produce could confer.

This art-in-advertising attitude persisted after the war, extended into the early 1950s. Shortage of goods possibly helped to lengthen its life. When real competition returned the business became more businesslike and there was less pretension towards art. Nevertheless there is still evidence of it today, except that the border has changed. The crossover occurs at a different point, namely film – by which I mean the filmed television commercial. I think there is a direct analogy between the situation of the advertising commercial director/producer today and that of the advertising art director of the prewar and immediate postwar period.

Here again the same person does both. Here again there is a community of interest, an exchange of technique and, above all, a mutual education. Just as the Bauhaus said much about art in general by approaching it from, among other aspects, the commercial one of display and industrial design, so the discipline of the television commercial has brought its own lessons to bear upon the art of film. Many of today's leading directors owe a debt to the commercial which isn't simply financial. They've learned what can be done in short time lengths and what can't, or rather needn't, be said or shown. The public has learned. They can take quick cuts, unrelated transitions, direct addresses to camera, voice-overs. Many techniques which were regarded as bad filming in 1955 are today standard practice. The language of the cinema has become terser, more elliptical. The necessary conventions of a decade ago serve little purpose today.

The interchange of people and ideas in the business of film could confuse us into thinking that advertising is as much an art form as the cinema, just as our other examples could align it with painting or design. But the fact that the two jobs use identical skills, techniques and tools does not make the occupations identical. Any professional advertising writer with an uncompleted novel in his drawer appreciates this fact when he turns from one task to the other. There are poets working in agencies, and very good copywriters they make, but though the skills and techniques may correspond the difference between the two tasks is fundamental. Exactly what is this difference?

Leibniz describes the appreciation of a work of art. He says it produces a peculiar satisfaction. 'No rational process of thought occurs but rather an intuitive apprehension.' The satisfaction is aesthetic. It pleases. How it happens is hardly relevant. *That* it happens is crucial. Asked to judge a work of art this intuitive apprehension is uppermost.

On the other hand, asked to judge an advertisement an 'intuitive apprehension' is by no means the most important reaction asked of us. The fact that we like it is of less weight than *why* we like it. We must give reasons. But even so, to explain why *we* like it may be irrelevant unless in so doing we explain why *other* people like it – if like is what we want them to do. Maybe it is, but probably it isn't. For what we want them to do is not to react aesthetically but to change, or be strengthened in, an attitude. So when faced with a work of 'advertising art' we ask ourselves not the simple question 'Do I like it?' but 'Do I think the audience to whom this work is addressed will respond in the required way – i.e. be moved to buy the product?' This is not intuitively apprehended. It demands a rational process of thought. The same reasoning powers are called for as in science.

Now I won't deny that advertising can be *created* intuitively. Hunch, inspiration, 'flair' – all play an important part in the creation of advertising. In fact the danger today is that we are discounting their contribution, with the result that advertising has a depressing sameness. But despite the fact that advertising can be created intuitively it must be subjected to critical analysis, and that is *not* intuitive.

The difference between art and advertising art – as must surely be plain by now – concerns function. Art must move. It arouses passions, opens eyes, reveals truths, stimulates concern, inspires, elevates, purges, intoxicates . . . its functions are many. But its purpose? Need it have one? No. Aesthetic satisfaction is an end in itself. Not that men have not been moved to action by art. They have been and will be. But eventual action is not essential to its nature.

Advertising on the other hand cannot afford the luxury of aesthetic satisfaction for its own sake. Ads are not designed to decorate walls or newspapers, though they may do so incidentally. Ads are designed to sell goods, or more realistically, to aid the process of selling goods. The adman – as all of us – likes being liked, is pleased if his work is appreciated, but the real criteria by which his work will be judged will be sales of the product whose worth he is advocating. The aesthetic context of his ad may win plaudits from the public but unless it also wins sales he has failed. Repeated failure and he's out of a job.

There's a very famous quotation about rhetoric (and advertising). Here's Adlai Stevenson quoting it at Los Angeles in 1960: 'Do you remember that in classical times when Cicero had finished speaking, the people said, "How well he spoke" – but when Demosthenes had finished speaking, the people said, "Let us march"?' There's the basic difference between advertising and art. And how often it's forgotten or wantonly ignored! Art is an end in itself: art-in-advertising is a means to an end.

11

The funnel . . . or a model, would you believe?

So far we have described advertising as 'an activity conducted by people who cannot agree upon a definition of what they are doing, the result of whose labours is submitted to others who are ill-equipped to judge it'. And have defined it for the benefit of the people above as:

● *The origination and/or communication of ideas about products in order to motivate people towards purchase*

We have looked at what advertising is not and have, I hope, thereby learned something about what it is.

Advertising is not a science – but an inexact science. It is not an art – but a bastard art. And since what science there is happens before the creative man gets to work (research, analysis of the problem, media planning, etc.) and after he has finished (more analysis, of the result, and research into the effect upon behaviour) then one could describe the business of advertising as:

● *A bastard art in the middle of an inexact science*

I first used this phrase publicly in a speech at an Advertising Association seminar at the Royal Garden Hotel.

A bastard art in the middle of an inexact science. Put like that advertising sounds just the occupation for a charlatan, opportunist, or failed academic. And today I am addressing you as all three.

The national press were there. The *Guardian* quoted me considerably out of context and minus my tone of voice. This was then picked up by the radio programme 'A Word in Edgeways' and three distinguished figures proceeded to criticise advertising, its charlatans, opportunists and failed academics.

This chapter will position the bastard art in relation to the inexact science, combining both in a model of the advertising process. It will not attempt to describe how advertising works: it will merely illustrate how advertising is produced, the stages gone through and the peculiar qualities involved. It may be a bit pretentious to refer to it as a model. When I first devised it I called it a chart or a diagram. Then the sophisticated term was visual aid. Now, to keep up, I refer to it shamefacedly as a model. Here, as if you need it, is further proof of the theory that the only changes in the advertising business are semantic.

It is a model based on experience and observation. It reflects the situation which exists in most advertising agencies today. It is true but it is not the whole truth. A later chapter is devoted to demolishing it, which you may regard as evidence of the author's scientific detachment, indecision or incipient schizophrenia.

Look at the illustration on page 74. An advertisement is a communication between two people. On the left, the manufacturer. On the right, the consumer. And the thing between them that looks like a funnel? This is called . . . a funnel.

Each advertisement is in fact a communication between the manufacturer and a *single* consumer. A lot of bad advertising results from treating consumers *en masse*, from regarding them as a body without individuality. Even though advertising communicates with a 'mass audience' it does so *one at a time*. You are less likely to write a compelling advertisement when your audience is seen as a grey mass. To come face to face with a single consumer, a sentient being, to imagine him (or her) in the round, is to improve your chances of making your message relevant and *personal.* An old trick – much beloved of creative directors when dealing with a subordinate – is to ask him how, face to face with a potential consumer, he would persuade her to buy the product. What arguments, what words, what gestures would he use? What questions would he expect in response and how would he, in turn, counter them?

The funnel is a two-way funnel. It emphasises the importance of 'feedback'. Through the funnel left to right the manufacturer speaks to the consumer. He does this through advertising.

But it is not by any means the only method of communicating open to him. Messages about the product bombard the consumer in many other ways. For example, the package says something

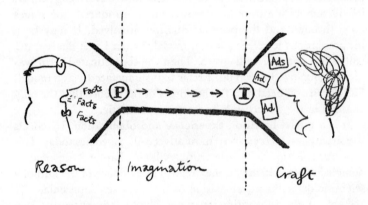

about the product. So does the price. So does the type of store which stocks it. So does its place on the shelf. So does the type of consumer whom our consumer sees consuming it. So may the behaviour of the manufacturing company – how its *other* products perform, how it treats its workers, even how the manufacturer treats his wife and children. Public relations, the transmission of the company's non-advertising communication to its public, clearly is important in this respect. And finally the loudest message of all is that delivered by the product itself ... PERFORMANCE.

Through the funnel right to left the consumer speaks to the manufacturer. She does this through research. We have already seen that market research is the message from the consumer telling the manufacturer if she buys and how often and where and in what quantities and when; and that attitude research is the message somewhat less direct telling him what she thinks of it, why she doesn't buy it and, with luck, why she does – and maybe why she is what she is.

There is another form of research which is more specifically concerned with the creative aspect of advertising: advertisement research. This provides a feedback of information concerned with the consumer's attitude, not to the product but to the way that product is or perhaps will be advertised. Advertisements are shown to the consumer in draft or finished form and the consumer reacts. This is as important an operation as it is delicate to perform. There are some major problems. First the situation is artificial. Advertisements are never seen in real life in anything like the same way. There is an examination room quality about the whole exercise. Careful deception has to be practised by the researcher – but even so the respondent is no mug and she realises that the interviewer isn't simply passing the time of day. The second snag is that respondents are put into a position of advertising experts. The last thing you want them to do – and unfortunately the first thing they want to do – is to pontificate on the advertising.

The consumer also speaks to the manufacturer by writing to him, either to complain about the product or its lack of availability or, more frequently, by completing a coupon or entering a competition. And of course she also speaks to him by buying or not buying the product. Just as the loudest message left to right is performance, so the loudest message right to left is . . . PURCHASE.

Sometimes the silence is deafening.

Our concern in this chapter is left to right. What goes into the funnel at the manufactuer's end? A lot of facts. About the product, the consumer, the competition, the market, packaging, pricing, methods of distribution, merchandising, and a great deal more. History, sociology, economics, psychology . . . these are some of the disciplines called in to help. These facts form the basis for the marketing and advertising decisions.

These facts are sifted, weighed, *weighted* by the advertising agency team and the client team. Who is on each team and who skippers varies from place to place. You can safely assume, however, that an account director will be in charge rather than a creative man at the agency end and that a 'brand manager' will run the whole show (the agency included) at the client end. Creative people though should be represented in the agency team and should participate in the original thinking. Particularly if you want it to be original.

From these facts we arrive at *P*. *P* in our model stands for Proposition. This is another overworked word and one for which there are several not-quite synonyms. It is perhaps easier to explain what it is not. It is not an idea. It is not a picture. It is not an advertisement. It could be a 'concept', a 'strategic intent', a 'brief' even. The terminology varies even within the same company or agency.

The word 'proposition' (which I'll define my way in a moment) suffers from a plethora of dictionary definitions. 'Premise' will serve. Shakespeare uses it in the sense of 'offer' which is also appropriate. Our friend Chambers defines it as 'the thing proposed' and defines propose as '*to offer for consideration*'. That's not bad. The work leading up to this stage has been concerned with determining what exactly should be offered to the consumer for her consideration. All we need to add is the commercial purpose behind it all.

Thus a proposition is in my book 'that one thing about the product which is offered to the consumer in the belief that it will motivate her to buy it'. In other words, the proposition is *related to a consumer desire*.

But take note that at this stage of the proceedings all we are talking about is a concept. And we have arrived at this concept largely through cold reasoning from established data. Through analysis, knowledge, understanding, common sense. But not, as a rule, through creativity. 'As a rule' because there are occasions when the 'creative' determining of a proposition is the most important contribution of all. Indeed, a whole school of advertising is built on this belief. The USP adherents insist that the really creative work occurs *before* the proposition.

We can't sell a product [Reeves[1] says] 'unless it's a good product and even then we can't sell it unless we can find the
Unique Selling Proposition. There are three rules for USP.
First, you need a definite proposition: buy this product and
you get this specific benefit. Pick up any textbook on advertising
and that's on page one – but everyone ignores it. Then,
second, it must be a unique proposition, one which the
opposition cannot or does not offer. Third, the proposition
must sell. Colgate was advertising 'ribbon dental cream – it
comes out like a ribbon and lies flat on your brush'. Well,
that was a proposition and it was unique, but it didn't sell.
Bates gave them 'cleans your breath while it cleans your teeth'.
Now, *every* dentrifice cleans your breath while it cleans your
teeth – *but nobody had ever put a breath claim on a toothpaste before.*
That USP is eighteen years old now. Using it, Colgate has
had as much as fifty per cent of the whole toothpaste market;
even today, against the toughest kind of competition, Colgate
still has the largest share of market in the toothpaste business.
And every time anybody else advertises that *his* toothpaste
cleans your breath he's really advertising Colgate even though
he doesn't know it.

USPs are found in the first part of the funnel. They come out of
the product (and who's going to knock that?) and once found are
seemingly never let go of. For example, 'Pal Meat for Dogs
Prolongs Active Life, Because it Contains Marrow Bone Jelly.'

One's objections to USP are directed chiefly at those blinkered
disciples who follow, or rather push, it into areas where it does
not belong. Reeves's *Reality in Advertising* is still a stimulating
read but the laws it describes are not universally applicable to all
product areas. The chief objection to USP, and this applies even
in those areas which are more naturally its province, is that it is
in danger of extolling uniqueness at the expense of relevance,
and reason at the expense of imagination. If the only difference
you can find between your product and the competition as far
as product composition is concerned is a minor and irrelevant one,

---

[1] *Madison Avenue U.S.A.*, quoted by Mayer.

do you magnify it or do you turn your attention instead to the manner in which you convey the truth about your product, regardless of the fact that your competitor's product has the same constituent ingredients?

Rosser Reeves claims that what makes his agency different from any other (Bates's own USP as it were) is that it applies reason to advertising. What I take exception to is this denial of the possibility that imagination has a role to play once the proposition has been found. In a world of similar products the creativity with which an identical proposition may be treated may differentiate that product in the consumer's mind, on the shelf and in the sales graph, far more than the playing up of an insignificant uniqueness. I do not criticise the USP disciples for their belief in uniqueness: I simply question their apparent assumption that uniqueness exists only in the proposition and not in the *manner* of its projection.

To return to the funnel. Creative people as we have seen will almost certainly already have been involved in the preliminary work but the determining of P is rarely a creative act. Creativity *starts* with the proposition. It is the job of the creative people to take that proposition and interpret it creatively. To turn the proposition into an advertising idea. To turn P into I.

How this happens we shall attempt to describe in the next chapter. Meanwhile let's complete the model. We've gone from manufacturer through facts to a propositon to an advertising idea. The idea is not yet an advertisement though it may have been conceived in a form closely approximating an advertisement. What happens after the idea has happened is the transmission of that abstract idea to the consumer in the form of physical advertisements.

The funnel is divided into three sections (pre-P; P–I; post-I) because different skills are required (perhaps of the same people!) at these three stages.

- The proposition is arrived at through *reason*.
- P becomes I by the application of *imagination*.
- The idea becomes an advertisement largely as a result of *craft*.

The dividing lines, you will note, are broken since this is no simple relay race, the baton being surrendered for ever at a particular point. Creative people are involved, for example, in the preliminary thinking and they are involved, inevitably, in the writing of copy, the direction of the art, in the mechanics of getting an advertisement, a script, a poster into the shape in which it finally appears. *But* the really creative work happens in the narrow bit of the funnel, when you are turning dead propositions into living ideas. And though the final execution is important and demands hard work, talent and imagination, it calls for none of that white hot intensity which brings into being something which wasn't there before.

This funnel is as accurate a visual representation of what I believe happens in the production of advertising as any I have seen. As such it can help you examine the progress of any job through the agency or the client organisation. More profitably it can be 'overlaid' on your own time sheet and those of your colleagues. If the top creative talent is spending little time in the narrow part of the funnel then something is wrong. If, on the other hand, the successful transforming of P into I is being managed by the junior staff then you had better double their salary before JWT does.

12

The narrow part of the funnel . . . or
the art at the heart of the business

This chapter concentrates on the narrow part of the funnel, the turning of P into I and the relationship between them. The relationship is a subtle and a variable one. For a start, a great proposition may preclude you from needing to seek an idea.

If you are selling brand A considerably cheaper than the very similar brand B, then you almost certainly don't need an idea. In fact you may not need advertising, though it is by no means axiomatic that a significant product advantage precludes the need to advertise. For one thing, advertising allows you to communicate that advantage immediately, comprehensively, graphically and (particularly in television) demonstrably. For another, although you may enjoy a product advantage at launch, your lead time over competition may be very slight. Thus to launch primarily on the basis of P could mean trouble if the competition launches $P+$ when you have no I: or launches $P =$ by means of an I.

But usually the world we are concerned with is the tough world not of major competitive advantages but of small though significant differences. Differences which the advertising seeks to *intensify*. Competing brands may have virtually identical compositions – and, for very good reasons, virtually identical propositions. Differentiation, the establishment of a clearly defined identity, is a function of the idea. Often the idea is the *only* differentiation. But not always (cf. USP). Also there is the means by which you present your message, media selection: and, more significantly, the particular stance you choose to adopt for your product in both the consumer's mind and the market place. These two aspects will be dealt with more closely in the chapter on Identity.

You will notice that the creative (P to I) is the most concentrated part of the funnel. This is no accident. The preliminary work has intensified our thinking, crystallised it into one expression of intent (P). Furthermore, it has provided a strict discipline. For, above all, an idea must be not only novel but *relevant!* The discipline is provided by the brief (the requisition or start-work-order) which states the proposition with strict limitations. It also requests its interpretation by a fixed date – another discipline. Now this discipline is not just a business necessity, an administrative necessity, it is also a creative necessity. Discipline provides not a prison but a stimulus. Of course it's a limitation. As the sonnet form is to the poet, the frame to the painter, the two-dimension screen to the film director. But the artist's job is to *exploit* his limitations not surrender to them!

In advertising a creative man unrestricted by an open brief *may* come up with the answer. It is moreover possible that his answer could change the whole nature of the problem, not to mention the product. The possibilities which that opens are looked at towards the end of this book. However, in the normal agency routine such activity is 90 per cent of the time a luxury. Moreover, discipline not only provides a positive creative stimulus, it also helps the creative people in a negative way by setting up a system by which their ideas cannot be rejected for reasons they knew nothing about when they started.

Exactly what the difference is between P and I we shall attempt to discover by analysing several advertisements and inducing certain characteristics. Before then, though, what *happens* in the narrow bit of the funnel?

I *think* this: The creative man looks at the proposition and then works *backwards*, re-examining all the facts which have helped the team arrive at *P*. He will almost certainly also look at other facts: this is fine provided that he bears *P* in mind. Secondly, he searches among those facts for *relationships*. Relationships which have not so far been recognised and which are therefore *original*. The second stage may be a conscious act. The actual discovery, however, may *not*. If he is totally immersed in the problem, the solution (i.e. the original relationship) will rise to the surface seemingly *without conscious effort*. Spontaneously. Maybe while shaving (which may sound like a cliché but some of my best ideas happen in the bathroom: one of them paid for a week's holiday for two in Moscow which is not bad for ten minutes' effortless endeavour – and another story). The act is more likely to be spontaneous for the simple reason that your unconscious mind has a free rein and makes associations which might not be made by your conscious mind. Might in fact be rejected by it. Anyway, consciously or unconsciously, associations happen, and, with luck, one of these relationships will produce an idea. (Not all relationships are original. Not all original relationships are ideas. Not all ideas are worth having let alone printing. However . . .)

The idea is the imaginative expression of this relationship. The advertisement provides the form. The form the expression takes will depend largely on the person having the idea and the requirements of the brief. It should never be taken for granted that the expression will automatically be verbal. It is for this reason that I prefer to use the term creative man rather than copywriter, unless I am referring specifically to words.

What is the job of the creative man? To turn *P* into *I*. *P* was reached through a process of reasoning. *P* becomes *I* by the application of imagination. *I* is *P* 'once more mit feeling'. It is the feeling, the emotion, which the individual creative mind brings to the proposition which turns it into an idea – and, differentiates *I* from other identical propositions.

We mentioned earlier two matched samples of executives reaching the same conclusion and two matched samples of creative men reaching very different conclusions. One may go further. Reject the executive's conclusion and ask him to reconsider it and, if his thinking is right and he is strongminded, he will come up with the same answer. On the other hand, reject the creative man's solution, ask him to reconsider and, unless he is overly stubborn, he will produce a totally different answer. He may be happier with the earlier work but the chances are that he now favours the second attempt. Push your luck and ask him for a third interpretation and you may get it. Then ask a different creative man to have a go . . . ask a different agency . . . and so forth . . . and you begin to realise the complexity of the decision problem which the client has to solve. How does he know that the solution is the correct one? He does not. What he may find easier to solve is the question: which of these two solutions is better? One method of solving that is to apply the continuum.

Another is pre-testing, advertisement research. There are pragmatic rules of thumb which may be applied. But faced with *one* idea (maybe one which has survived the qualifying rounds of earlier comparison with other ideas) how does the client begin to judge?

We need to go back. The agency team has worked with the client team. After a while they agree on a strategy. The strategy either is, or is part of, the marketing plan, it determines the target audience, the long term objectives possibly, the short term goals undoubtedly . . . and what the advertising campaign is supposed to do. The proposition is part of this. If this sounds vague it merely reflects a far from uniform situation. No two companies work in exactly the same way and the terminology is ambiguous. There are marketing strategies, media strategies, creative strategies, merchandising strategies. Within a creative strategy you can have a thing called a copy platform. Procter & Gamble had a very good three paragraph 'strategy document' which concentrated the mind wonderfully. The three points are, in fact, answers to questions:

1. What do we want to tell the particular audience?

2. What is our justification for the claim we are making in (1)?

3. What is the *tone* of the advertising?

This can be summed up as:

● Claim
● Reason-why
● Tone

as good an aide-memoire as any: it won't write the advertisement for you, nor will it judge it. In the hands of the wrong people it can stifle creativity. But used wisely it can make sure that the basics are being observed.

Creative people are fairly relaxed about strategies. They allow the executive his moment of importance. They accept the odd subordinate clause which tactfully acknowledges the contribution of one particular member of the committee: they look simply for the claim and the reason-why. They want to know 'what are we saying?' and 'what do we base it on?' They know that if they can transmit *that* in a striking and original way the subordinate clauses in the strategy document become *very* subordinate.

The trouble with the word 'claim' is that it is a manufacturer's word. Strategies used to begin with the statement: 'We shall aim to convince all housewives between 18 and 35 . . .' Some avoided such selectivity: 'We shall aim to convince *all* housewives . . .' Some avoided all reticence: 'We shall convince . . .'

The so-called 'marketing revolution' (something which happened more in textbooks than in the real world) switched the emphasis from the manufacturer to the consumer. Things weren't simply made and customers found to buy them. Instead consumer needs and desires were studied and products were made to meet *them*. Marketing had become consumer-orientated rather than manufacturer-orientated. Consequently strategies were phrased from the recipient's point of view. Not 'what do we tell them?' but 'what do we want them to believe?'. This is far more than a semantic switch. It can affect the whole approach of the advertisement, particularly the mood, the delivery and the wording of the 'claim'.

'Claim' is an off-putting word. It smacks of bombast (e.g. *de*claim) and deceit. 'Benefit', another word taken from insurance, is more consumer-orientated. However, it doesn't matter too much how the overall strategy is worded provided that the central proposition is firmly rooted in a consumer desire. If that happens then the idea (and the advertisement which expresses the idea) will put the consumer's interest first. If it doesn't it has gone off strategy. The creative people have been working outside the narrow bit of the funnel.

Thus – to return to the client and his criteria – the first question he has to ask himself about I is 'does it fit P?' Because in one sense I is the same as P. If the client has agreed with the agency's definition of P (and, after all, the client team had helped to determine P) then his assessment of I must be confined strictly within the parameters already imposed.

Indeed, one could go further and say to the client: 'You agreed P. I is the imaginative interpretation of P. Therefore, you will accept I.' Sometimes these words are implied rather than said and creative presentations are accordingly short, the air thick with trust.

I said that in one sense I is the same as P. The fact of the matter is:

● *I is the same as P only different.*

I shall explain this in chapter 14. But before that we shall, with luck, discover what I am talking about as we examine some advertisements, their propositions and their ideas.

13

Proposition to Idea . . . some instances

This chapter looks at several advertisements, at each proposition and idea, and more particularly at the difference between them. At the *characteristics* of the idea. In so doing we shall lift the curtain on the creative process and, if not learn to do it, at least better understand it. If you want to get the most out of this chapter, however, you need to join in, to stop at each proposition and ask yourself how you would interpret it. (A blank plain postcard would be handy both to cover up the text after each proposition and to scribble your creative solution on.)

Exercise A: Löwenbrau

Proposition.

Löwenbrau is very expensive but it is the best quality beer you can buy.

(Note, however, that I have both here and subsequently cut the strategy down to the barest detail. Also I am in most cases post-rationalising the proposition wherever I was not involved in the account. The strategy for Löwenbrau would almost certainly have defined the consumer and his motivation. Nevertheless, for the sake of brevity in this chapter of practical exercises I state merely the essential fact about the product.)

The Löwenbrau proposition gives you little to work on. If there were a 'product plus' – an ingredient, strength or price advantage – an idea would be easier to arrive at. Indeed, in that case *P* could be *I*. If you were launching the first ever German beer on the domestic US market you could simply state that fact. *P* equals *I*. But if you accept that premise in this case you end up with a headline such as:

'Löwenbrau – supreme quality'
or
'Löwenbrau – when only the best will do'
or
'The mark of excellence'

And so on. *Ad nauseam* (which is a good name for this sort of advertisement). Brian Palmer has a favourite all-purpose headline for this proposition. 'Preferred by those who like it best.' It has the merit of sounding impressive and being totally acceptable to Weights and Measures Inspectors.

But to return to the Löwenbrau proposition ... and the idea.

Idea
'WHEN THEY RUN OUT OF LÖWENBRAU ORDER CHAMPAGNE.'

Observations

1. The idea re-presents the proposition. It says that Löwenbrau is a top quality beer without saying 'Löwenbrau is a top quality beer'.

2. The idea is a relationship. The product has been associated with another, more accepted, symbol of quality. The association moreover justifies the price.

D

3. The idea is a reversal of normal thought processes. Instead of the beer being an acceptable alternative to champagne it suggests the reverse. (An interesting comparison can be made with an advertisement for Gold Label – a UK barley wine. Looked at as a beer it is expensive. But the advertiser chooses to associate it with Scotch.

'As strong as a double Scotch – less than half the price.')

Exercise B: Dreft

Proposition

Dreft is a synthetic detergent. Whereas in hard water soap forms lime scum, Dreft does not.

Therefore it does not clog the fibres of delicate fabrics such as wool.

Idea

'DREFT LETS WOOL BREATHE'[1]

Observations

1. The idea re-presents the proposition. $I = P$ (Since all the examples which follow share this characteristic we shall not list it again.)

2. The idea re-presents the proposition in a highly concentrated form. Just four words.

3. A relationship has been perceived (between the fibres of wool and breathing). And note that 'breathe' is not simply an emotive word but an appropriate one when you consider a living fibre such as wool. The association must be relevant otherwise it does not belong inside the narrow part of the funnel.

4. The thought is original. To say that wool breathes is essentially a new thought which an idea ought to be. After all, the word create means 'to bring into being' – something that wasn't there before.

---

[1] The campaign featuring this slogan began in 1961.

5. A reversal has taken place. *P* is essentially the absence of a negative (does not clog fibres). *I* is the positive ('lets wool breathe').

6. Something strange has been made familiar. (Clogging lime scum has become 'lets wool breathe'.)

Exercise C: BOAC VC10

Proposition

BOAC look after their passengers in their special quiet plane.

Idea

TRY A LITTLE VC 10-DERNESS.

Observations

The pun is essentially a relationship. Two thoughts come together in the one word – namely, the new plane and BOAC's care. ('BOAC takes good care of you.')

The BOAC headline is the only one so far which does not mention the name of the 'product'. In my first week in advertising Robert Caplin gave me three rules for headlines:

1. Isolate the consumer.

2. State the name of the product.

3. State benefit use of product confers.

It was many months before I was allowed to show him an advertisement which broke any of those rules. Like most rules they can be broken – but knowingly. And it is only the letter of the law which is broken. The spirit remains intact. When the name of the product is absent from the headline of a good advertisement it either does not need it, the style says who is advertising, the illustration does it for the advertiser, or the uniqueness of the message points to only one possible source. The last is the case with BOAC who were the only airline to fly VC10s across the Atlantic. By concentrating on VC10s BOAC played its strength, a quieter plane uniquely their own. They also flew 707s – almost as many in fact – but they hardly featured in the advertising. Yet somehow the aura of the VC10 rubbed off on to the 707.

An interesting predicament arose when the Jumbo lumbered on to the horizon. How would the VC10-derness airline maintain its identity? The answer is in the advertising now running. However, one advertisement which was rejected did in my opinion come closer to solving the problem. By the time BOAC got the 747 it was no longer a novelty. Pan Am, TWA, Air France and Lufthansa were already flying Jumbos. Thus to scream 'New!' would be a bit silly, not to say out of keeping with the image. The rejected solution was to show the huge aircraft from a low angle (to make it even more enormous) and caption it thus:

'You'll remember the little things.'

This says that BOAC has the Jumbo but also that BOAC is maintaining its standards of customer care. It does so by a reversal – a switch of emphasis. It makes the strange familiar – and thus personalising the claim it says in effect that the airline which gave you the VC10 is bringing all that special service to bear upon the 747. The advertisement which actually ran said:

'All the 747 needed was BOAC service.'

I think this was a mistake. For the simple reason that it represented a major change of mood. It was boastful. It was explicit of course. There was no question of the message not being comprehended immediately. Criticism could be levelled at the VC10-derness type posters (e.g. 'Hush hour travel', 'Slip across the Atlantic on the quiet', 'Love at first flight') that their meaning had to be worked at. And the same 'failing' could be levelled at 'you'll remember the little things'.

Leaving aside for a moment the question of communication and the part played in it by the recipient (see chapter 15) there remains the nature of the message which is so explicitly communicated. The line ('All the 747 needed was BOAC service')

represents not so much an idea as the proposition. The rejected
line ('You'll remember the little things') represents an idea which
means it also re-presents the proposition. They are the same only
different. The difference is one of feeling: the feeling initially of
the creative man for the product, the feeling (which the advertisement transmits) of the airline for its customers.

Exercise D: Birds Eye Sliced Beef

Proposition

Birds Eye Sliced Beef is very good – just as good as cooking a
roast yourself but far less trouble.

Idea

A BIT OF SUNDAY ON WEDNESDAY.
(This line was used in a commercial which showed the product
being served by a housewife to her husband.)

Observations

Here again is a relationship, an analogy. It describes something
in terms of something else. But the really significant fact is the
oblique nature of the communication. What makes this such a
knock-out idea is the route it chooses to take.

What the commercial is communicating in fact is – what else?
– the proposition, namely that Birds Eye Sliced Beef tastes as
good as the real thing but is far less trouble. But instead of
showing it as the main dish when 'the real thing' is normally
served, that is Sunday, it shows it being served on a Wednesday
when presumably the woman of the house has less time. Thus the
consumer has an excuse, a rationalisation for purchase, a justification for serving what in her heart she regards as second best.
Thus: 'It would be nice to have roast beef in the middle of the
week but it really is far more trouble than chops. And I don't
have the time. But these beef slices don't look too bad and if they
taste near enough like the real thing well ... that's not a bad
idea for tomorrow ...' That I maintain is what went on in many
a viewer's mind. The justification (the housewife is busy) is

presented implicitly. In the case of VIOTA, a pre-mixed cake mix, the justification was overt. 'Viota for busy mothers.' Of course it could be said that the real reason for using prepared foods is not the saving of time but a dislike of work – in which case the Viota commercial is also oblique.

Note that the consumer is not oversold. It is not suggested that she should serve the product on Sunday instead of the real thing (a concept she would probably reject) but on Wednesday. When you think of some of the ways this problem could have been tackled (e.g. 'Just as good as a Sunday roast', 'Make Sunday dinner in half the time') you may share my enthusiasm for the idea. Note too one other characteristic which we have met already – concentration. The communication route may be oblique but the idea is succinct. Finally, stylistically, consider the language. 'A bit of Sunday on Wednesday' is colloquial. You can hear people saying it – *people* as opposed to advertising men.

Exercise E: British Rail

Proposition

British Rail have electrified most of their routes. All over the country you can now get to destinations far more quickly.

Idea

THE OVERGROUND.
(This was a poster displayed mostly in the London area.)

Observations

This poster deservedly won a number of awards. It is one of those advertisements which if you are in advertising gets better each time you look at it and, if you are a member of the London travelling public, gives you more information each time you look at it.

First of all, note the association between London tube travel and British Rail. By adopting the style of the London Underground map and changing the name, it makes its point immediately. It says British Rail travel is fast, that places are easy to get to. Note the trick of reversal : it makes the strange familiar or the familiar strange according to your familiarity with London. Note the amount of information actually conveyed by the poster. Try to imagine a briefing session at which the client had not simply outlined the proposition (above) but had stressed that sixty destinations had to be shown and the travelling times listed. Could – should – all that be attempted on a poster? We may have had serious doubts. Yet the solution sweeps them away.

The poster works on two levels. The message is immediately conveyed graphically. The details are comprehended according to the individual reader's (geographical) area of interest and the amount of time he has in which to read. Remember this poster was displayed on platforms in and around London so presumably there would be time.

Exercise F: Knorr Stock Cubes

Proposition

Knorr Stock Cubes are concentrated chicken flavouring.
They can be used to add richness to gravies.

Idea

A headline above an illustration of cooked chicken –
'WHY ADD WATER TO CHICKEN WHEN YOU CAN ADD CHICKEN TO CHICKEN?'

Observations

The advertiser chooses to position his product not against the competition where he has no specific advantage but against water (i.e. the normal gravy from the cooked chicken). In so doing he creates an identity for himself. The copy could merely have read 'give your chicken extra richness'. 'Add chicken to chicken', associating the stock cubes with chicken, is a new way of looking at the same thing. Somehow the change of words gives a new dimension to the promise. The meaning has been made more meaningful.

Exercise G: National Savings Premium Bonds

Proposition

A premium bond gives you the excitement of gambling, the opportunity of winning a lot of money for a small stake and at the same time helping the economy of the country.

Idea

(Illustration of small man and big Union Jack.)
HAVE A FLUTTER IN THE NATIONAL INTEREST.

Observations

Again a relationship – two thoughts (the little bet and the national economy) come together in the audio/visual pun (flutter/flag). Note too the economy of the headline. An idea is almost always more compressed than the proposition.

Exercise H: Volkswagen

Proposition

VW introduce a truck new to the American market where its car has had a great success.

Idea

(Illustration of car and truck side by side.)
WILL HISTORY REPEAT ITSELF?

Observations

The headline could have said:

'From the makers of the sensationally successful Volkswagen comes the new VW truck.'

Instead it manages to say all that in its distinctive way. And in far fewer words. Note too the method of communication. As with many of our examples the communication route is *oblique*.

14

Proposition and Idea . . . the same only different

The advertisements examined in the previous chapter were chosen primarily to illustrate the journey from *P* to *I* and the difference between the start point and the destination. This chapter collates the characteristics we observed.

I is the same as P only different

I re-presents *P* but it does not simply restate it. A change takes place not in the fact but in the feeling, in the intensity with which the proposition is restated. Meaning is made more meaningful. This is not the same as exaggeration. Exaggeration is cheating. It is the overclaim which is meant to be literally believed (and rarely is – and then only once since trial of the product leads to rejection thereafter). Exaggeration is different from hyperbole, the overclaim which is not meant to be literally believed, the thing for which it stands, however, being meant to be believed. Advertisements which use fantasy situations for example (e.g. Fry's Turkish Delight) don't ask you to believe the fantasy but the thing for which it stands (an 'exotic' luxury chocolate). The question is: Does the idea re-present the proposition? Here is a luxury sweetmeat, delicate in texture with a scented taste, a somewhat self-indulgent chocolate bar. Is this truly re-presented by 'Full of Eastern Promise'? Undoubtedly.

'Oxo adds a rich flavour to meat dishes which husbands appreciate' is re-presented by 'Oxo gives a meal man appeal'.

Very often the difference between I and P is the visual. To illustrate the proposition gives it a new dimension. Illustration can be the most potent way of emphasising an implication in the proposition. Sometimes the difference between I and P resides in the finished art. The choice of photographer or location or model can make the proposition more meaningful. The execution in certain cases is the idea. But it is a dangerous philosophy since it leads to an attitude in which a second-rate idea is accepted in the belief that the execution will make it all happen. Nine times out of ten a second-rate idea becomes a beautifully shot second-rate idea. (The one out of ten exception is the world of fashion and cosmetics.)

Sometimes the difference between I and P is merely in choice of words. This does not mean playing with words for its own sake, being 'clever-clever' at the expense of the product. Many words become used up, their meaning becomes the opposite of meaningful. Advertising tries to redress the balance by neologisms, often disastrously, sometimes successfully, e.g. Lux 'gentles its way through your wash', 'drinka pinta milka day'. But it would be misleading to say that the idea is just an arbitrary change of words. Paraphrase is not invention. Moreover, since words represent thoughts and English is the richest language, the vocabulary allows you to choose from a variety of subtly different shades. But the basic truth of a proposition is there and the idea communicates it. It does not distort. It transforms.

I is a relationship

Advertisements are invariably associations of thoughts (generally called association of ideas but this book restricts use of the word 'idea' to advertising ideas). Sometimes it is an analogy. An analogy may be implicit. For example, John Player Special Cigarettes show the product next to an 'upmarket accessory'. Each is captioned: 'Diamond by Garrard. Cigarettes by John

Player'. Analogies may be explicit. These are either direct similes or metaphors : a simile (one thing is said to be *like* another) or a metaphor (one thing is described in *terms of something else*). A metaphor is really a simile in overdrive. (This last sentence is a metaphor.) Some analogies are like tea from China – farfetched. (This last sentence is a simile.) It is typified in the sort of advertisement which says 'Nine-tenths of an iceberg is hidden below the water. This is a fact. It is also a fact that Belvedere Multi-Flange fittings ... etc., etc.' Similes must be relevant. 'The Triumph 2000 has the fine parts of a great aircraft.' Atlas lighting relevantly compare their Kolorarc lamp with a cocktail – 'a subtle blending of vaporised metals that balances its lumen output happily along the spectrum producing a light uncannily close to daylight'. The illustration shows the lamp surrounded by cocktail glasses and a coupon offer. The Atlas atlas of cocktail recipes. When London Transport introduced its one-man buses delays while people fed the turnstile with the correct change were affecting schedules. To counteract this London Transport said 'This is a bus but think of it as a phone box'. A metaphor is more concentrated. The thing is not described as like another thing but as the thing itself. In 'a Bit of Sunday on Wednesday' the word Sunday refers to all that Sunday means. The action of wool is not said to be like the breathing of a living being – wool breathes. Libresse sanitary towels equals 'Women's liberation' (headline). 'Every woman has a right to use new Libresse' (baseline).

An idea happens when two thoughts come into collision. Koestler (in *The Act of Creation*, 1964) talks of the bi-sociation which takes place when two frames of reference coincide. He chooses to call them matrices. The creative act – whether it is the creation of a work of art or a scientific discovery or the making of a joke – depends on two matrices coming together. In the case of art they confront each other in an aesthetic experience. In the case of science they fuse into a new intellectual synthesis. In the case of humour they collide and the shock finds release in laughter. I believe Koestler's subdivision is for our purpose unnecessarily complex. I believe that collision is the key factor in advertising. The exercises in the previous chapter provide several examples (overground, breathing wool, VC10-derness).

I is more concentrated than P

Invariably the idea, by saying it in fewer words, says more than the proposition. The *New Statesman* decided that its competition could well be the quality Sunday papers and that therefore the proposition should position the journal against them and tell the potential reader that he will find items in the pages of the *New Statesman* which the Sundays don't cover. So much for *P*. The *I*: '*New Statesman*. Things you wouldn't find in a month of Sundays.' This says it all – and more. It also adds dimension to the phrase. It implies that you can look for a long time before finding material similar to that found in the *New Statesman*. And, more subtly, that the posh Sundays can be big and boring. The idea says more than the proposition.

It is no coincidence that the theme of concentration occurs throughout the process of making advertisements. The facts have to be condensed to a single simple statement. Otherwise it cannot 'go through the narrow part of the funnel'. This provides the creative stimulus, forces in turn the intensity of feeling from the creative man. The idea, concentrated into a tight ball of meaning explodes once it is expelled from the funnel. Einstein describes matter as frozen energy. A proposition is a frozen idea. Imagination does the de-frosting.

The Idea is a result of looking at the Proposition in a different way

We have already met the switch, the reversal, the bipolarity of negative/positive in Dreft, of beer/champagne in Löwenbrau, of the familiar/strange in British Rail. British Leyland provide another example of this. The Mini has now to compete with small rivals from the Continent. It countered by showing a Mini alone in a street, beneath it a caption 'Before you buy a foreign car, check what the foreigners are buying'. On close examination you see that the Mini has an Italian number plate. The proposition probably went something like this: 'The Mini is better than its foreign competition.' The creative man looked at the problem the reverse way, turned it on its head.

Veet is a depilatory. It gets rid of hair from girls' legs and armpits. Hair in certain places is thought of as unsightly. The proposition therefore is the correction of a negative. The idea turns this about by offering a positive phrase: '*All* of a girl should be beautiful'. Pimms No. 1 is a powerful drink despite the lemonade and all the foliage and paraphernalia. In an attempt to get away from the tennis club image the writer looked through the glass from the other end: 'Pimms No. 1 – the world's longest short'. He has repositioned the product, thus making its high price more reasonable.

Another device is to choose one aspect of the proposition, dig in among all the facts which led to it, grasp a word or thought or ingredient of the product composition or a piece of trade terminology not known to the general public and work it to its utmost. This is not exaggeration. It may be hyperbole. It may be fanciful. But it is relevant. The Atlas example does this brilliantly. The word 'cocktail' was said by the man at the laboratory bench in the hearing of the writer of the advertisement. He pursued it to the limit.

Just like Harry, Charlie and the Senator

Only Atlas know how to mix metal vapours to get the Kolorarc cocktail. Just as only Harry of Ciro's could shake an authentic Monkey's Gland, just as no one but ol' Senator Fairbanks ever grasped what you do with Noyau and Vermouth to achieve a Fairbanks Cocktail, just as it took Charlie at the Racket Club to conjure the H.P.W. out of what ought to have been a Gin and It, or Sidney of the Cecil to realise you could graft Grenadine to Dubonnet and come up with a Rose, so you'll have to go to Atlas and Kolorarc if you want to look at a mercury lamp and see daylight.

The strategy behind the Canada Dry trade advertisement[1] presumably underlined the fact that Schweppes has the major share of the off-licence market through exclusive representation in the majority of outlets. An attempt must be made to force

---

[1] See illustration "h" in the fold-out.

distribution by suggesting that stockists offer an alternative. The proposition honed this down to an offer of a second mixer drink for those many customers who prefer Canada Dry and whom the stockist would otherwise be missing. The idea arises from the creative man pursuing this thought of two types of drinker. He decided to show the one-type outlet by picturing the one-type drinker as one individual crowding himself in the store.

A not dissimilar problem faced the creative man concerned with army officer recruitment. The strategy demanded that the advertising attempt to correct the impression that the army forced all its officers into the same mould. One obvious way of denying this graphically would be to show the various activities enjoyed by various officers. The solution was to do exactly the reverse, to present the negative and let the copy refute it. There was an arresting headline – a statement echoing the thoughts of potential recruits: 'Army officers. They're all alike' How to illustrate it? The Canada Dry solution could have worked here. Instead the artist chose a simple, more telling visual – painting by numbers. A graphic bombshell. The idea is a result of looking at the proposition in a different way.

The chief talent of the creative man is his ability to shift gears, what psychologist Donald McKinnon calls 'conceptual flexibility'. He sees things as if for the first time – and makes you see them that way. He should elicit the reaction 'Good Lord I never thought of it that way before' from the person asked to judge the advertisement and from the ultimate recipient of the message. I am sure this is what happened when the advertisement for Coty Emeraude[1] perfume was first seen: 'Want him to be more of a man? Try being more of a woman.' Unigate started selling other things than milk from the milkman's float. The creative man looked at the proposition and at one implication of it. He reasoned that if there were more things to sell, then the milkman would have to get up earlier to sell them, so he scripted a commercial featuring a milkman waking from a romantic dream very early in the morning. Later he is yawning at the doorstep. The point is made. Moreover, the idea enlists the sympathy of the viewer.

---

[1]See illustration 'm' in the fold-out.

Very often the creative man has to look at something in a different way after that something has been looked at for several years. He has periodically to re-invent the wheel. Credit cards are no new thing. Barclaycard hold a large share and a long lead in the UK. When the other major banks joined forces to introduce Access, a virtually identical service, it put the onus on the creative man. He had to find a new way of saying the same old thing. He came up with 'Access takes the waiting out of wanting'. Not bad. But the trouble is it is a generic claim. It applies to all credit cards. It is interesting to note that at the time of the launch of Access, Barclaycard were attributing powers of financial wisdom and management to their customers: 'Barclaycard Holders are Masters of Money.' In other words they had progressed to an advanced position. The basic proposition of the credit card had been reinterpreted by the established brand leader. It was Barclaycard who 'reinvented the wheel': all that Access seems to have done is to paint it a different colour.

We have defined four characteristics of the idea.

1. The idea is the same as the proposition only different. It differs not in fact but in feeling. The meaning through the use of words and illustration has been made more meaningful.

2. The idea is a relationship or association. Ideas happen when two thoughts come into collision.

3. The idea is more concentrated than the proposition. The discipline is a creative necessity: it produces an intensity of vision in the creator which he communicates to the reader.

4. The idea is a result of looking at the proposition in a different way. The creative man (through a switch, a reversal, hyperbole, extension, pursuing a fact in the proposition or its implication to an extreme yet essentially truthful position) shows us the often common-place object in a new light. This is the real task of the creative man – in the narrow bit of the funnel.

It alone justifies advertising's use of the pretentious word 'creative' and of Koestler's definition: 'the defeat of habit by originality'.

15

Communication . . . or How they brought the good news from P to I

There is a party game where guests stand in a circle and whisper a message to each other. The last guest says the message aloud. The originator repeats aloud the original message. The difference is striking. A proposition needs to be singleminded: 'a single fact about a product which we believe will motivate the consumer towards purchase'. (According to 'experts' the average consumer is bombarded with anything from 500 to 1,500 commercial messages a day.)

Surely the most effective distance between two minds is a straight line? Not necessarily. The shortest, undoubtedly, but that is not always the same thing. If communication is the transmission of a message one must distinguish between simplicity of message and simplicity of route. Jeremy Bullmore, Creative Director of J. Walter Thompson, summed it up once when discussing the much praised campaign for Campari. The message which those advertisements were communicating was 'It's smart to drink Campari.' But no advertisement ever ran with the words 'It's smart to drink Campari.' Instead, certain other words we use such as 'cryptically bitter' and 'macerated'. If you knew (or thought you knew) what they meant you were smart. And therefore wasn't Campari possibly your kind of drink?

Piccadilly No. 1 cigarettes were an expensive brand. In the heyday of motivation research it was discovered that people who smoked 'ordinary' cigarettes during the week would switch to Piccadilly No. 1 during the weekends. This was only partly a question of economy, restricting the expensive outlay to two days in the week when furthermore a luxury could be properly enjoyed and enhance the pleasures of the weekend. The roots went deeper. Dig beneath the top soil of many an answer to a research question and you'll find 'class structure'. Respondents felt diffident, not about *buying* Piccadilly No. 1 but about *offering* them. 'I couldn't take out a packet of them on the factory floor, could I?' The cigarette was an embarrassment. Or rather the pack. Cigarette advertising is a mystery but one factor is key: the pack and the smoker's identification with it. Mike Savino, who has observed the scene for many years said: 'The only thing I really know is that when somebody takes out a pack of cigarettes he is showing his card. He's saying that's the kind of club I belong to.' And the bloke on the floor or in the office did not want to appear to be putting on airs. But the weekend was a different matter altogether. A different environment with different people. And, reasoned the agency, Piccadilly No. 1 could help him feel superior to his workday colleagues – and even his workday self. The proposition was clear – Piccadilly No. 1 would help you feel superior. The creative team produced a commercial. A well-heeled gent emerges from an exclusive London club. A uniformed flunky salutes him and opens the rear door of the expensive car. The chauffeur drives away, our hero sinks into the leather, takes out the packet, puts a cigarette into his mouth and with an elegant lighter lights it. Until then nothing has been heard. Then the discreet voice: '*Significantly* he smokes Piccadilly No. 1.' That's all. Fifteen seconds of what used to be known as soft-sell. When the film was shown in a rough-cut version the account team got angry. It wasn't explicit. Despite valiant rearguard action by the creative people, the endline was changed to ... you guessed it ... 'You feel rather special when you smoke Piccadilly No. 1.'

Now it could be argued that *that* was what the commercial was meant to communicate. It was undoubtedly. That was a proposition but (cf. Campari) the proposition was the last thing you wanted to *say* – it was what you *wanted the consumer to believe*. And between these two lies a chasm!

What the commercial succeeded in communicating – by a literal and overt transmission of the raw proposition – was: 'Feel more important than you really are, you poseur you.' The commercial, based on intensive and costly research, had fallen into the very trap which that research had in fact pointed out. As with 'It's smart to drink Campari', overtness boomerangs. Marketing as we know must be consumer orientated. It discovers consumer needs and desires and seeks to satisfy them. Leonard Hardy in *Marketing for Profit* writes: 'Profit is the business objective, but the objective can only be reached if the purpose is fulfilled. The purpose is the creation and satisfaction of customers.' By the same token the advertising message must be consumer orientated: not what we want to tell him but what we want him to believe or, better still, *take out of the advertising*.

Obviously not all communication must be indirect. Most of it in fact should be direct. It depends on the nature of the product and the nature of the message. As a general rule the greater the appeal to reason the more direct the route; the greater the appeal to emotion the less direct the route. Consumer-orientated advertising involves the transmission of a message concerning a product. But the message is not always, as they say in intelligence, *en plein*. It often has to be 'coded'. The use of the code does two things. First, it protects the advertiser and the consumer from the embarrassment of an overt message: the advertiser from the consumer's hostile reaction to an appeal which he considers has insulted his intelligence; the consumer from fear of being conspicuous, of having his motives for subsequent purchase being questioned by his friends. Second, it invites active participation by the consumer in the advertising message, in the communication process.

The ever-present word in theories of advertising is 'action'. One task of the creative man is to move any advertisement towards the 'action' end of the continuum. It is fatuous to believe that advertising 'works' by the impregnation of messages into consumer heads or that the incessant repetition of a slogan will result in anything but the recall of that slogan (and then not always that) or that recall has a direct relationship with sales. What I believe is that a message in which a recipient participates is far more likely to result in action than one in which she is regarded as a piece of absorbent material. And I am surprised that the newspaper industry, facing increasing competition from the more 'fashionable' medium of television, hasn't in its dealing with agency media buyers played its one major strength, namely that a reader is not a passive receiver of messages (part of television's 'captive audience') but a *selective perceiver* – an active searcher after things she is interested in.

The sad fact is that people do not buy newspapers or turn on their television sets to look at advertising. They must be attracted by what they only partly see and, once attracted, involved. (The first two acts of *Aida*.) If everything is spelled out the only reaction may be indifference. But if they are intrigued, and comprehension is not immediate, they may go on to participate in the advertising. It is not too fanciful to suggest that this is what happened with the 'VC-10derness' poster. The first time a passer-by saw that message he may not have understood. But people see posters more than once. If he puzzled over it we were still in business. If he rejected it, then the next time perhaps it annoyed him. But when he 'got' it – when he cracked the code – he had *participated*. More importantly he had *contributed*. He had played an active part in the creation of that poster. So that the next time he saw it he felt that part of *his* work was on display.

In the Army Officer advertisement in the last chapter we saw an example of a proposition being communicated by the statement of its exact opposite. The Army wanting to stress the individuality of its officer product, grasped the nettle of disbelief by saying: 'All officers are the same.' The message intrigued the very people who believed it. What they found intriguing and incredible was that the Army were saying it! Moreover, they contributed by their understanding of the painting by numbers device. They understood the illusion. Another example of uttering the opposite comes from Guinness. They want readers of women's magazines to try the product. They show the face of an attractive and real 30-year-old female. Her hands are holding a partly consumed glass of Guinness. The headline reads: 'Nice girls don't drink Guinness.' It is a trick – but not for its own sake, as with so many headlines. The acid test when presented with a trick headline is to see what happens when you compare it with the straightforward message which it is meant to impart. 'Army officers aren't all the same' would evoke a yawn. 'Nice girls do drink Guinness' would sound smug and yukky. Neither would intrigue or invite participation. The headline would do it all.

There is one interesting difference between the Army and the Guinness advertisements. In the first the caption and the headline agree: in the second they conflict. The technique of showing one thing and saying something else may boomerang. You may try so hard for effect that only you appreciate the paradox. The relationship of words and pictures in press advertisements, of sound and vision in television commercials, is a complex one. If the illustration is self-explanatory a straightforward caption seems redundant. The Army caption is not redundant since it echoes the thought of the recruit in words he would never imagine the Army might use: yet, having said that, it is certainly less crucial than the caption in the Guinness advertisement where the picture and the caption are clearly in conflict.

Often an advertisement arouses interest by means of the tension between words and picture. For example imagine a television commercial which begins with a shot of a bowl of soup. If the audio says simply 'this is a bowl of soup' its contribution is minimal. 'This is a bowl of tomato soup' takes us further and a woman's voice saying 'tomato is your favourite' begins to involve us. But hearing a man's voice saying 'I don't think I can eat it' could very well rivet us. But in interplay, as with trick headlines, there is a real danger. There is all the difference in the world between intriguing the recipient so that she participates and fooling her, between getting her to take part and taking her in. There is a picture of a sullen man holding a glass. The headline reads: 'Samantha Brown drinks Appleton Wine.' Ah, you think, a sex change. You read the copy. It begins 'So does her boyfriend Bert . . .' You stop reading. And how about this headline for a Givenchy perfume? 'There's always been one place a woman couldn't put perfume.' A stopper – even in the permissive pages of Nova. One place? The copy tells us where. 'In direct sunlight'.

The public like to be intrigued. They don't like to be fooled.

I once formulated a pseudo-scientific definition of the effect the BOAC posters had on a passing mind. I called it the 'Mmm? ... Aah' syndrome. The initial reaction was puzzlement but elucidation followed soon after and the recipient, instead of cursing the advertiser, complimented himself. Several years ago *The Times* ran a campaign 'Top people take *The Times*', one of the most memorable and least effective slogans of all times. It was, like Piccadilly's claim, overt and embarrassing. Some four years later *The Times* wanted to communicate that people who read the paper were well-informed. But to say 'well-informed people read *The Times*' would be to fall into the same trap. The chosen approach was deliberately oblique. A campaign ran in the London Underground. The tube cards featured sentences uttered by non-*Times* readers, e.g. 'Why should I read *The Times*? I know Chou-en-Lai is crispy noodles and bean shoots.' The reaction is 'Mmm ... Aah?' People get involved. This was proved by one of the advertisements: 'Why should I read *The Times*? I know J. Edgar Hoover invented the vacuum cleaner.' Which provoked a letter from an irate managing director reminding *The Times* that Goblin had invented the vacuum cleaner. (One of the series was cancelled since London Transport do not allow political advertising: 'Why should I read *The Times*? I know all about Barbara Castle. I'm taking the kids there Easter weekend.') The campaign illustrates the virtue of the oblique approach mentioned earlier. First, it eliminates the embarrassment of an overt message and the hostile reaction by the insulted consumer. Second, it invites active participation by the consumer in the communication process. The reader says 'Mmm ... Aah!'

A public service advertisement for Mobil in its 'We want you to stay alive' series showed a boy driving a car with his arm around his girl and oblivious of oncoming disaster. The caption: 'Till death us do part'. Sometimes the message is simply and directly communicated, particularly if it is an appeal to reason. At other times the best route is an indirect one. Indeed in a business where so much is being shouted the only way to be heard may be a whisper: where so much is being communicated one way the only way to get your message across may be to invite your recipient to talk to you. In a business which sets such a premium on originality it is hardly surprising that its practitioners should seek to break the mould of habit not merely in the area of ideas but in methods of transmitting those ideas.

16

A new way of looking . . .

Who said this about the creative job? Who called it 'The power of so dealing with things as to awaken in us a wonderfully full, new and intimate sense of them and of our relations with them'? David Ogilvy? Bill Bernbach? Jeremy Bullmore? It was Matthew Arnold and he was writing about poetry. And what he said about the poet's task applies equally well to that of the advertising creative man. This chapter pursues the comparison in the belief that it will throw new light on the dark part of the funnel and amplify some of the points made in previous chapters.

The task (P into I)

We have seen that an idea re-presents a proposition. That I is the same as P only different. The difference is significant. I is not a paraphrase. It is an intensification. It makes meaning more meaningful.

Here is a proposition:

● 'Beautiful women must bear daughters and those daughters in turn bear daughters . . . in order that beauty may be perpetuated.'

Reason has produced this proposition. Apply imagination to it. Let emotion work upon this thought and this happens:

> From fairest creatures we desire increase
> That thereby beauty's rose might never die.

It happens of course if you happen to be Shakespeare. There we have in the first lines of Shakespeare's first sonnet a re-presentation of the proposition. Not just a paraphrase but an intensification. Emotion has worked upon the thought. What is, in fact, not much of a thought becomes transformed by the feeling and vision which the poet brings to it.

Concentration

The creative advertising man is controlled by a tight brief. It is determined by the nature of the marketing and advertising objectives – the whats, whens, whys and to-whoms. The brief states the proposition – itself a single entity – and requests its interpretation. This discipline is a creative necessity.

The budget may not allow a large space and the resulting compression acts as a stimulus. I remember being told by Robert Caplin to write copy for a two-inch double-column advertisement. He would get me to draw the actual size of the advertisement – and to write the words inside it. It was hard work but as a result the words you wrote also worked hard. A lot of advertising copy today spreads itself. It is flabby and shapeless. It is like a football team which starts an attack but then after a succession of square passes gives the ball back to the goalkeeper. Copy has to move. It cannot afford to tread water.

The restraints of the medium are essential. Any creative man who rebels is neither a professional nor a true artist. For a true artist respects constraints. The task of the artist is not to succumb to limitations but to exploit them. The painter exploits the limitations of his frame. The film director exploits the limitations of the two-dimensional screen. The poet exploits the limitations of the sonnet form or rhyme. Here is Dryden comparing rhyme and blank verse: 'The easiness of blank verse renders the poet too luxuriant: the labour of rhyme bends and circumscribes an over-fruitful fancy.' Creative advertising men have over-fruitful fancies. Set them free to have solutions about problems they have not been set and they will bring you a dozen bright ideas. But ideas must be not only bright but *right*. (I don't know who said that first. But I'm sure it wasn't Dryden.) 'Restrictions', 'limitations', 'bends and circumscribes'. Here is Voltaire on the subject of concentration: 'One merit of poetry few persons will deny: it says more and in fewer words than prose.' Concentration has been called 'the very essence of poetry'. It is certainly the very essence of good advertising. Concentration in the sense of a tight brief. Concentration also in the sense of the restricted space or fraction of time in which to tell a message. And this concentration is, of course, a prerequisite of the intensity we mentioned earlier. There is no intensity without concentration.

There is another related meaning of the word 'concentration': the direction of 'exclusive attention upon the matter in hand' (*Chambers*). Walter de la Mare once told Stephen Spender (though not in my presence) that he thought 'the desire to smoke when writing poetry arose from a need, not of the stimulus, but to canalise a disturbing leak of his attention away from his writing towards the distraction which is always present in one's environment'.[1] My own canalising medium is the music programme of Radio 3. Spender also explains the nature of concentration.

Concentration, of course, for the purposes of writing poetry is different from the kind of concentration required for working out a sum. It is a focusing of the attention in a special way so that the poet is aware of all the implications and possible developments of his idea, just as one might say that a plant was not concentrating on developing mechanically in one direction but in many directions, towards the warmth and light with its leaves and towards the water with its roots, all at the same time.[2]

---

[1] Stephen Spender, *The Making of a Poem*, Norton Library.
[2] *Ibid.*

This is the prerequisite of the power of which Arnold speaks. The poet having directed his attention to a single thought then forces himself to become 'aware of all the implications and possible developments'. It is exactly what the creative man does when examining the proposition and the facts which it represents.

But note too the paradox in Spender's description. 'Developing . . . in many directions' is hardly how one would normally define concentration. But the paradox is 'true' nevertheless. In advertising as in poetry. A poem is at one and the same time simple and complex. The concentration imposed by the limitations of the medium and the 'concentration' or intensity self-imposed by the poet, means that the simple-to-understand expression is in fact compressed. It is rich in meaning. In meanings perhaps not immediately recognised. It is like a Japanese paper flower when dropped in a glass of water. Try it yourself with this poem 'Armistice' by Paul Dehn:[1]

> It is finished. The enormous dust-cloud over Europe
> Lifts like a million swallows; and a light,
>
> Drifting in craters, touches the quiet dead.
> Now, at the bugle's hour, before the blood
> Cakes in a clean wind on their marble faces,
> Making them monuments; before the sun
>
> Hung like a medal on the smoky noon,
> Whitens the bone that feeds the earth; before
>
> Wheat-ear springs green again, in the green spring,
> And they are bread in the bodies of the young:
> Be strong to remember how the bread died, screaming;
> Gangrene was corn, and monuments went mad.

A rhetorical polemic against the horror and madness of war or a prayer to remember the dead . . . this poem says as much as both in a mere twelve lines. There is a special kind of ambiguity in poetry. Not the sort which leaves you wondering what is meant but the sort which gives you more meaning than you bargained

---

[1] *Poetry of the Forties.*

for. The poet's choice of words and juxtaposing of thoughts creates this ambiguity. The Japanese flower unfolds. Perhaps not all at once. The second time you read it you may get the significance of certain phrases. Take the beginning of the second verse. Replace the first five words with 'And now when morning comes'. It fits. It scans. It says the same thing inasmuch as it depicts the identical time of day. But bugles mean reveille, a call to wake. The noise is juxtaposed to 'quiet dead' in the previous line. Meaning is made more meaningful. 'Gangrene was corn, and monuments went mad.' Poetry is more compressed than prose, more highly charged.

Paraphrase a poem. Turn it into prose. You not only spoil it: chances are you double its length. Look again at the Shakespeare sonnet. And Bill Bernbach's advertisement for the Volkswagen truck – 'will history repeat itself?'

Relationships

The creative advertising man first looks at facts and then relates them. Until he went to work these relationships were not yet made (at least, not yet recognised) and so merit the term 'original'. Cullen in his book *The Poet At Work* says: 'The primary activity of the poet's mind is that of imagination which may be described as "the entertainment of new entities". The poet relates ideas hitherto unrelated, and in so doing makes a synthesis which we call a poem.' The synthesis is apparent in the Paul Dehn poem. For example, the apt simile of the 'sun hung like a medal on the smoky noon'.

Here's T. S. Eliot describing London fog: 'The yellow fog that rubs its back upon the window-panes.'

Obliqueness

What is the reader's reaction to Eliot's metaphor? A misprint perhaps? Not fog but dog? But the 'Mmm?' is soon followed by 'Aah!' Fog *is* like a dirty furry animal rubbing its back on your window. The reader's reaction is surprise. The poet's job (as that of the creative advertising man) is to stop the reader short.

Koestler, you remember, defined creativity as 'the defeat of habit by originality'. The idea causes a sudden awakening. Stephen Spender says that the reader of a poem is 'startled out of sluggish associations'. Too many of our associations (or relationships) are tired. Clichés are habits of language we take for granted, the original force of which has been spent. Sometimes you can imagine the original force and full meaning of the cliché. For example, I saw a packed football crowd rolling behind a goal like an ocean. A moment later I recalled the expression 'a sea of faces'. Not only did I appreciate the cliché's full meaning but for a moment I felt as if I had invented it!

The associations a poet makes may seem strange but they are never inappropriate. Here's Robert Herrick using a word from physics in 'Upon Julia's Clothes'.

> Whenas in silks my Julia goes
> Then, then (methinks) how sweetly flows
> That liquefaction of her clothes.

'Liquefaction' stops us short. But, on consideration, it tells us a lot about Julia. How she dresses and how she walks.

Here is another poet approaching us obliquely and surprising us:

> Son, you have two more months
> to live. On the sixteenth of December
> 1963, if the hospital has guessed
> right, you will begin to die.

Only when you have read the whole of Edwin Brock's 'D-Day Minus' (and perhaps not even then) do you realise that the poet is writing not about death but birth. 'Mmm? Aah!'

Individuality

We have seen that the distinction between the received impression of one product and that of another may reside not in the proposition but in the idea. The same P can result in several different I's. The differentiating factor is the creative interpretation. This throws the onus on the creative man, on his individual appreciation of the proposition. On the application of the individual imagination to a fact which may be commonplace.

Every so often one has to bring new meaning and reveal an importance never before suspected in non-exclusive areas. One has to re-invent the wheel.

Here's Robert Frost describing a rough sea:

> The shattered water made a misty din
> Great waves looked over others coming in
> And thought of doing something to the shore
> That water never did to land before.

I've seen a few rough seas. Asked to describe one I might have rabbited on about its might and mystery and noise and terror. But Frost . . .! The fusion of thoughts. The synthesis of 'shattered water' and 'misty din'. Whereas I would have spoken of waves as big as houses, he speaks with deceptive quiet (in simple English, notice) of 'great waves' which 'looked over others'. Thus personalising them. They are not just waves but living beasts. They can look. The next line confirms it. They can also think. And the terror they have in store for those on the mainland is darkly hinted at in words which again underplay in their simplicity:

> . . . doing something to the shore
> That water never did to land before.

If a young copywriter ever says to me 'look, I've been working on this soup account for three years. What can you say that's new about a tin of soup?' I recite those four lines and tell him 'Robert Frost was twice your age when he wrote that. And the sea has been around longer than your tin of soup.' 'A poem', says the American critic Donald Stauffer, 'is an individual imaginative experience recorded . . . by an individual poet.' Frost looks at the raging ocean and sees what we cannot, until that is, he shows us. You or I hear a quiet automobile engine. Someone else hears a ticking clock. You or I think how short life is. Shakespeare sees 'And summer's green all girded up in sheaves'.

Poetic truth

Byron said:

> Poets and painters as all artists know
> May shoot a little with a lengthened bow

(which is probably no defence against the Federal Trade Commission).

When Edmund Waller says in his poem 'On a Girdle'

> That which her slender waist confined
> Shall now my joyful temples bind:
> No monarch but would give his crown
> His arms might do what this has done.

none of us takes it literally – but we accept the essential truth of the message. And here are some other words 'on a girdle': 'What you feel in a Warners isn't the girdle.' Neither Waller nor Warner is concerned with strictly factual representation. As an advertisement McCann-Erickson wrote for itself said, 'The girl you love is 70·2% water, 25% oxygen, carbon, hydrogen, nitrogen and 4·8% mineral . . . but she won't love you any better for telling her!' The poet is not concerned with the detailing of objective facts, what we might call clinical truth. But with the expression of subjective feeling aroused by those facts. Honest feelings sincerely expressed. What we might call poetic truth.

The poet knows. But what of his critics? 'Poetry,' said Saint Augustine, 'is devil's wine.' And the criticism of poetry quoted and obviously subscribed to by Sir Philip Sidney four centuries ago has a familiar sound: 'It is the mother of lies . . . infecting us with pestilent desires.' I offer it to Ralph Nader.

To summarise. The poet turns a proposition into an idea by the application of imagination. Concentration is vital. It contributes a framework, limitations which must be exploited. The disciplines ensure the intensity of the idea. The idea is arrived at by a process of association or relationship, the fusion of thoughts. The communication route is often oblique. The initial reaction is surprise, a perplexity which in the words of Leslie Williamson 'contains its own elucidation'. The poet's individual vision makes the reader see anew something he may have regarded as commonplace. Finally there is such a thing as poetic truth which differs from clinical truth only in intensity of feeling: the expression of that feeling is just as 'truthful' as the facts. The idea *re-presents* the proposition. Only when it *misrepresents* is one's poetic licence endorsed.

Note I am not saying that copywriters are poets or that poets make good copywriters (though some do, for instance Edwin Brock). Nor am I trying to give the business a dignity to which it is not entitled. No. All I am saying is that the nature of the two jobs is similar and that the study of poetry helps the study – and practice – of making advertisements.

The creative advertising man's job and that of the poet differ in many ways. With the adman persuasion is paramount and diversion at best secondary. And we measure by commercial results – a move towards purchase – rather than aesthetic satisfaction. But at the very centre of the advertising business, in some tiny cell perhaps, sits a creative man intensely looking at a product and exercising what Matthew Arnold calls 'the power of so dealing with things as to awaken in us a wonderfully full, new and intimate sense of them, and of our relations with them'. That's what the bastard art is all about.

Maybe for *this* I went to Oxford?

17

Naming of names . . . estate agents and others

Have you noticed what funny names estate agents have?

Giddy & Giddy. Jackson Stops. Brown & Merry (sounds like the ideal holiday). Gascoigne Pees. Friend and Falcke (halt who goes there?). Hetherington and Secrett and Swanell and Sly (that used to be two firms but I feel sure they joined forces in order that Mr Secrett could meet Mr Sly). It might be an idea if two others of those mentioned also got together. Jackson Stops and Gascoigne Pees. Or should it be Jackson Stops *while* . . .? But my favourite is a firm on the South Coast – Reason and Tickle. If they didn't exist I would have had to invent them. Reason and Tickle. The twin poles of an advertising creative man's existence. Reason and Tickle. It's what the central part of the funnel is all about. For every advertisement contains both. Some advertisements are almost all reason. Some are almost all tickle. But no advertisement can be all one or the other. The proportions vary, of course, but both ingredients are present in every advertisement.

Another name for tickle is emotion or feeling. However, tickle is a more active word. And we are in favour of active words. It says *contact*. In order to tickle the tickler has to be near the ticklee. The word puts the consumer first in the creative man's mind. He has to know when to reason, when to tickle. He has to gauge reason. For to tickle when reason is called for or to reason with a consumer when she is expecting a tickle can frustrate both advertiser and consumer. An interesting occupation is to flip through the pages of a magazine and give reason and tickle percentages to each of the advertisements. One might assume that a financial prospectus is an all-reason advertisement and a cosmetic advertisement is nothing but tickle. But though they are fundamentally reason and tickle respectively they are by no means exclusively so. Examine the wording of the financial advertisement, the appeal to cupidity, the way the typography is used, the photograph perhaps and you begin to appreciate how far it has departed from all-reason. Conversely, despite the glamorous photograph, the exotic situation, the suggestive name, there lurks beneath the fashion or cosmetic advertisement some hard core of fact and justification.

The previous chapter demonstrated the difference between clinical truth and poetic truth. It is almost impossible and utterly barren to live a life of absolute reason. Reason equals fact, clinical truth, needs. Tickle equals emotion, imagination, poetic truth, desires.

I was involved in the launch of a malt whisky. When the distiller came to us he brought a small medicine bottle of it complete with cork and simple label printed with the name of the distillery. Today that whisky is available 'in the more exclusive outlets' in London and around the country. When people visit the office I offer them a drink of the whisky as it is today. First I show them the outer square packaging with the illustration of the Highlands where the whisky is distilled, then I take up the bottle again with the brown on black illustration and dignified lettering, remove the small booklet attached to the neck of the bottle. I leave the cap on and bring the original 'medicine' bottle from the cupboard and pour from that. The effect is interesting. The whisky in the two bottles is, of course, identical but it looks like a switch-sell. The difference between the two bottles is, in microcosm, the job we did for our client. It involved a great deal of marketing thinking (reason) and advertising, promotion and packaging (reason and tickle). The medicine bottle is an all-reason package of the product. It is perfectly functional. It holds the product.

E

The label says what it is. The cork keeps the product from falling out and losing its alcoholic strength. The bottle in which the whisky is now sold is also practical. It has an even more functional screw cap plus a seal which is broken only by the customer. It has a label which tells him the name of the whisky. It also shows him a picture of the part of the Highlands where the whisky was distilled. Tickle has entered. It is not absolutely necessary to show that. Does it make the whisky any better? Factually no. Yet there is a certain mystique surrounding the whole product.

Why, for example, is it impossible to recapture the myth and character of the Scotch anywhere else in the world? The Japanese have even built an exact fascimile of an old Scottish pot still into a Japanese landscape which itself has been made a facsimile of Scotland – and produced only a fair imitation. Why is it that a whisky from one distillery on the Isle of Islay, say, has a different feel from one a mile away? The ingredients are the same – to all intents and purposes. But the quality of the peat in combination with the water from a particular burn, both peat and water coming from the immediate vicinity of the distillery, is what separates one Scotch from its neighbour. And all this magic happens here in this piece of countryside. That's why we show it on the label. Not just because it's a pretty picture. Not just because it will undoubtedly motivate more people towards purchase. But because it happens to be relevant. Of course it's more expensive than a plain label with a typewritten name on it. Of course that money has to be allowed for in the distiller's costs. On the other hand if the plain label inhibits people from buying the whisky would the retail price stay where it is? Wouldn't the saving on packaging be eaten up in increased retail cost? But this is not cited as an economic defence of advertising but as an illustration of the purpose of a pack design and to distinguish between the absolutely functional and the decorative, between reason and tickle.

If you have a baby you invariably desire to give it a name. The fact that he has got one already (your surname) will not have escaped your notice. Nevertheless, to distinguish him from his mother and father you give him a first name. You could, of course, call him son of Smith (or whoever) which is how names such as McTavish came about (Mac: Gaelic son of) or O'Connor (Irish patronym for descendant of) or Smithson for that matter. Alternatively, you could give him a letter or a number. This would fulfil absolutely the need for a distinguishing sign. But in order to conform with accepted practice you decide you will give him a name. How about Thatch? That would distinguish him not merely from all the other boys in his class but all other boys in the country. It may also cause him embarrassment in later life. So you open a book of names and dip in at random and come up with Rosemary. This won't do apparently because all those other people who don't have your sense of absolute logic associate the word Rosemary with girls. 'Look Rosemary old man,' you tell him, adjusting his school blazer 'your mother and I believe that what you are is all that matters, not what you are called.' No – there are certain conventions. You need a boy's name. Any one will do. All you need is a signifying mark. You plunge again into a book of boys' names and come up with Evelyn. No? Look on the same page. Esmé? No. It seems that as soon as you start giving him a name other considerations arise. Pictures happen in your mind. Something plain then – John? 'But there are a lot of Johns – sort of defeats the object.' Algernon? 'Sounds too pretentious.' Andrew? 'There's not a drop of Scottish blood in him.' Luke? 'But we're agnostics.' Jonathan? 'I knew a boy called Jonathan once. He was blond.' The point I am labouring is that the moment you name a child you decorate him. Tickle has happened. Of course there is every reason why he has to have a name but from that moment on it does more than stand for the thing, it brings with it associations from outside the thing. Subsequently characteristics of the thing itself affect the name. A continual interplay happens. I have two daughters called Jane and Lucy. They could equally have been called Lucy and Jane. But not now. The associations of the name 'Jane' at Jane's birth are less important than the characteristics of Jane which now affect the word 'Jane'.

This analogy is very relevant to the subject of advertising. For advertising as we know it today began with the branding of products. When all goods were simply commodities – tea, coffee, flour, horseshoes, etc. – there was very little advertising. Today there are few commodity products and even those are advertised occasionally by appropriate authorities (e.g. the Milk Marketing Board). A simple definition of advertising is 'to make known'. When the earliest manufacturer or retailer wanted to make his wares known he soon realised that he had to put a name on them. Initially he put his own name. This not only helped in directing the public attention to his product or shop, it also helped the consumer since if the product or service was inferior the consumer would know whom to complain to and whom to avoid. Hence such expressions as 'My name is my bond' or 'our name is your guarantee'. In September 1658 appeared this advertisement:

> That Excellent, and by all Physicians, approved, China drink, called by the Chineans Tcha, by other nations Tay alias Tee, is sold at the Sultaness Head Cophee-House, in Sweeting's Rents, by the Royal Exchange, London.

Much advertising even today consists simply of name identification. We look at this whole subject in some depth a little later on. It is fashionable to attack so simplistic an attitude to advertising. Nevertheless it remembers a fundamental rule, it answers a question we raised earlier: 'Who is advertising?' Football grounds today are littered with one word advertisements, hoping to catch the passing gaze of the television eye. There is an old saw handed down from poster designer to poster designer: 'he who runs may read'. In the case of football grounds it is amended to 'he who watches he who runs may read'. Single names like Virol, Bovril, Oxo, Mazzawattee, decorated railway stations till quite recently.

One of the problems when advertising was very young was the illiteracy of the general public. A name may be a guarantee but what if people could not read? As G. H. Saxon Mills recalls in *There is a Tide*, this produced an interesting resort to the use of visual symbols. Thus a shop owned by someone called Harebottle would exhibit a sign showing a hare and a bottle, while one owned by someone called Cox would have a sign showing two male fowls. This technique is still used today. The Bowater Group's symbol designed in the 1950s is a stylistic representation of a bow and water (lines of waves) though whether half the people who see it 'get' it is another matter. Why should Bowater adopt this rebus device? I don't know. Unless to communicate their name piecemeal (as with Hare-Bottle) to uneducated masses in foreign parts who, it seems to me, are unlikely to be their customers. A single illustration of a name which is also a word in its own right is one thing: a contrived representation of two separate words is something else.

Here is an advertisement from the very first *Sunday Times* (reprinted on the occasion of their 150th anniversary in 1972):

> John Burgess and Son's long established and much esteemed ESSENCE OF ANCHOVIES, continues to be prepared by them after the same manner that has given the greatest satisfaction for many years. Warehouse 107, STRAND, corner of the Savoy Steps London. (The original fish-sauce merchant) Burgess' name is his bond.

Of course, when people learned to read, then name identification and visualisation of the name could exist side by side. But soon products were given names other than that of the seller. Products were branded. Although we generally think of 'brand images' as a recent phenomenon, the brand image is as old as the use of a brand name. As the naming of a baby has shown, the act of choosing a brand name by itself begins to create an image. Again the same interplay occurs: the name affects the thing and the subsequent characteristics of the thing (its performance chiefly) affect the name. Perhaps the best definition of brand image comes from the *Harvard Business Review*.

> The image of a product associated with the brand may be clear-cut or relatively vague; it may be varied or simple; it may be intense or innocuous. Sometimes the notions people have about a brand do not even seem very sensible or relevant to those who know what the product is 'really' like. But they all contribute to the customer deciding whether or not the brand is the one 'for me'.

These sets of ideas, feelings and attitudes that consumers have about brands are crucial to them in picking and sticking to ones that seem most appropriate. How else can they decide whether to smoke Camels or Lucky Strike; to use Nescafé or Borden's instant coffee; to drive a Ford or a Chevrolet or a Plymouth?

Justifying choice is easier with cars; there at least the products have clearly visible differences. But the reasons people give for choosing a brand of cigarettes (and soap and bread and laxatives) are pretty much the same. Thus you find drinkers of any brand of beer justifying their preference in identical terms: 'Schlitz is better because it's dry.' 'I like a dry beer, so I prefer Bud to Schlitz'. Something must make a great difference; the conception of the different brands must be compounded of subtle variations in feelings about them, not necessarily in product qualities. A big problem in this area then, is what kind of symbol a given brand is to consumers.[1]

Note that this chapter is concerned chiefly with the naming and branding of products, rather than advertisements in general. The very act of naming a product involves the use of tickle. Indeed so can the very naming of a type of product. Often it is more than a simple denotation (denote: 'to signify or mean') it is a connotation (connote: 'to imply as inherent attributes'). The word radio for example denotes a 'wireless communication' but the word wireless means strictly 'without a wire or wires', that is 'pertaining to telegraphy or telephony without wires' (*Chambers*). So the very denotation of radio involves a connotation, a criticism of the accepted method of communication on which radio is an improvement. The term 'horseless carriage' is in the same category. The 'Trade Descriptions Act' was so called because the advertising industry objected to the original name of the proposed legislation 'The Consumer Protection Bill'. The former denotes, the latter connotes, the implication being that all the activities of all manufacturers are such that the consumer needs protection. A similar battle has been joined recently, though the parties are in different roles, over the so-called 'Fair Rents Act'.

---

[1] Quoted in *Marketing for Profit*, by L. Hardy (Longman).

Thus if it is difficult to prevent tickle from playing a part in the naming of product types or inventions, let alone products, it is impossible to prevent connotations attaching to any brand name which the manufacturer chooses to append to his product. Early advertisers were aware of this. They therefore invented names. They put together combinations of letters which had no denotations (i.e. they were not in the dictionary) and therefore, they assumed, had no connotations. They did this for one or both of two reasons. First, they could begin with a clean sheet, the consumer could approach their product with an open mind. Any impressions subsequently imprinted upon that were the result of the product's performance, the consumer's experience, the manufacturer's advertising etc. Second, they could distinguish their products from all other products, from all other product categories. It was much easier to register an invented name. Whereas if you were Mr Johnson and you made a baby powder you couldn't be sure that another Johnson wouldn't do the same. Or if you called your product 'Lion' or 'Rose' there was no guarantee that a product in a similar field couldn't also advertise under that name. And even if the confusion which arose with a product with the same name in a totally different field (e.g. Johnson's wax) were slight as far as the consumers were concerned, there was always the problem that confusion in the trade or the media could prove embarrassing, even costly. There are several common names around today. Cresta is the name of a soft drink, a car and a sewing machine. Singer is also the name of a sewing machine and a car. Lee make jeans: so do Lee Cooper. But with an invented word you were your own man. Register it and anyone using it would be prosecuted for 'passing off'.

OMO   DAZ   KODAK   EKCO   FAB

These are all invented. Nevertheless, assuming one had not heard any of them before are they entirely free of connotations? Daz and Fab clearly not. They betray their origins. You may tell me that Ekco is an abbreviation of E. K. Cole and Company but that's not what I hear. (There's a margarine with the same sound.) Omo may suggest all sorts of things. Kodak of the five examples is unique. It is a jealously guarded name and is almost synonymous with popular photography. It must be the single most important asset in the company! The name today has a host of connotations which together form a favourable image. When it first appeared the name probably connoted nothing at all. But Kodak is an exception!

Let us suppose, however, that you have discovered the ideal non-denoting, non-connoting word. Beware – the situation changes as soon as you commit that word to print. The moment the word appears as a design you have begun the act of communication and tickle (connotation) has joined forces with reason (denotation) or to put it positively, the image of that product is in your hands and those of the package designer. The style of lettering and typography, the choice of type-face, the size, the weight, the space, etc. . . . all this says something about the company. Putting the brand name alone on a poster does more than simply keep the name before the public. The manner of so doing must say something about the company.

Compare for example the current BOAC logotype with the one it replaced a few years ago. Is the change one merely of fashion? It could be so argued. Yet a good case could be made out on rational rather than aesthetic grounds for the change. The early design portrayed lightness and speed – italics to suggest flight. Those letters look as if they could take off. The latter design on the other hand, is meant to show stability, solidity, reliability (BOAC takes good care of you, remember). The last thing you expect those letters to do is to take wing.

As an exercise I took a collection of letters with, as far as I know, neither denotation nor connotation:

KAZON

The word 'Kazon', plainly typed on plain paper, was shown to several people. The word meant nothing to them. They were asked to guess what sort of product or company it was. There were as many different answers as respondents.

Two art directors then designed eight logotypes. A leading research company, Market Behaviour Limited, presented these to a total of twenty-six consumers – eleven of them in an individual interview situation, and to one group of seven and one group of eight people in a group interview context. Respondents were presented, one at a time, with between two and eight of the different logostyles. In each case they were asked to give their impressions as to what sort of product they would expect with that name. When shown additional logovariants of the same name they were then asked . . . 'and if you saw it presented like that, what sort of product would you expect?'[1]

The logotypes (see illustration page 128) vary from the plain to the seemingly explicit. The reactions to the plain logotype 'L' were almost as widespread as those evoked by the typewritten word. 'Respondents were unable to see Logo "L" as a product in most instances, because the effect of the lines surrounding the name suggested a sign or nameplate so strongly. In group and individual interviews the most consistent and frequent associations were of this type – nameplates, railway station signs, labels on jars and the name of a house.'

All the other logos, however, produced more consistent responses. Logo 'F' used the type-face known as Tea-chest. 'Response was simple, straightforward and very consistent. The "stencil" style of lettering in the logo was readily recognised and produced associations with names on car tyres, and a name on a tea-chest.'

Logo 'H' also employed a simple letter-form but surrounded it with an intricate border. 'Several people thought it could be the name of a game or a puzzle, building and building products were mentioned a number of times, and because the letters were touching this sparked off Greek associations in the minds of two respondents in quite separate interviews.'

Each of the remaining five logos owes everything to the designer and nothing to existing type-faces.

Logo 'S' produced two sets of responses. 'The first association seems to result from the lack of a hard outline to the letters and the consequent "soft" impression given by the word. This "softness" about the logo leads to associations with flour and water softeners. The second association created by the "blurry" effect of the lines seems to be that of something which you can't see

---

[1] The extracts are from the MBL report.

through because it's dirty. This produced suggestions such as window cleaners, a detergent and glass.

Logo 'P' similarly 'generated two sets of associations, one of power and the other, also with power implications, of American comic heroes. Again these associations were quite consistent across both types of interview, giving suggestions of Batman, fireworks, a powerful cleaner, and a design of a T-shirt.'

L

F

H

S

P

M

U

E

Logo 'M' evoked the same reaction as Logo 'P'. 'It, too, produced associations of American comic heroes and of power. To some extent however, it seemed to stimulate more ideas and associations than had Logo 'P'. With Logo 'M', Tarzan and Superman were added to Batman, and Strength and Reliability were added to Power.

Logos 'U' and 'E' incorporate 'realistic' as opposed to 'symbolic' cues. The reactions are immediate, the impressions more clearly defined. However, the lines in Logo 'U' produced alternative images: (i) the letter was on fire, (ii) the letter was moving very fast. 'These two concepts – of fire and speed – produced different sets of associations. However, these associations again came up quite consistently in both the group and individual interviews. Firelighters was the most frequently mentioned product association with airlines, oil and petrol and cars following the speed link as another set of associations.'

There was minimal confusion with Logo 'E'. 'Response ... follows a very similar pattern in both the group discussions and the individual interviews. The main cue for respondents seemed to be the "grass" base on which the word was standing. The presence of the grass led to associations with the garden, weed-killers, pesticides ...'

This simple research shows that a name with no obvious denotation nevertheless attracts unto itself *connotations* by virtue of the design and the logotype. Kazon can be Greek or American, powerful or soft, a detergent a weedkiller or a range of male toiletries. It depends upon the logotype. But the connotations received by the respondents weren't always those intended by the designer. Logo 'M' which was meant to represent a shipping line suggested no such thing. Logo 'E' which, I was firmly convinced, said fertiliser was seen almost universally as a weedkiller.

The search for a collection of letters which has no connotations whatsoever is extremely arduous. For if the word means nothing or suggests nothing to the eye, the ear may transmit impulses to the brain. It is virtually impossible to separate the sound of a word from its meaning (whether denotation or connotation). When people speak of a word having a beautiful sound how can you be sure they are not influenced by other factors? Is 'sweet' any sweeter to the ear than 'sweat'? If so why? Why should 'ermine' be all right and 'vermin' not? I remember reading about an Italian who thought that the most beautiful word in the English language was 'cellar-door'.

I was involved in the launch of Ajax scouring powder in Italy. Colgate conducted some preliminary research into the name. How did Italians react? First of all there's no J in Italian, so this was changed to a small i. AiAX. Did it mean anything to them? Not really. Hardly any of them connected it with the legendary hero. One or two, however, thought it had something to do with Ajaccio, capital of Corsica, and resented an Italian product being given the name of a French town, particularly since Corsica once belonged to Italy! Otherwise the name meant little. The sound, however, did ring bells. Did they think it would be a good product? No. Anything which sounded as scratchy as Aiax would harm the bath. Colgate studied the research and launched the product with the name . . . Aiax. In about six months it was brand leader, a position it retains to this day. What this proves I'm not sure. Possibly that the product makes its own associations so that once it is on the market, and tried, the image is being created by *performance* and that initial connotations (if any) are being replaced. (In the UK about the same time, Colgate were launching a soap-filled scouring pad. They thought of calling it Trojan. The Americans were sceptical. In the US it was the name of a well-known contraceptive. Rarely if ever filled with soap.)

Names do reverberate with meanings. And it is as well to do a little research, though not to get your knickers in a twist for several months and do nothing. Massey-Ferguson launched a new tractor worldwide. Instead of giving it a name they gave it a number. Now that, one would imagine, would need no preliminary research. They thought not. They had everything printed when the management of their German subsidiary made frantic noises. The chosen three-digit number was the code number of legislation recently enacted concerning homosexual behaviour and had become the accepted slang word for homosexual. The number was changed. But would you have pretested?

Context is important too. Move a name out of one environment (product category, audience classification, country) and it begins to have different connotations. I remember hearing laughter emanating from a Dutch lavatory and an Englishman emerging clutching a toilet roll with the name 'Special Krepp.' Crêpe paper is not funny to Dutchmen. Nor is the celebrated distiller Wynand Fockink, though it may sound a pleasant enough way to spend a weekend in Amsterdam. I was once stuck at Bordeaux airport for a couple of hours. It was only then that I realised that it meant edge of the water. And on the subject of wine names why does Chambertin sound marvellous and 'Chamber tin' somewhat less so? Could it have anything to do with meaning? The French word for 'crack', so I was informed by a biscuit manufacturer, is 'tuc'. That is why the Belgian biscuit has the name and this is what the holder of the UK licence intended to call Tuc in this country. But here the letters TUC have a different connotation. There are two possible relevant questions. First, do people appreciate any second meaning of the letters TUC? Second, and more important, if they do does it matter? In the event the product was launched without researching the name and zoomed to brand leadership in the savoury biscuit category. The subsidiary name is ignored: United Biscuits were quite right to resist the suggestion of would-be copywriters to run the slogan 'TUC – light as a Feather'.

But I digress . . . All this chapter has attempted to do is point to the part played by tickle *at the very beginning of a product's life*. For as soon as a product is named emotion of some sort enters on the scene. If it happens then it follows that no subsequent advertisement can be devoid of it. You can still do the advertisement which is 99 per cent reason. But none will be thoroughly devoid of tickle. I searched far and wide for a comparison. I chose eventually a common product, common salt. Here are two advertisements for salt. Both are quite old. One for Cerebos (1896), the other for Morton. And though my reason for including them here is to contrast the reason approach with the tickle approach you may also care to look at them in terms of Proposition and Idea.

Cerebos

Seven Reasons for Using
'CEREBOS' SALT
Instead of common salt

——oOo——

1. BECAUSE it contains the valuable nutritive ingredients of Wheaten Bran which are almost entirely wanting in White Bread.

2. BECAUSE it is more *natural* than common salt, which is never found either in the body or in plants, unless in conjunction phosphates, &c., as in 'Cerebos' Salt.

3. BECAUSE it forms the actual substance without which the bones and teeth cannot grow – hence its importance in the diet of CHILDREN.

4. BECAUSE it stimulates the changes which result in the growth and repair of brain, nerve and general tissue – hence its value for ACTIVE WORKERS.

5. BECAUSE it is cheap. All the food (meat, vegetables, bread, soup, stews, &c.) can be made more nourishing and strengthening by using 'Cerebos' Salt instead of common salt, without appreciably increasing the cost.

6. BECAUSE it is the only Nutritive Salt. Common Salt is only a seasoning: 'Cerebos' Salt is a splendid Food.

7. *BECAUSE it is beautifully fine and dainty for table use. It does not readily cake, and can be sprinkled like sifted sugar.*

'CEREBOS' NUTRITIVE TABLE SALT.

In Large Tins   From All
6d. and 1/-   Grocers and Stores

Morton

'When It Rains It Pours'
(illustration of girl holding umbrella pouring the salt into the
name Morton)

You will have noticed that the reason ad is, not surprisingly, full of
P, that the idea (or ideas) are within the proposition. And that
the tickle advertisement (Morton) takes as its *P* item No. 7 and
applies imagination to it to produce a memorable and relevant
and indestructible pun. Finally, would you have believed there
were 160-odd words to be written on behalf of salt?

18

The job, the department . . . Surprise! Surprise!

In this chapter I want to explore the implications of something we touched on in the discussion on poetry.

'What', I have been asked, 'is the job of the creative director?' Creative director is a management role. In common with all other leaders of people, the creative director has to plan and budget. He has to organise – or so organise things that he gets an organiser to organise, but he still has to organise the organiser. He is responsible for selection and training of staff. He has to control, he has to encourage and set examples. At the eleventh hour he may have to do it himself to prove to the staff that he can, to prove to himself that he *still* can, because frankly there's nobody else who can do it. He has to cajole and lift up. He has to represent the company to its clients, to potential clients, to the trade, to the media and even the world outside. He has to innovate.

Now much, if not all, of this is the stuff of which general management is made. But there is one additional characteristic which he shares with none of them, though it is a characteristic to be welcomed in other executives who are put in the position of approving advertising. *His job is to be surprised.*

When the young Jean Cocteau used to walk into Diaghilev's

room, Diaghilev (one of the world's best creative directors) would greet him with the words: 'Jean, étonne-moi.'

How often were you astonished last week? How did you react to the last piece of creative work which was shown you? Did you say 'Good, that was just what I was hoping for?' or 'Good lord! I never thought of it that way before'? Did you say 'Mmm' or 'Mmm? . . . Aah!'? All good advertising surprises. Just as good poetry surprises. Not because the statement is bizarre or incredible or outlandish (though occasionally it may be) but because the poet has managed, to use Spender's words, to 'startle us out of sluggish associations'.

The first job of an advertisement is to surprise. But the surprise must be relevant. The result of irrelevant surprise is rejection. The result of relevant surprise is revelation. The job of the creative director is to be surprised. Who then does the surprising? The Creative Department.

If we look at what this term connotes we may, via another route, arrive at the same destination. The term creative department or creative management or creative business is a paradox. It is really a surprise in itself. It is the juxtaposing of two opposites, the collision of two frames of reference (matrices, as Koestler calls them). It is in the same league as 'shattered water', 'misty din', 'gangrene was corn', the 'yoking together' as Doctor Johnson called it, referring to the metaphysical poets, of apparently diverse matters, words from different worlds.

If we turn to Roget's *Thesaurus* and examine those clusters of words, the structured associations which Roget bequeathed a nation, what do we find? Take first 'creative'. This word leads Roget immediately to imagination. And this subdivides. Type of imagination. Vivid, highly coloured, bold, wild, fervent. Thence to originality. And rubbing shoulders with it, frenzy, lively and other spiced adjectives – enthusiastic, extravagant, preposterous, and just in case you (as managing director) are thinking 'Oh lord, should I employ creative people at all?', a word to convince you you should not – impractical. Could one list a worse roster of characteristics for a successful business enterprise? Turn now to Roget on business. We're in a different league. All severely practical.

● *Function:* 'What one has to do' (no nonsense about that!) Capacity, duty, office, business life, terms of reference (none of your frenzy and extravagance here). Job, concern, care, look-out.

Look out indeed. So the creative department is by definition a paradox. A disciplined anarchy.

Now if we approach the question from the opposite direction (i.e. not by defining the existing term but by examining the nature of the work the creative department *does*) we do in fact arrive at the same point. If creativity occurs as a result of serendipity, random association of thought, relationship, fusion of matrices or (the word I prefer) collision, then it is absolutely appropriate that the form of the organisation set up to provide those ideas should be anarchic. Or, to put it another way, if an idea happens when two thoughts come into collision, a creative department must be structured to encourage collision.

The structure of the typical creative department in any medium-to-large agency owes as much – or more – to the influence of business as to the influence of creativity. It is a structure designed to get the work out rather than to stimulate the random association of thoughts. When I first became a creative director my very first job was to decide who in my department should have coathangers. I decided that art directors, senior copywriters and above should have coathangers. (Big deal!) I thus made two important discoveries. One, there were things called hierarchies. Two, fundamentally my job as creative director was to create not advertisements, but environment. I was concerned with the environment of the department (not to be confused with the Department of the Environment which came later).

Hierarchies and environment. I decided to do something about both but first to determine what exactly the department had been set up to produce. Advertisements? Yes but what was advertising? Clearly it had something to do with ideas. Clearly too a business based on the production of ideas would be unlikely to be structured in the same way as an ordinary business or industry organisation. Since ideas, unlike tangible end-products such as pots, pans, tractors, bras or marketing plans for that matter, are not produced to order. For ideas in my experience occurred at the unlikeliest moment and in the unlikeliest people and bore little relevance to the titles, job descriptions or the status of the people concerned. As the man said, an idea doesn't care who has it.

The rigid horizontal divisions of hierarchy (seniority) seemed repressive. The rigid vertical divisions (craft skills: copy, art, etc.) though necessary, were also restrictive, causing demarcation disputes. In fact the more I examined the structure of the department the more archaic I found it. The second of these two problems (the vertical craft division) was the easier to deal with. The writer and the artist instead of working apart were encouraged to work together. The art director had been a second-class citizen.

It's difficult sometimes to recall those days. The pendulum swung quickly and violently away from the domain of the word to that of the picture. But in 1960 it was still the exception in an agency for any but the senior art director to be concerned with the initial thinking. It was common for the writer to write his copy and then take it to the visualiser for a layout. Indeed, the copy was often not taken but sent. I remember in the late 1950s, writing a full-page advertisement for a junior flavoured aspirin. I decided to show the benefit: a picture of a young mother closing the door of a child's bedroom and putting her fingers to her lips saying to her unseen husband: 'Quiet, he's sleeping now.' Beneath this were two or three paragraphs of copy. And at the bottom a picture of the product and the logo of the manufacturer. For some reason the budget was cut and instead of a full page we were left with a two inch double column. Moreover, the client insisted on a picture of a baby's head and another of the bottle of aspirin and the logo. My role was to sum up the main advantages of the product. There was just room to do this. The headline was simply the brand name and the copy a list of the four points, each marked by an asterisk 'safe, soluble, stable, raspberry flavoured'. I did the copy while the account executive waited. And as he rushed it to the visualiser I turned to my next task (writing the Lord's Prayer on a grain of rice). The next thing I heard was that the client didn't like the word raspberry. 'He thought it was rude and a lot of people don't like raspberries.' So we just left it out. And we left out the asterisks to give more room for the words. Another revised layout was done. I didn't catch it until it was about to go to press and then only by accident. I happened to see a proof on the art director's desk. It read:

SAFE

SOLUBLE

STABLE FLAVOURED

Art directors came into their own in the 1960s with the emergence of pop groups, designers, photographers, entertainers and other manifestations of a youth cult which owed more to innate talent than training in the hitherto accepted manner. A Cockney or northern accent was no longer an impediment: in fact the reverse. And people who had striven to hide their origins were belatedly flaunting them. Art directors were becoming articulate, finding their opinions taken notice of, proving that ideas were no longer the sole prerogative of the writer. The visual could also express the proposition and motivate the consumer. Television was getting into its stride and that was clearly a visual medium. Art directors were taking their own photographs and becoming photographers. They were on the floor during shooting of commercials and before long some of them were discreetly directing, even becoming fully-fledged and union-recognised directors. And, final accolade, many were also writing headlines.

Now he was encouraged to write headlines officially, to break down barriers. At the same time the writer was encouraged to draw layouts. And for the same reason. However, one discovered that some art directors were bringing a new vitality to advertising prose. They were blunter in their speech and far more colloquial. Copy was gradually becoming closer to actual speech. The impetus was television. It benefited the art directors. Writers on the other hand were not contributing to art direction though they were learning more and more about it and began co-operating in television. Initially the old procedure was adopted:

the writer wrote the words (here called audio) and the artist drew the pictures (video). They learnt that this was not simply copy with moving as opposed to static pictures or a series of illustrations accompanied by captions, but something requiring an interplay of spoken words and moving pictures throughout a period of time. The medium was virgin territory. They had to conquer it together and their past training could in fact prove a severe handicap. Indeed, the most immediately successful workers in the new medium were the comparatively inexperienced creative advertising men, those who had learned sufficient of its ways but were not restricted by its static techniques. Many people in top positions today, some with agencies of their own, were at the right place at the right time when commercial television arrived. If not the most likely to succeed, they were assuredly those least likely to fail.

So television helped to break down the barrier between copy and art. They learned together. The copywriter's storyboards (the commercial drawn in comic strip form) were more often of more use than the artist's. Since he couldn't really draw he would draw only the essentials. The artist's words were often better than the writer's. Since he wasn't a 'writer' he would talk – which is what the medium needed. But though they cooperated, a new barrier grew up between them and the rest of the agency: the television department. And new methods of infiltration had to be devised. It wasn't difficult. It demanded from the creative director and his immediate associates a certain vigilance and, from the department itself, an eagerness to participate in everything. This attitude was, of course, encouraged and stimulated by the creative director.

The horizontal division was – and still is – a different matter. Hierarchies, pyramids, organisation charts, have a greater sense of permanence than the lines of demarcation between one job and another. And obviously, since advertising is a business, some ordering of society is necessary. People have to report to other people. People have to train and be trained by other people. 'Neighbour Verges ... an two men ride of a horse, one must ride behind.' Someone has to be made copy group head, for example. The choice narrows down to the best writer and the best administrator. With luck both qualities will reside in the same man. But if they don't?

In the term 'copy group head' as with 'creative department', you have the paradox in a nutshell. The conflict of idea and organisation. How do you structure a department whose main function is to surprise? In my opinion you begin by separating the creative hierarchy from the administrative hierarchy. The person in charge of a group of *people* is not necessarily in charge of a group of *accounts*. A horizontal group structure seems to spell out a permanent order of ability *in all things*. A is above B is above C on all matters whether administrative or creative. Whereas in truth B is better than A in some things, C is better than A in others. So, although you put the best administrator in charge of the day-to-day running of the group you allow the best person on a particular account to control the creative work on the account, irrespective of his place in the administrative hierarchy, and irrespective of whether he is an artist or a writer. You then have to decide whether you need groups at all. Certainly they serve a purpose as administrative units but aren't they perhaps restrictive? In some big agencies the groups are so self-sufficient that the members of one group don't know the names of those in another group, let alone their calibre. Don't groups restrict creativity? Undoubtedly – in three ways.

First, they exclude the involvement of a person outside the group whose knowledge – or even whose ignorance – of that product could be vital.

Second, they inhibit collision, the number of associations, the coming together of minds.

Third, they create an inward looking society. There is an understandable tendency, once a writer-artist team has been formed and found to produce good work to keep it together permanently. They enjoy working together. They 'spark each other off'. The attitude of management is 'why change a winning team?' My reaction is to change it before they stop winning. A two-man team especially needs to break up if only occasionally. If they live together too long they know each other too well. They cease to surprise each other. It's a marriage. Often the communications are wordless. Each person knows the other's answer before he asks the question. Furthermore, if they are so good then it is essential for the health of the department (let alone their own) to work with outsiders, to spread their influence and to be stimulated by other influences.

In short, if one accepts the idea that ideas happen as a result of collision and that the raw material for ideas is thoughts and often thoughts which are disparate (i.e. they don't normally exist side by side or in the same mind or pair of minds), then you have to structure a department which encourages collision and bring thoughts from all over in order that there is a state of flux, a state of anarchy.

So the creative department is a paradox. It is a disciplined anarchy. It is the creative director's job to maintain that state of disciplined anarchy. He has to institute controls and procedures while simultaneously encouraging the utmost flexibility. If he has chosen the right people they will assist him by accepting their responsibilities and by exercising self-discipline. But he must not rely on that. Nor should he go to the other extreme and, having found his formula, strictly enforce it. He can afford neither policy: neither *laissez-faire* nor dictatorship. If he wants a quiet life he can draw up an organisation plan and a *modus operandi* and sit atop the pyramid. But if he wants a quiet life he has chosen the wrong job in the wrong business. It is not easy to explain to a visiting dignitary that there is no organisation chart or that 'we have as many organisation charts as we have clients' or that 'we are in effect a repertory company rather than a department – the guy who plays the lead in *Charlie's Aunt* doesn't play King Lear'. It is not easy to keep things in a state of flux, to call to your aid the questionable authority of Mao Tse-tung ('change is the only constant'), to tell an account director that the writer who was on the product last year has been taken off. 'I say,' he'll say, 'we must maintain continuity.' But it's the easiest thing in the world to maintain continuity. Show me the Sahara Desert and I'll show you a perfect example of continuity. Continuity is often another word for security. In fact no matter how much a creative department is restructured, permanence is there imbedded in the woodwork, ingrained in the contact reports. No. If the function of the creative department is to provide ideas, and ideas are a result of collision, then the management of that function must recognise the essential paradox (which the term 'creative department' by definition proves) of a disciplined anarchy. Obviously too much anarchy and you go out of business. But too much discipline and you get no ideas. And you go out of business.

19

Tickle . . . or advertising as a joke

There are two main reasons for devoting a chapter to humour. One, a lot of advertising is funny (some of it intentionally). Two, an examination of the mechanics of the joke may reinforce the point about how ideas happen and how they are communicated.

The joke is the simplest example of an idea. Koestler tells one about two prison wardens playing cards with a prisoner. The prisoner cheats so the wardens kick him out of jail. Koestler explains that two matrices have collided. The first matrix: prisoners must be confined to prison. The second matrix: people who cheat must be expelled from their immediate society. The two matrices collide because they cannot be fused.

'Waiter there's a needle in my soup.'

'No sir, that's a typographical error. Noodle.'

Here two possible realities come into collision. It is quite possible that a needle could be found in a plate of soup and that such a typographical error could occur. But when the two events take place simultaneously you have collision. Note that each of the two examples contains a key word. In the first it is 'prisoner', in the second it is 'needle'. The key word is the point of collision.

Or you can look at it another way. A joke takes you up one path. Suddenly you find you are up another. The key word is the intersection. It is the button you accidentally step on which instantly changes the scene around you. Watch where you step in the next joke.

A cartoon shows a man leaning on a gate looking at a bull in a field. Only, on close examination the bull is a 'pantomime bull', shoes are to be seen sticking out of the rear half. There is a sign on the gate. It reads: 'BEWARE OF IMITATIONS'. You will have noticed an underlying logic. The needle in the soup could have been caused by the error in the menu. The prisoner could have been kicked out of jail according to normal rules of behaviour. If there were such a bull in that field it is quite 'logical' that the sign should read as it does.

Surprise must be relevant. The joke depends on the relevance of the dénouement to the preceding event, of the answer to the question. Here are two actual remarks I heard at football matches. A centre-forward who had been having an off day had the ball at his feet and was making clumsy progress up the field. He was at a loss what to do next. A voice from the crowd shouted some advice. 'Use the empty space!' 'Between your ears,' said another voice. The second piece of advice was as relevant as the first. It was not what the first man had meant but it was equally appropriate. The next remark I heard at Charlton. They used to have a player called John Hewie, a versatile South African who had played for Charlton in every position on the field. One Saturday with their first and second team goal-keepers both injured, Charlton decided to play Hewie in goal. It was the first time in the history of the game that a man had played for his team in all positions. I was standing behind the goal. About five minutes before half-time a man behind me said to his companion, 'Hewie's got to go off now'. 'What do you mean?' said the other. 'He's got to change. He's in the band.' This joke is an example of extension. If A and B and C therefore Z. It begins with a fact and pursues that fact beyond literal truth to a fanciful but nonetheless meaningful conclusion. If Del Monte tinned fruit is fresh fruit picked the moment it is ripe and canned the moment it is picked then the label belongs on the tree with the pineapple and the copywriter can say 'peel a can today'.

Campbells introduced a range of ready-meals in cans. What

was there to say about ready-meals? Not much, frankly. It was a case of telling the same story differently and better. 'What oft was thought but ne'er so well expressed', as Pope so well expressed it. The commercial shows a supermarket check-out. A middle-aged man has a collection of packets and tins and one plate of steaming meat and vegetables. He carries it nonchalantly past the check-out, down the street, past a perplexed policeman and an incredulous neighbour to his home, sits down and eats it.

'Funny' has been defined as 'incongruous', 'not fitting well together'. Incongruous comes from the same root as congruent 'capable of coincident superimposition'. The joke does superimpose, only along *part* of its length (i.e. that intersection where all hell breaks loose). The same techniques which a joke writer employs are used by the ideas man in advertising. Whether or not he wishes to make a joke. Often the result is quite serious.

We have just seen an example of one of these – extension. The most common is the reversal or switch. 'When they run out of Löwenbrau order Champagne'. Sometimes the surprise is effected by bathos – the expected extension stops short. 'Volkswagen leaps into the present.' Compare this with Alexander Woolcott's remark: 'The English have an extraordinary ability for flying into a great calm.'

The *double entendre* is rampant in advertising. Though advertising's critics often see meanings which were not intended, undoubtedly today the number of 'permissive' joke headlines has grown. Santigo is a light rum. Its market is young. The headline is 'Santigo. One day you are going to be too old for it.' The illustration shows a party of early twenties' fellers and birds and two old fogies looking on disapprovingly. The copy knows its audience. 'You're at some party . . . you look at the drinks table . . . the spirit bottles are the oldest faces you've seen all night. With one notable exception. Santigo . . . it's not old, it's new. Not been round for ages. Only just begun.'

Often the shock is brought about by the juxtaposition of a picture and a caption. The elegant girl in the luxury car and the line 'Marcia isn't wearing panties' (she's wearing tights, get it?). The heartwarming news 'Fresh food is flying into Biafra' beneath the picture of a locust. The first of these is meant to be funny.

The second is serious in intention and effect. The technique is identical.

The pun is a common device in advertising and the most obvious example of a collision since the two matrices come together at a single word. A good pun is more than a self-conscious display of verbal dexterity but a felicitous coupling of appropriate thoughts. John Donne watching his mistress unrobe beseeches her:

> To teach thee I am naked first: why then
> What needs thou have more covering than a man?

In advertising, the best puns work on both levels at once. The two meanings are contributing to the selling story. The acid test for the advertising pun is 'would you want to say both these things if they weren't combined in a pun or is it merely a play on words for its own sake?' 'Player's Please' was presumably one of the best known puns in prewar advertising (though whether everybody appreciated it as a pun is another matter). Both meanings work for the product: the request at the tobacconist and the pleasure of the cigarette.

An advertisement for *The Economist* told up-and-coming business men that reading the paper would help them get to the top but it acknowledged that the task of finding enough time to read was not easy. It showed a managing director looking out of his window at his factory. *The Economist* is on the desk. The caption reads: 'I made it my business . . . to read *The Economist*.'

Product names can be puns. A new cereal in test market as I write is called 'Quake-Up'. It tells you what it does and who makes it.

Puns are not merely verbal. Schrafft's coffee ice cream is made from real coffee. The advertisements showed the tub of ice cream with a coffee pot handle and spout. Noxzema skin cream put the word 'pimples' in the headline, dotting the i with six dots. The German newspaper *Die Welt* advertised to advertisers on bus sides: one word in big Gothic type: GOTTERDAMGOODREADERSHIP. Smirnoff Vodka is exciting and odourless: 'Smirnoff leaves you breathless'. But puns don't have to work on both levels to achieve their effect in advertising. 'My Goodness My Guinness' fails our acid test. But the colloquial expression (My Goodness) allows the advertiser to equate in an easily assimilable way the product name and the benefit. Another prewar pun appeared in football programmes. 'Bovril feeds the inside right.'

Perhaps my favourite advertising pun was coined by Gray Joliffe for an airline, which was promising disembarking passengers immediate transport to their hotel: 'Out of the flying plane into the foyer.'

There are people who say that humour is out of place in advertising by which they mean it does not work. At least I think that's what they mean. (I don't believe they would criticise it for being improper if it worked.) It depends how it is handled and how relevant it is to the selling job. After all, nobody would say 'Is photography in advertising a good thing?' Out of context the question is meaningless.

A joke is high explosive. It is a hand grenade. It could win you a street fight: it could also go off in your own hand. Better maybe to leave it alone. Humour is subjective. Some audiences get a joke which others do not. Moreover, a joke often doesn't misfire, it backfires. Irony which is not appreciated as such is self-destructive. It is the very power of humour which scares people off. The joke becomes more important than the product. The medium takes over from the message. People remember the joke and forget the product. Often the advertiser has a joke at the expense of the product or he has been too subtle or too broad or he misreads his audience or he doesn't know when to stop. But these are examples, not of humour spoiling a good joke, but of *bad advertising*. The same faults can be made without the presence of humour. They are indeed made frequently every day . . . not identifying the name of your product, forgetting your audience, talking to yourself. And they often go unnoticed. The point about humorous advertisements is that they *do* get noticed. *Humour amplifies your mistakes*, increases the visibility of your errors. Some people could be afraid of being funny for fear of being made to look a fool. Just as some people prefer not to use direct response advertising for fear of being shown up. It is a high explosive weapon but the fact that it has to be used with care is no reason not to use it at all.

There is another criticism which goes like this: if the seller is not serious about his merchandise how can he expect the consumer to take him or his merchandise seriously? This view is summed up in Claude Hopkins' famous phrase 'people don't patronize a clown'. This seems to be about as relevant as saying people don't buy from typographers. There is all the difference in the world between taking your product seriously, which by definition any advertiser must do, and projecting an aura of seriousness. Of course it is a serious business making a product and planning its marketing. Of course it is a serious business when the prosperity of the employees is affected by the sales of the product. When £250 000 has been spent on an advertising budget. Bill Bernbach told me a story once when we were judging commercials at the Cork Festival. Doyle Dane Bernbach had just been appointed to the Chivas Regal whisky account. The agency were working on their first campaign. The label had recently been redesigned. DDB thought that this would make a good subject for the advertisement. They showed a photograph of the product and captioned it 'What idiot changed the Chivas Regal bottle?' The agency visited the client. The president looked at the advertisement and then at Bill Bernbach. 'Mr Bernbach, *I* changed the Chivas Regal bottle.' Bill Bernbach smiled and said, 'Call yourself a genius and people don't like you. Call yourself an idiot and everyone's your friend.' The ad ran. It was far more effective than a straightforward announcement of a label change. By admitting that not everybody will like what has been done it disarms the critic, enlists friendship and, of course, also announces the label change.

I believe people oppose humour in advertising for another reason (which is rarely expressed but hidden behind rationalisation). A sense, if not of guilt, then of discomfort. The puritan ethic teaches that if you enjoy something it can't be right. Work is serious. An advertisement has to work. If the client reacts to an advertisement by laughing it can't by definition be said to work. (Possibly the reverse is true. The advertisement has produced a reaction and if the joke is relevant to the product brief the advertisement can be said to have 'worked'.) The client (or agency executive) who smiles has exposed something of himself and feels vulnerable. Yet if an advertisement manages to get a reaction – any reaction – in today's crowded market place it has achieved *something* . . . something which the vast majority of single advertisements rarely achieve. The biggest enemy of advertisers is indifference – the public yawn. And advertisements help to create that indifference. The world is full of boring advertisements. Humour is a way (by no means the only way – but as valid as the others) of breaking the boredom barrier – of provoking a consumer into involving himself with the advertisement.

The advertiser could justify rejecting a humorous advertisement by saying 'I find it funny but I don't believe it will appeal to everybody.' He likes it therefore they won't. And not everybody does find the same thing funny. Thank goodness! You don't get the identical response from all of your audience. But you're not going to do that anyway! You're only going to reach – really reach – a certain part of your audience whatever you do. And by trying to go after everyone you may find that though you will reach everyone superficially – you will persuade none of them. Greed produces undistinguished advertising. And if a client believes that only he and a few others will understand the joke (i.e. that the general public won't) his belief can easily be put to the test with some communication research.

Another criticism of humour in advertising is also really a criticism of bad advertising. People say humour is irrelevant. Which is nonsense. Irrelevant humour is irrelevant.

Now advertising creative people have brought this criticism upon themselves. Much of the fun has been perpetrated at the expense of the product and much of the amusement has been had by creative people themselves and their colleagues in other agencies. The 'sophisticated' creative man can often force his 'superior' sense of what is funny past a timid client (who wants to appear sophisticated himself) and on to a bemused and indifferent public. The ad world is very small. If a writer is not careful he lives where he works. Home is a *pied-à-terre*. And almost certainly unlike the homes of the people he is addressing. He watches television as they do but not in the manner they watch it. He flips through the magazines to see how they printed his advertisement and he doesn't read the editorial, the stories, the features, the recipes. He jokes about the North starting at Potter's Bar but it is a double bluff. He means it. What's more the 'North' in the sense of the unknown is all around him. What does he know of the lives beneath the roofs he sees out of his commuter train window? Of the people in the houses which line the streets he back-doubles through towards work? He knows more about New York where he probably hasn't been. He reads their advertisements.

We were working on a campaign for a tomato sauce. An art director came into my room with the layout, with a picture of the product and the headline 'Stop Hunting'. What did it mean? He explained a little sadly. Hunts produced a tomato sauce and their headline was 'Hunt for the best'. The fact that it was an American product unknown in this country had either not occurred to him or had been dismissed as irrelevant.

Some television commercials contain odd asides from one creative man to another, little nudges in the ribs. Even Homer nods. In a Doyle Dane Bernbach commercial for Crackerjack popcorn a man is rummaging around his attic and comes across a sledge (he also finds an old packet of Crackerjack) and as he blows the dust away the name is revealed, 'Rosebud'. This is a reference to Citizen Kane. Sometimes the aside becomes a whole commercial. For a frozen food recently a very talented director made a series of pastiches of well-known films. The coterie went wild. I don't know what it did to the general public – or to sales – but to me the humour was irrelevant. The same people who find it 'terribly clever' would no doubt turn up their noses at what the public at large finds funny.

'I'm only here for the beer' has become a catch phrase. People repeat it at all sorts of odd moments but it doesn't make your actual creative genius laugh. It's not an in-joke. (More of an inn-joke really.) It embarrasses him. Mind you, many of the jokes that embarrass him embarrass other more professional advertising people just as much but for a different reason, namely that they serve no purpose. They attract attention perhaps – but to themselves and not to the product. But when a slogan or phrase passes into the language and takes the product with it, the advertiser has a bonus of publicity. This in my book is distinct from advertising. Publicity is advertising you don't pay for. 'Drinka pinta milka day', 'tiger in your tank', 'sinking feeling', 'My goodness my Guinness', 'that's Shell that was', are examples of publicity. And it is no accident that all of them are humorous. Indeed, the majority of popular advertising is funny.

There are advertisements which are 'just plain daft', which insult the intelligence of the average consumer, which are banal. But, to repeat, those are criticisms which might be levelled at any manifestation of bad advertising.

Humour probably is not suitable for all products though the range for which it is suitable has widened over the past decade (banks, insurance companies, charities, medicines, are using it). However, the decision whether or not to use humour must rest not simply upon the product but upon more immediate factors. One looks at the proposition, at the job the advertisement is supposed to do and then sees if a humorous idea can re-present that proposition. It may then be ruled out but it is far better not to preclude it from consideration at all.

There are three advantages which humour provides. First, and it is the obverse of a point we discussed earlier, not everyone laughs at the same thing. A joke in an advertisement flatters the receiver. As a result, second, the advertiser has established a *rapport* with the consumer. The consumer has identified himself with the product. He has joined the particular club which that product represents. The late Roy Brooks began running property ads in the posh Sundays which broke all the accepted conventions of estate agent advertising. It amused people so much that the ads became as much a sought-after feature of the paper as the editorial and certain, though not all, readers identified with his company. They liked the style, the understatement, frankness and occasional arch charm; they said 'that's my type of estate agent – he doesn't take me for a moron and therefore won't take me for a ride'. (I question the view which states that if a person likes your advertising he will automatically like your product and therefore buy it. But I do have a feeling that if he doesn't like your advertising he is far less likely to like or buy your product.) The third advantage brings us back to our continuum. The

F

closer the ad to the action the better the chance of a sale. An advertisement stands more chance of moving a consumer towards purchase if it gets him to do something. Very few advertisements get the consumer to do anything. We also discussed the oblique route which communication in advertising can take. A joke is always oblique. It does not make its point overtly. It invites the recipient to participate. The recipient has to decode the message. And, having done so, is more likely to remember it.

If I tell you something you may listen. If I tell you a joke you not only listen – you take part.

20

'Say something, if it's only Goodbye'

I was at a presentation to a client organisation not long ago. They had been subjected to twenty minutes of advertisements, a new campaign for their product. There followed the usual pause. Then the senior client turned to the marketing director and asked him:

'Do you have an opinion?'

The director looked at the work still on display, then at the agency, then back at his senior colleague and said: 'No.'

It is at moments like this that I remember the cartoon of the army squad marching over a cliff and am tempted to shout as they did to their sergeant in the rear: 'Say something if it's only Goodbye'.

Often clients are inhibited by the 'presentation' aspect of the presentation. They feel perhaps that they have been oversold. They need to reflect. Some clients have a policy of saying nothing except thank you. You leave the work, they take it away and a few days later a lengthy document thuds on your desk with all the comments which have tumbled out of the client since you turned your back. Emotion recollected in tranquillity.

A client once said to me very politely, *à propos* of some ads I had presented: 'Mr Bernstein would you now criticise the work you have shown us.' Contradictory feelings raced through me.

He had spotted something which I had not. He thought it was all marvellous and therefore *I* had to discover the faults which he could not find. Perhaps his way of doing things was by reasoned argument, by dialectic not showbiz. But was the real reason somewhat less complex? He did not know where to start?

Procter and Gamble give you a formal reaction. They have a book, a bible, a code of practice. They can judge any piece of work against a set of commandments. They also have a strict procedure. The most junior client representative begins. He begins by thanking the agency for the work, for the amount of work, for the thinking behind the work. For anything in fact but the idea. He then picks on certain aspects of the work and examines them against the canons of the P & G bible. What he invariably says is 'very interesting'. After all, there are probably at least two more senior colleagues to go in to bat after he has finished. Nobody, however, says 'Great!' or even 'Bloody awful!'

Other companies have other methods. The more methodical check the advertisement against the proposition, the agreed strategy. They ask the sort of questions we looked at in a previous chapter (what is the product? what is the idea being communicated? etc.). But after that they are in an uncharted sea of subjective opinion. Nevertheless they are in a better position than those who have no check list at all. Of course they bring to their task a great deal of special knowledge – informed opinion about the product, the competition, the market, etc. But what if they are asked to judge an advertisement out of the blue? This is the task facing a member of an advertising awards jury. Can you be expected to judge an advertisement in isolation without benefit of background knowledge. Are there in fact absolute criteria?

Absolute criteria do not exist. Any book which holds that advertising is a bastard art in the middle of an inexact science is hardly likely to advocate absolute criteria. Nevertheless there are signposts. This chapter and the five which follow, while not pretending to give universal laws for a good advertisement, attempt to determine some common criteria by which each piece of advertising may be judged irrespective of type of product, type of consumer or type of market. They constitute an *aide memoire*, an index of what seem to me to be the four crucial qualities every advertisement must possess. If nothing else they allow you when faced by a previously unseen advertisement to begin to think constructively about important matters rather than comment superficially or criticise inessentials or simply say 'very interesting'. The four qualities each advertisement must possess are:

● Visibility
● Identity
● Promise
● Simplicity

Their initials form the mnemonic VIPS which is an *aide memoire* to help you remember the *aide memoire*.

This chapter and the next deal with visibility. If an advertisement isn't seen nothing happens. Visibility could be said therefore to be the most important of the four qualities. One of the many dictionary definitions of advertise is 'to draw attention to oneself'. When you realise how many advertisements the average consumer is subjected to in any one day you realise too how difficult it is to gain attention and you wonder how successful some of those advertisements you see (blushing violets all) possibly can be, let alone those advertisements you don't see.

In the eighteenth century when newspapers were small, 'trade announcements were almost more interesting than the news. But when the papers increased in bulk and advertisements became common it behoved those who wished to attract special attention to resort to contrivances which would distinguish them from the surrounding creative competition'.[1] Doctor Johnson in 1759 said: 'Advertisements are now so numerous that they are very negligently perused and it has therefore become necessary to gain attention by a magnificence of promises and by eloquence sometimes sublime, sometimes pathetic.' Getting attention is the creative man's first problem. But attention from whom? The people to whom he wants to sell the product. The target audience.

---

[1] Sampson quoted by Mills, *op. cit.*

One of the tips that was taught me as a writer was to try to have the actual product on the desk or, failing that, a picture of it. If it does not actually inspire you at least it reminds you of the name of the product (and not all advertisements do that). But you should also try to keep in front of you a mental picture of the consumer. Impact is fine provided it is hitting the right target. Unfortunately too often impact is rough, unselective, hits everybody.

When advertising was young shrieking headlines and 'stopper' pictures had a novelty which no doubt attracted attention. Today such 'pathetic eloquence' falls on deaf ears. The noise is so loud, the clamour so general, that the only hope of communicating is to be specific, to remember the consumer you want to address and design your advertisement for her (or him). The funnel, remember, showed a manufacturer talking to *one* consumer. Advertising is messages one at a time. If you think of your audience as a grey impersonal mass you end up with grey impersonal advertising.

Leo Burnett in a memo to his writers:

Best attention comes from the entirely natural interests of the reader, built around the results of the product advertised. Being different from others is not an asset if the others are right. An ad may get attention and fail completely in getting anything else. An able show window designer once said 'The one thing to avoid is drawing a crowd. The hard thing is to catch the eye of every possible customer and keep the others walking past.' It is better to attract the serious attention of possible buyers than through an exaggerated and clever headline to attract other possible readers who won't be interested in the message anyway.[1]

There are many ways of attracting notice. We shall examine several. Each has to be judged on its merits. And remember these are only techniques. Ideas are more important than techniques. And an understanding of and sympathy for the consumer will help you choose the technique which is appropriate for the

---

[1] *Communications of an Advertising Man.* Leo Burnett, 1961.

advertising task in hand. This point is crucial. We met it earlier in our discussion of the continuum. *There is no divine order of effectiveness of media.* Once you accept that 'television is better than press' you have sold your birthright to a computer. Moreover, there is no law which says that 'a full page advertisement is better than an eleven-across-four'. A full page advertisement in a national newspaper may be 'lost' just because it is a full page. The reader says 'that's an advertisement' and turns the page: whereas a smaller advertisement, sharing a full page with an editorial which the reader wants to look at, has longer to attract and hold his attention.

Have you ever noticed two women in a noisy factory talking to each other? You can't hear a thing yet they are carrying on a conversation *without shouting.* An advertisement has to do this – know whom it is talking to, have something interesting to say and maintain a very high sound-to-noise ratio. The continuum taught us that all advertisements are calls to action and that each advertisement to be made more effective should be moved along the continuum. The study of communication showed that the best form of communication is one in which the recipient actively participates. If you know your audience, have something relevant to say to her, express it in emotive and active terms, she will stand more chance of seeing your message.

Note that I use the term visibility rather than impact. Impact is a manufacturer-orientated word. Impact is all one way. Visibility presupposes the participation of a consumer. It is the difference between slapping the consumer on the back and shaking her hand. You stand more chance of her not merely seeing your advertisement – but *seeking it out.*

At first sight this seems extraordinary. People tell you, 'I don't look at advertisements.' You nod knowingly because results tell you they do. However, you would accept 'I never look *for* advertisements' as more indicative of consumer reaction to advertising. Yet this does happen. Not merely with classified ads where people are consciously looking for a job or a secondhand car. But in display advertising where the seeking out is unconscious. Nobody except marketing and advertising people opens a newspaper and looks for advertisements but, having opened it, part of them is seeking satisfaction of needs and desires or information about topics which are of interest. The Rover 2000 owner will see a Rover 2000 advertisement in the *Daily Express*. The Triumph 2000 owner will probably see it too. The Fiat 127 owner may see it. The non-driver will hardly know it's there. Their participation in the advertisement will depend partly upon the interest inherent in the ad itself and partly upon the degree of interest *which they have already* and which they bring to the perusal of a newspaper. Selective perception takes place. The eye sees all manner of things rather as a magnet runs at random over a collection of objects but only those which are magnetic will be attracted. In advertising it is not essential to shout your message to be heard, to write your message in large type to get it read. The coupon-clipper can spot dotted lines from a hundred paces. Similarly the hard of hearing will see the headline 'Deaf?' in ten-point type in a two inch single. Media choice also affects perception. I lived opposite a man for about ten years. We never spoke. One day I ran into him in Derby. We spoke as old friends. It's the same with media. If you live in Croydon the word 'Croydon' in a headline in the local paper is unlikely to arouse interest. But in *The Times*, be it buried beneath a column of type, you will seek it out and read every surrounding word.

Though part of your task in writing the advertisement for the Rover 2000 must be to reassure existing owners (and this must never be forgotten) that purpose is unlikely to be primary. Should your target consumer be a Fiat 127 driver the advertisement must be designed with him in mind. Greed, as has already been emphasised, is one of advertising's deadly sins. Too many advertisements are addressed to everybody. Mass communication is a necessary adjunct of mass production. But even in an age of mass-consumption not everybody buys the same thing. J. B. Priestley coined the term 'ad-mass' to illustrate how manufacturers and advertising people view the millions of sentient individual human beings who see their messages. It is an indictment and we stand guilty as charged. It is time to do something about it. Not merely because we have to prove that our trade has become a reformed character and we have earned our parole but for the purely commercial reason that to think of the public as ad-mass is unprofitable. 'We shall aim to convince everybody' is no way to start a strategy for any product no matter how general its distribution, how potentially large its custom. 'Who likes to be thought of as "everybody"?' asks Jeremy Bullmore in the film *Risk and Responsibility*. He quotes an advertisement 'Everybody's talking about Shepherd brand mini-castors'. And comments: 'I happen to know that that statement is a lie.'

My earliest mentor, Robert Caplin, used to say 'Isolate a customer. If you want to talk to one-legged men in Manchester you can't do better than use a "strap-line" for your ad – "News for one-legged men in Manchester".' Similarly if you want to hire a French-speaking telephonist it makes sense to write your ad in French as the Post Office do. The people who can't understand it are the people you don't want anyway. Rank Xerox some years ago wanted intelligent salesmen. The ad could have said 'wanted – intelligent salesmen to join Rank Xerox'. This has the merit of simplicity and directness. However, a lot of salesmen consider themselves intelligent. The actual advertisement featured an illustration of the machine and beneath it some brief cases. The headline, in two parts to correspond with the illustrations, said: 'Successful copier seeks six originals.' Here was a deliberately oblique approach. It could be criticised for being too clever by half, for not getting to the point, but it appeared on a page of situation advertisements so the reader knew automatically that a job was being advertised. The approach demanded participation of the reader. The participant was exactly the type of person sought, i.e. someone who appreciated the style of the advertisement, the original mind which understood it. Instead of asking for intelligent salesmen it invited salesmen to *prove* their intelligence by decoding the message. The advertisement worked. Though in sheer volume of applicants the advertisement was less successful than others run by Rank Xerox, in *quality* of response it was superior. The advertisement got its six originals, the upper echelon, and since the people who did not reply were presumably not the sort of salesmen they wanted, it was just as well the advertisement was too clever *by half*.

Grabbing everybody's attention, as Leo Burnett's show window designer pointed out, may be counterproductive. Put a coupon in your advertisement and you're back to coupon-clippers. It is quality of response that matters: the number of conversions. Although you want action from your consumer it may be necessary to make it a little difficult for him to react in order to test how genuine his interest is (e.g. by having him send a stamped addressed envelope or pay for the catalogue). Attracting attention which results in action is pointless if the advertisement has not selected its audience and given sufficient information about the product. If people are invited to write away for more information this presupposes that *some* information has been imparted. Too often the information is either insufficient or in its attempt to attract, misleading. Either way the advertisement has failed to be selective, to act as a first filter: the result is a waste of printed material, company time and postage. Furthermore, if you appear to be offering something which, through no dishonest intention of your own, the consumer subsequently realises you are *not* in fact offering, you have lost not only sales but customer goodwill. (You are in the position of the advertiser who runs a message 'Hair falling out? Send one pound and I'll send you something to keep it in' and sends each applicant a matchbox.)

It is almost as essential to filter out the people you don't want as to select the people you do. Not every advertising man will accept this as fact. The number of ads containing lines such as 'Everybody reads . . .' or 'all the world knows . . .', bears witness to this. They believe that if the product can be used by everybody the advertising should be aimed at everybody. A beer was once promoted with the line 'People like X'. I can imagine the presentation to the client. 'This is a simple colloquial phrase, easy to remember and true. It mentions the name of the product, isolates the consumer (everybody) and gives reason for purchase, i.e. people like it. What's more we have stolen a march on our competitor Y with his masculine image campaign. Research has proved, gentlemen, that there are more people than men.' Cheers. This is the impact school of thinking. Whereas the visibility school says that since the product can be used by everybody then everybody should be able to purchase it. If, as advertising's proponents preach at every opportunity, advertising offers the consumer freedom of choice then for heaven's sake allow her to *choose*. Allow her to come up to your barrow and choose her wares. Use every device to persuade her but don't hit her over the head. Allow her to express her individuality. In choosing your product she is not simply responding to the hectoring demands of the ad-mass communicating advertiser but expressing something of herself. She is making an individual decision.

And by being selective in defining your audience you may get a surprising extra bonus. You may, in fact, interest everybody by talking only to some. The trouble with going after everyone is that you may satisfactorily reach none of them.

There was an examination question in English Literature which said, as far as I can remember, 'Shakespeare was not of an age but for all time – Discuss.' It was something of a nonsense question. It suggested that the two statements were alternatives, mutually exclusive. Whereas Shakespeare, by being so deeply an Elizabethan, reaches into all time. No other age could have produced Shakespeare. He responded to his environment, the limitations of his medium, the demands of his patrons, the desires of his audience, the state of development of the craft . . . responded as he thought fit, calling upon services which were then available. If Shakespeare had sat down and said to himself, 'Bill, with a genius like yours, mate, you ought to write something for the centuries to come', what sort of insipid, general and uninspired work would have resulted?

Similarly, by rejecting a general approach, the lower common denominator type of advertisement and homing in on a specific target, you not only produce a more definite advertisement but the individuality of that ad, its distinct and clearcut persona, attracts others who may not be the immediate audience for whom you are writing but whose custom is nevertheless welcome. The *New Statesman* boasts a lot of Tory readership. It does so because it is essentially a left-wing publication. Should it decide to go after a wider spectrum of political adherence it would lose its character and therefore cease to attract Tory readership.

Greed is the enemy of visibility.

The Post Office wanted to get people to use their phones more often – particularly in the evening. They ran a general campaign.

> Don't forget to phone your friends
> After six and at week-ends.

A simple, catchy rhyme which told people *en masse* when to ring (at the cheaper rates presumably) but not why. And, it was addressed to everybody. But the Post Office was also careful to specialise, to go after target groups. For example, getting off a train at Birmingham I was accosted by the following:

> Hey you with the briefcase,
> Ring your wife tonight.

That was me they were talking to and I rang her. But being presented with that idea in rough form many clients I know would have paused and made certain observations. 'What about the man who isn't carrying a briefcase?' 'What if he's not married?' 'What if he is on his way home anyway?' Don't laugh. These are typical reservations made by those who judge advertisements. *Remember, any advertisement can be rejected on rational grounds.* Show me any successful advertisement and I can give you one good reason why it should never have been run. In an inexact science I cannot, of course, prove that I am right but neither can anyone prove that I am wrong. If you try to accommodate objections to the ad the ad becomes weaker with every compromise you make. Whereas by making the specific approach you will without doubt attract the attention of people who, though neither male nor married, neither businessmen nor away from home, will be provoked into ringing someone that night.

People are interested in people. The prime motivator of consumer behaviour – self interest. Which of the following is Mr Blenkinsop most interested in?

- Football
- Sex
- His Job
- Mr Blenkinsop

No prizes for the solution. But if the advertisement is not specifically addressed to Mr Blenkinsop it is far better to address it to

Mr Jones or Miss Smith because next to himself he is interested
in other people and unless that advertisement is clear cut, defines
its target audience and itself projects a distinct personality,
Mr Blenkinsop won't bother to look, or pry perhaps.

People can be divided into two categories: 1. Those who
currently are using your product, and 2. Those who currently
are not using your product. (For the sake of this exercise I have
departed from the usual triple classification of users, non-users
and lapsed users.) Even suppose you wanted to talk to both
categories it would be more prudent to address just one and who
knows, if you're smart enough, you will get home to both. Here's
how Dial deodorant soap does it.

> Aren't you glad you use Dial?
> Don't you wish everybody did?

Non-Dial users, excluded from the advertisement may resent
being excluded and do something about it. *People are more
inclined to read messages specifically addressed to someone else than
messages addressed to everyone in general and no one in particular.*
Black Magic ran a press campaign for over twenty years consisting
of extracts from handwritten letters. Basildon Bond, more pre-
dictably, did something similar. Granada ran a campaign aimed
at getting more advertisers to use commercial television by
naming only one target consumer per advertisement. Naturally
everybody else read this private correspondence and got the
message.

The same principle holds for television. Many straight-talking
commercials with an announcer addressing everybody in general
arouse little positive reaction. Far better to use a 'story' technique
which tempts the viewer to eavesdrop. Or to address a specific
sector of the viewing public. Food manufacturers occasionally
talk to grocers telling them to stock up with a new product. It's
expensive if calculated on a cost-per-grocer basis. But, since
eavesdroppers are presumably potential purchasers of the
product, the 'waste' viewership is a considerable bonus!

Finally, a word about visibility on television. All the models of
the advertising business discussed earlier were designed before
television became an advertising force. It could therefore be

argued that the need for visibility is far less when you have a captive audience. If one interprets visibility solely as getting attention, then I would agree. However, though the viewer in his armchair, passive rather than active, is unlikely to get up and switch off the commercial or shut his eyes and ears, he is just as unlikely to participate in the commercial unless you do something to provoke him. The fact that you have been provided with a recumbent viewer does not excuse you from the advertiser's task of arousing his interest. You will have noticed that I am using visibility to cover both the first two acts of *Aida* – attention and interest. Too many advertisers assume that because the television medium has made them a present of the first they don't have to work at the second either.

This discourse on visibility – the gaining of attention and arousal of interest – has been concerned primarily with the question of selectivity. Which means knowing who your market is and understanding what motivates them. It is impossible to deal adequately with the latter point without discussing promise which we shall tackle later.

How do you know if an advertisement has visibility? Maybe the next chapter which details some techniques to help you achieve it will also help you know which advertisements have got it. Alternatively, answer this question: 'What advertisements do you recall seeing in the past twenty-four hours?'

21

Some techniques

Remember. This chapter is not a list of finite golden rules. They are not finite, nor golden, nor rules. Simply a few observations in no particular order on the art of attracting attention and arousing interest.

● An idea is more important than any number of techniques. Ancient rule of Chinese painting: 'If the idea is there, the brush can spare itself the work.'

Remember, too, that all mention of benefit, the motive power o any advertisement, is postponed to chapter 24. It's a bit like Hamlet without the prince but you might find a use for Osric.

Get the ad off the page

An ad has little time to attract attention. This does not mean that once attention is attracted, the reader won't spend much time studying it. Just don't rely on a complicated entrée. Don't, for example, put a full-stop in a headline for the sake of symmetry or because it looks like a Bernbach ad. (There was a very good reason in the original. Bill has been worse served by his imitators than by his detractors.) Full stops say the end. They hold up communication. Copy must move. Don't tread water. Paraphrase and you stay where you are. Each sentence must take the action forward. You're not writing a reflective poem: you're writing farce.

Use short sentences and some a little shorter. And light and shade. And succinct paragraphs. And active rather than passive words. And words that conjure up pictures rather than abstractions. And Anglo-Saxon. And simple language. Maurice Smelt, in *What Advertising Is*, says: 'Most advertising calls for pace, simplicity and urgency. Kai Lung is right when he says "When you are asking a way of escape from a pursuing tiger, flowers of speech can assume the form of poisonous bindweed."'

Don't set out to make an advertisement

If you set out to make an ad you will probably end up with something resembling all the other ads in the paper or on the box. Set out to try to motivate somebody towards purchase.

Don't use copy as a design element. Of course being part of a design it is just that. But its primary purpose is to put across the proposition in the most effective way. Form follows function. The purpose of the advertisement should dictate the shape. Don't make it too difficult to see or read. Allow plenty of room for the illustration.

Don't think in terms of laying out. It's what you do to corpses. Don't think that because the advertisement appears neat it will attract greater attention. The supermarket manager knows better than that. The end-aisle displays are rumpled before any customer enters the store. Discordant elements can help. Too many commercials are so polished that they slip down unnoticed. They have an almost too perfect shape. Conventions of form arise because fashion not function has dictated. The pack-shot, the freeze frame, the closing burst of music, etc., etc.

An advertisement should be more like a burr than a pebble.

Make the layout say 'Action'

Enough has been said about action already. Remember every

advertisement is designed to move somebody towards purchase and every advertisement can be made more effective by moving it along the continuum to the 'sharp end'. Leo Burnett said: 'Consider every ad like an approach golf shot – try to hole out – don't merely shoot in the general direction of the green.'[1]

Make sure the words and the pictures work together

This does not mean that they have to do the same thing. Or that the sales message is the sole responsibility of the former and the presentation of the product the sole responsibility of the latter. Often they can swop roles and the ad thus stands out from those around it. Often they can conflict, gain attention. They work together in that jointly they contribute to the total impetus of the idea.

'Less is more'

Précis is to copy what pruning is to roses. Layouts are improved by concentrating on essentials. The mid-shot is better than the long-shot, the close-up better than the mid-shot. If you want to show the chef of the kitchen at the Savoy Hotel you could start with a long establishing shot and then move in or cut to the chef. Or you could show the chef in close-up from the start and super-impose the word Savoy or have him say it or have another voice say it. It's simpler, quicker, cheaper and better television.

Don't show off

Ads should draw attention to the product not the writer or artist. Typography should be unremarkable. The moment the reader notices the typography rather than what it conveys you're lost.

---

[1] *Communications of an Advertising Man.*

Remember the medium

Ads on your wall are one thing. Ads *in situ* are something quite other. Always put your press advertisement no matter how rough into a newspaper. See what it has to fight against – what it can work with. Each medium presents its own problems and opportunities. Limitations are to be exploited. Each medium, different examples of the same medium, offer unique chances to stand out. Just as you don't write an ad addressed to the lowest common denominator audience so you don't design a lowest common denominator layout. It may save costs simply to adapt a press ad for a women's magazine or a poster but if the ad is less effective where is the saving? Even if the identical ad could make sense in all three media there are sufficient differences to question such a policy. A full page magazine, for example, has advantages and problems of a truly different nature from an eleven across four press-ad. If you tackle each medium on its merits you will almost certainly find better ways of using the same amount of your client's money. Instead of one advertisement on a right-hand page how about two advertisements half the size on opposite or successive pages? If your client has agreed to pay for colour and it isn't necessary you could spend the colour premium on a separate advertisement on a facing page listing all the stockists of the product for example.

If you are in *The Grocers' Gazette* don't headline your ad 'News for Grocers'. Remember the medium.

Move the goalposts occasionally

This isn't cheating. It's being creative, looking at things differently. For example, you may be selling a middle-of-the-market item to housewives in the 25–35 age group. Experiment. See what happens if you choose a medium addressed to older women. What seems ordinary in one medium may seem young and adventurous in another.

Read the newspapers

An advertisement should be news. Newspapers contain news.
Read their headlines. How often do popular newspapers use
blind headlines? (Yet how common they are in advertisements.)
How often do newspaper headlines tell the whole story so that
you don't need to read on? How often do they provoke the
reaction 'so what?' Notice how the popular press gets you into the
story in few words. And, having done so, how it encapsulates the
story early on in the copy, amplifies it in the second section and
fills in details in the third. Journalism has much to teach the
copywriter.

My favourite newspaper headline: 'Bank clerk elopes with
vicar's wife.' There you have sex, religion and money in six plain
words. All it lacks is royalty and animals. ('Bank clerk elopes with
vicar's wife and corgi.')

And use subheads. Not for decoration but effect.

Write enough

There's no such thing as a minimum or a maximum amount of
copy. Simply an optimum and that will depend upon the job in
hand. If your target consumer is in the market for a Hi-Fi he'll
read every word. If you're the New York police and have something strong to say then twenty-five words is not too long a
headline: 'If this year's anything like last year Dave Spreng will
save two lives, return \$89,016 in stolen property, make 82
arrests and deliver one baby.'[1]

Surprise

Every ad should surprise. Check your ad with someone who hasn't
been involved in its planning or creation. Does he go 'Mmm?
... aah!' If he does you have got a visible advertisement. The

---

[1] *Creativity in Communications*. Edited by Robert Adams, Studio Vista 1971.

surprise may be in the product claim or the way it has been told or it may be the shock of recognition. 'That's me. That's the way I feel', or the surprise at the statement of the obvious which no one before has recognised. It may elicit the response 'Why has nobody thought of that before?' But remember that irrelevant surprise leads to rejection. Relevant surprise leads to revelation. 'BOAC – the all-America airline' surprised, probably because BOAC flies to a dozen US cities.

Don't fool people. It's easy to surprise irrelevantly. It boomerangs and people are smarter than some advertisers suppose. You can say black is white but you've got to have a good comeback when they say 'how come?' Don't imitate the whisky manufacturer who said his whisky was free but he was going to charge £2·60 for the new type cap on the bottle. It got him attention but very few friends.

This ad got attention – and results – an illustration of a rat. The headline read 'Cut this out and put it in bed next to your child.' It was for anti-rodent legislation. People were invited to write to their Congressmen in Washington. The baseline: 'It's time we stopped giving rats equal rights with people.'

Make tricks – but don't be vulnerable

The English language is rich in meaning and ambiguity. The pun can work for you. It can also make people distrust you. 'A lot of girls in this bus are expecting little tots' is an intriguing headline on the back of a London double-decker. You get closer and read the next few words 'Cherry Heering of course'. 'Mmm? ... Ugh!' On the other hand a picture of a driving glove and the headline 'Careful drivers have Dents in their cars' is justifiable. It is not contrived. It mentions the name of the product. The name is the subject of the word play.

You can gain interest by 'related items', i.e. by associating the product with other products, with greater interest to the reader. The association, however, must be relevant and the link forged. There are too many advertisements where the related item takes over and the reader or viewer is not sure what is being advertised. And the mistake is often repeated the next time the consumer sees the ad. (Of course, the mistake is not the consumer's but the advertiser's.)

You can gain attention by deliberately not mentioning the name of the product, or omitting all copy whatsoever, by running a preliminary teaser advertisement, by pretending it is not an advertisement but editorial or a news bulletin. They can all get attention and arouse interest but be careful. Ask yourself what your reaction would be were you the consumer.

Don't make it too hard for the reader – or the blockmaker

Remember not everybody has perfect vision. Some of your readers may have older eyes than you have. White type reversed out of black may look dramatic but if it is difficult to read who needs it? Sans-serif type similarly has a pleasing aesthetic effect. But do newspapers use it – in body copy? And if the ad looks OK on coated art paper that may be fine for your specimen book but on the newsprint of a high-speed rotary press . . . ?

Remember the holy trinity

When I interview a would-be copywriter I ask him to play my version of Desert Island Discs. 'You have an inexhaustible supply of lower-case six point body copy but only 8 upper-case fourteen point words with which to attract attention. What are they?' If omitted from the eight are NEW, YOU and FREE I begin to suspect we're both wasting our time. The words are overworked and often used when they have no right to be but they are overworked for a reason. They work over and over. Remember them every ad you write. You may not need them but merely thinking about them will constitute a discipline. Tell yourself why you haven't used them, what you have used instead.

Get the nod

Though you may attract attention with a surprise you very soon want people to agree with you. You must 'get the nod'. A list of points which do not accord with your consumer's experience will result in rejection. Note – this is not the same thing as simply telling consumers what they know already but making use of what they know already to persuade them of something they may not know (often because they haven't used the product, ever or recently).

You could always do it better

Colin Forbes in a lecture reproduced in *Creativity in Communications*[1] chose to demonstrate the scope and power of graphic design by limiting his examples to one theme, the human figure and the different graphic ways in which we can illustrate it. He had time for sixty-two points, but as he explained that was only a beginning. 'There are endless different tangents for any of the points which have been made . . . with a few permutations and a little imagination the possibilities are infinite.' Combine that with the richness of the English language and you begin to realise that with the tools at your disposal the achievement of visibility in advertising need not be another labour of Hercules. Or, to put it more simply, ask yourself this question. 'Why do advertisements have to look like advertisements?'

[1] Edited by Robert Adams. Studio Vista, 1971.

22

Identity . . . 'I'll never forget what's his name'

'We interrupt this book to bring you a message from our sponsor. FLAKO. FLAKO flour makes the flakiest pastry. If you want pastry that really flakes you need flour that's really fine. And folks that means FLAKO. FLAKO the flakiest flour. So ask for FLAKO. And remember . . . FLAKO spelt backwards is OK ALF.'

Radio may never have been quite like that in its early days in the US but it wasn't far off. You may laugh at its apparent naïvety but one thing is certain, you remembered the name of the product, how it was spelt and what it was for. Why did radio repeat brand names so often? Because that was its way of imprinting a trade mark. Radio exploited its limitations. Denied the power of a visual, it had to exploit whatever resources the new medium could offer. It tried to equate the radio commercial with the print advertisement. In the latter the trade mark (or pack or company seal or whatever) took up, say, 25 per cent of the total area. Therefore the brand name should take up 25 per cent of the time bought. The visual trade mark had a distinctive look or shape. This was one of the brand's main assets. The word 'brand' means signifying mark. Probably the 'brand' was as old as the brand. Suddenly along comes radio and if you're not careful all that investment brings you no return in the new medium. What do you do? Either you draw attention to the look of the product so that the listener will recognise it next time in a store, or in a magazine ('look for the blue and yellow label', 'reach for the can with the stars on top'): or you find ways of forming a trade mark in the listener's mind by means of the spoken word and sounds (e.g. spelled out names, character voices, singing trade marks).

Then a strange thing happened. Radio, which was a lap behind in the branding race, overtook the print advertisement. Radio, like another No. 2, tried harder. Print with all its resources relaxed. Ads became more refined in layout, dignified in copy approach. An advertiser, though he would never ask a news-paper to set his copy, often had to leave his commercial to the station announcer. Therefore he paid more attention to the essentials. Essentials which the print (particularly the magazine) advertiser had decided to forget or thought he had outgrown.

Radio – the poor boy – had to fight to prove its value to the advertiser. When a client wants to know if a creative man really believes in what he has produced he turns to him and says 'Mr Jones, would you run this campaign if it were your money?' Would he? If he were writing an ad to sell his own car would he employ some of the tricks and adopt such an elegance of style . . . ? One thing is certain. He would make sure the reader knew the name of the advertiser!

This chapter is about identity. At the end of chapter 20 I suggested that one test of visibility was to ask yourself what advertisements you recalled seeing during the past twenty-four hours. Though any ads you may recall will certainly have visibility, the test is not comprehensive. Whereas all advertise-ments you spontaneously recall are visible, not all visible ads do you spontaneously recall. (Moreover, I am dubious about the association of recall and effectiveness.)

A better test of visibility is to tell another person the name of the advertiser and see what playback you get about the advertising. Try the test in reverse – describe an advertisement and see if he can mention the name of the advertiser – and you have the perfect (and frustrating) test of identity.

I would like you to imagine two scenes. In the first an advertiser calls in an agency chairman and tells him he wants him to advertise his product X. He has £100,000 to spend. He hands it over in one pound notes. The agency man counts it and puts £20,000 on one side. He asks the client for an envelope and the name and address of the major competitor Y. He puts the £20,000 into the envelope, borrows a stamp from the client and posts it to Y. Of course nothing like that ever happens. Hang on.

In the second scene the agency has spent the £100,000 on an advertising campaign for X. The advertiser has commissioned some communications research. Twenty per cent of the respondents interviewed thought the product being advertised was Y.

I have yet to explain the difference between the two scenes. There is none. And yet twenty out of a hundred 'getting the name wrong' is not unusual. Much higher scores have been recorded. One meets it every day. In the business. A colleague comes in and says 'did you see that great cigar commercial last night? There was this bird walking down the street and this feller . . .' And you ask the name of the brand. He pauses, mentions a name and then 'or was it . . .?' If this happens among advertising people what must be going on out there?

I went to a party once where we all got to know each other by playing party games. Advertisements had been cut from newspapers and magazines, pinned on the wall and the product names had been removed. We had to list the twenty or so missing names. I came first, as indeed I should have done, being the only advertising man there. But my score was about fifteen. The majority of the others got less than half right. And they had presumably seen all of the ads before and could make the odd intelligent guess.

Long-in-the-tooth account executives, often admittedly at a loss for something to say when presented with an ad, would ask the art director to put his hand over the product name and then turn to the writer and say: 'You know, the competition could be saying that.' To which the reply is either 'they wouldn't say it the way we're saying it' or, more petulantly, 'Aw – you can do that with any advertisement.' But can you? More to the point – should you? Failing to imprint the personality of the product on the advertisement is writing a letter and forgetting to sign it. Worse, it's writing a letter and signing it with the name of somebody else. Unidentified advertising is responsible for the most frightening waste of company money. Unless, that is, you happen to believe that each advertisement in a product field by advertising generically and not specifically contributes to a total increase in the sales of that product field. But this does seem a bizarre way of going about it! Most profligate of all – in percentage though not actual terms – are the corporate and prestige advertisements. As an earlier chapter has shown, the further back along the continuum you are the less concerned you are with the factors of an advertisement which contribute to action. Had my party host chosen all his examples from *The Economist* or *The Times* the scores would have plummeted, not simply because the guests would not have seen the ads as often as those for packaged goods, but because the copy would afford them few clues and the slogans would seem interchangeable. One day I asked an executive what she knew about a certain shipping company. Her knowledge was scanty but she did remember the advertising. She described it to me. I remembered it too. A simple and elegant commercial for a different shipping company.

Now when people make mistakes (unless they happen to be directly involved in that product field) it is no cause for shame or embarrassment. Often I have seen creative men look at a bad communications research score and hear them blame the respondent for her incompetence as if she had failed a simple test. Whereas it is he who has failed to observe a simple precept which, if he was trained at all, was taught in his first month of advertising. I was so taught by Robert Caplin. One of his three rules for headlines: *State name of product.*

As one develops one 'grows out of' rules. One graduates, puts away childish things. If all advertisements followed the same rules all advertisements would look the same and where would be identity then? However reasonable this attitude may appear it is valid only if the rule-breaker understands the underlying reason for the rules and makes sure that though he may have broken the letter of the law he has upheld the spirit. When you are taught that the headline should state the benefit use of the product confers you may decide that since the illustration is doing that superbly the headline, instead of reiterating it, should be amplifying it. And your decision would be justifiable – for the purpose behind the rule has been observed. Similarly, to return to identity, it is not absolutely essential for the brand name to occur in the headline – provided that it occurs in the consumer's mind as a result of looking at the total advertisement. Art directors will tell you that it is not simply a matter of putting a logo at the bottom of the page or at the end of a commercial, but that 'the whole advertisement must be a logo for the product'. This is a statement with which I utterly concur. If the whole advertisement has an unmistakable personality then one has indeed projected a full page or thirty second logo. And the promise has been inextricably identified with the brand name. Unfortunately the argument is too often used to justify inferior work, to defend the omission of the logotype without a compensating branding by means of distinctive design. Repeat – distinctive.

Some art directors hate some logotypes. It would be surprising were it otherwise. Nevertheless to reject a logo, to pretend it doesn't exist, is to lessen the chances of the advertisement being effective. A logo is untidy. It clashes with the rest of the advertisement. (The fact that this one 'discordant' element may in fact help the ad achieve visibility is conveniently ignored.) Certainly to put it in the headline will hold up communication. But to leave it out completely while not replacing it with a unique identifying total design is to push arrogance to the point of disaster. For the design of the advertisement will probably owe more to current fashion than to the character of the product.

One of the more regrettable consequences of advertising awards is the growth of mimicry. A prize advertisement, no doubt deserving of its accolade, will, twelve months later, have spawned a dozen imitators. An original solution to one product situation becomes, the following year, a not wholly suitable device for different products. Yesterday's idea becomes today's technique, tomorrow's cliché. I have already warned of the danger of imitation, of adopting mannerisms from other advertisements, of aping a style without comprehending the reasons why that style came about, how it developed as the solution to a specific advertising problem. The consequence is a general application of one hand-me-down graphic solution to all manner of advertising problems. So the very art directors who reject the rules because they lead to uniformity of visual approach adopt instead a graphic design indistinguishable from the competition and from products outside their product field.

It is no recent phenomenon. Here is Leo Burnett describing the practice in a speech made to the Tea Council in Bretton Woods. Having reminded his audience that 'advertisers were deeply conscious of the need of planting a visual symbol of the brand into the public consciousness in the old days' he goes on:

> One agency was largely responsible for the junking of this concept during the 'thirties. They did it by convincing their clients (who were followed by hundreds of others) that the ornate, cumbersome, hard-to-read logos were ugly and difficult to handle in an ad. So before the war, you could rifle through a copy of *Life* and see dozens of identical looking brand names, each neatly centered at the base of the ad, each set in 36 point Futura Demibold.[1]

Now the art director reading this – or the one you work with or employ – would never be guilty of such a crime. If he drops the logo he replaces it with a distinctive total look. So that when people see the ad they recognise it as an ad for that product and that product alone. Right? This is an improvement. Yet there is still a difficulty to be overcome. By replacing one logo with another (the 'ad/logo') the advertiser now has *two* logos. And since the original was rejected presumably for being old-fashioned, or ugly or somehow unsuitable, the two logos will therefore be very different. Thus the consumer is faced with confusion of images. The art director would be better advised to use the existing logo and to occupy his spare time with a *total redesign* of the company's corporate identity and planning a gradual phasing out of the old and introduction of the new. At least this way he would be able to prove his point and not cloud the issue while doing so.

Another factor contributing to lack of identity is a search for

---

[1] *Communications of an Advertising Man.*

identity. By the agency. Looking for a house style. 'Le style est l'homme même,' said Georges Louis de Buffon. It is virtually impossible to avoid projecting a personality when you are writing or designing an ad. It will have your trade mark. As opposed to your client's trade mark no doubt. When an agency has at its head a powerful and single-minded practitioner the influence is felt in every advertisement that agency produces. A strong creative director may put his style on everything his department turns out – even without knowing it. For often the members of the department prepare work which they believe he likes in what they believe is his style. The work of a few agencies can be recognised instantly from the pages of a newspaper or magazine or from the television screen, occasionally even when you are out of the room. And indeed, I expect many an advertiser has gone to a particular agency because he likes what they have done for X and wants something just like it for Y.

I believe the deliberate formation of an agency style is immoral. It is using the client's money to advertise yourself. This is not to say that each advertisement you do should not also be an ad for yourself (i.e. an advertisement you are proud of and which you can present to an interested purchaser of your services on your show reel or reproduced in a booklet). Nor am I against a 'style of the house' similar to those which publishers adopt (i.e. the stylistic rules concerning capital letters, quotation marks, indentation, punctuation, spelling, etc.). This is commonsense business practice: establishing conventions in communication. But to extend such conformity to layout, amount of copy, typography, style of headline, size of logotype, size of space, choice of media, is to substitute formula for thought. Top creative people who would no more use a cliché in their copy than wear pin-stripe trousers and a bowler, commit these far bigger clichés of total design. (The origin of the word cliché is worth reviewing. It is a printing term. Individual metal letters were put into a slug by a printer. Certain combinations of letters recurred: these frequently-used words were then cast in metal as entities. They were called clichés. It saved the printer from the labour of putting the letters together. Just as a cliché saves the writer or artist from working too hard.)

In the previous chapter I advised: 'Don't set out to make an advertisement.' If you set out to make an ad you will probably end up with something resembling all other ads in the paper or on the box. Indeed, you can take the advice more stringently and before setting out to motivate the consumer towards purchase you can ask yourself if that is the correct or only solution to the client's problem. By tackling the task from the very beginning and freeing yourself from all prejudged solutions and premature media constraints you are more likely to arrive at a unique answer to your client's problem. It won't guarantee identity but it will considerably reduce the chances of people forgetting the brand name.

23

Identity . . . some techniques

This chapter will review a few methods to assist you to achieve identity.

A. '*I'm only here for the beer.*'
B. Great slogan.
A. Which beer?
B. Er . . .
A. Try this (sings) 'A Double Diamond Works Wonders.'
B. You're flat.
A. The beer isn't. Which beer?
B. Don't be ridiculous. Double Diamond, of course. You said so. It's like asking me who wrote Beethoven's 5th.
A. How about this? 'That's Shell that was'. Which oil company?
B. Mobil.
A. Come on cooperate.
B. This is silly.
A. '*We try harder.*'
B. Avis.
A. Very good. Now you try harder – '*You'll never be the same again.*'
B. Gordon's Gin.

A. India.

B. The tyre company?

A. The country.

B. The country?

A. You can take it anywhere.

B. White Horse.

A. What do beans mean?

B. Heinz.

A. What prolongs active life?

B. Pal.

A. Fortifies the over forties?

B. Phyllosan.

A. I'm only here for the beer.

B. Mmm . . .

A. Clue . . . it also works wonders.

B. Double Diamond?

A. The same.

B. Good luck – and goodnight!

As we saw in the last chapter it is never too early to begin thinking about identity. The identity of a product must enter into the preliminary discussions before the proposition is formulated. If possible the proposition should be unique but the uniqueness should be relevant. Otherwise uniqueness will have to be a function of the idea. The advertising itself will by its translation of a non-exclusive proposition communicate a distinctive idea. In all this the advertiser must remember to ask himself 'does the image I am projecting set me apart in a meaningful way from the competition?'

The vogue word for this today is positioning. Claims are being made for positioning which suggest that it is second in line to the Reformation and a step ahead of sliced bread. In the swing away from 'creativity' which apparently was the OK word for the 1960s (just as 'marketing' was for the 1950s) 'positioning' is presented as the panacea for all the advertising manager's problems. I don't attack the concept – merely some of the claims made for it. That plus the idea that it is new. Advertisers have been practising it since the century began. Unknowingly maybe, like Monsieur Jourdain in Moliere's play who suddenly realised that he had been speaking prose all his life! Indeed, many of the examples the proponents of this new faith use in testimony are the very same advertisements which were recognised as 'creative' in the previous decade.

The furore in *Advertising Age* in 1972 was yet further evidence for my theory that the only advances in advertising are semantic. Positioning is identity writ large. Identity is more, certainly, than signing your name. Here follow some observations.

Identity comes out of the product

Start out believing this even if at the end you have to apply identity almost as an afterthought. Has the product a unique feature? If not is there a feature which it shares with others which you can pre-empt? If the competition then claim they also have this feature they will be doing you a favour unless, of course, they outspend you by a considerable amount.

The nature of propositions and the ideas they inspire has already been described. The whole subject of promise is dealt with in the next chapter. What follows are techniques which can be applied irrespective of promise. They should not be regarded as alternatives to a unique idea but as additional reinforcement. The first group are visual, the second verbal.

Make the whole advertisement a logo

If this rule is observed – and not merely paid lip service – you have no problems. It requires skill rather than genius, craftsmanship rather than imagination. And it requires tenacity. The number of possible ingredients in an advertisement is infinite (see Colin Forbes's point in chapter 21). It should not be difficult to select a distinct combination of photography, typography, lettering, art and copy styles. Why ads have to look like other ads baffles me. The trick, of course, is to maintain your ad/logo. It is too easy to compromise, to let the controls slip when you have a specific job to do (e.g. include a coupon, address the trade, run a promotion) but with a little ingenuity the style can accommodate such a tactical diversion. Look at the US Volkswagen advertising. Each ad is unmistakably a VW ad and though there is a small VW logo, there is no continuing slogan. The whole advertisement is a logo.

Some critics will say that if you reveal the name of the advertiser people will not want to read the advertisement. This reveals not only a lack of faith in their powers to arouse and maintain interest, but confused thinking and inability to distinguish form from content. The form (i.e. the ad/logo) merely identifies the name of the advertiser: the content can communicate any of a million messages.

If you own a logo make sure people know it's yours

A little preliminary communications research will tell you if what you know, they know. It is not very smart to spend a lot of money advertising a symbol if the symbol isn't inextricably linked in the public mind with your company. Otherwise you may have to undertake a two-stage campaign – associate the claim with the symbol and the symbol with the company. Mobil used to have a flying red horse. It is now gone to that great stable in the sky. Why? Because Mobil conducted some research and found that though the horse was known, its parentage wasn't recognised. Mobil's new symbol is simply their brand name in blue with the O in red. I am not advocating that all symbols should simply be the brand name. This inhibits flexibility of usage (see later). But there is one great advantage. Nobody takes it for anyone else's trade mark.

A logo must be read before it can be recognised

Ideally your logo – whether it's a name or a symbol, a combination of letters, a distinctive type face, a few pencil lines – will communicate immediately no matter where it is, what size it is or how far away the consumer is. All this must be of major concern to the designer ... and many designs which look good at presentation look less happy *in situ*. Nevertheless, there is always a preliminary stage to be gone through. The logo must be 'read' before it can be recognised. If there are words make sure that in its early life the logo is presented sufficiently boldly for those words to be read. For example, suppose you are designing a label. Eventually a shopper will take that can off the shelf without reading the name: she has merely recognised the label. But what she is recognising is a shape or collection of elements or colours or words which she had previously studied. See the Campbell's story later in this chapter. Do not assume because the brand-leader can sell on sight that you as a newcomer can dispense with the need to convey information.

Make the logo work

Our friend remembered the White Horse slogan because it contained the name and also because the symbol was part of the advertisement. The series of ads featuring the white horse in various civilised situations could be advertising no other whisky. Certainly not Vat 69 who also brand their advertisements just as effectively as they brand their whisky. Here the logo becomes a subject of a conversation between the advertiser and the public. Other examples of working logos are the shadow-man for Sandeman's Port, the 'woolmark' for the International Wool Secretariat (the beam of light in the commercials), the Green Giant, the Little X for Silhouette (where the name of the product is the logo), St Ivel, with the logo stamped in the countryside.

I wrote a commercial once with Peter Langford. The client had said to us a few weeks before: 'What I'd like to see is our trade mark on the screen for all sixty seconds.' We had smiled politely. Later we set to work. And unconsciously answered the brief. We had an oval face singing a jingle. There were four characters representing different countries. Each sang a verse of the jingle : in between the oval face became the Esso sign. The song was 'The Esso sign means happy motoring'.

Remember – a press ad is also a poster

People both read and scan newspapers. They read and scan newspaper ads even faster. An advertisement, therefore, exists on two levels or two time scales of attention. To the reader it is a press advertisement: to the scanner it is a poster. If you manage to create an ad/logo at least the form of your ad will be communicating the name of the brand. Whereas if your advertisement is not distinctively designed it will communicate nothing. Remember this the next time you feel the ad you do or are shown may look less than unique.

Change your style at your peril

'What are all these people doing on my account?' asked the client visiting the agency.

'Well those five over there actually plan and create the ads.'

'And the other fifteen?'

'They make sure you don't change it.'

Once you decide upon something give it a fair chance. That goes for form and content. But remember you can change content without necessarily changing the form. Coca-Cola's advertising has changed somewhat since the last century but the can would be recognisable to a ninety-year-old lapsed drinker. And no one could accuse Coke of being old-fashioned. Certainly a brand style needs to be updated but the method and timing have to be assessed with care. Lyons changed the fascias of their tea-shops to Jolyon (Joe Lyons – get it?) just when the ornate Victorian lettering was coming back into vogue.

If you have no reason to be dissatisfied with the directly attributable sales results of your advertising for heaven's sake don't change its form until you have tested it, comparing it, for example, with the standard version in a carefully controlled test area.

A logo is more than a name

If you decide that all you need is a simple typeface remember anyone may use that typeface. Whereas if anyone uses your combination of colours, shapes, letters or symbol you can sue him for passing off. And that applies equally to advertisements and labels. A propos of this I want once more to quote Leo Burnett.[1]

Not long after the war Campbells conducted 'some exhaustive package tests':

> A certain proportion of cans in the test stores were marked 'Gongdotte'. This combination of letters was used in a style resembling the familiar Campbells' script lettering on the familiar red and white Campbell cans. Another group of cans in other test stores were identical in design to the regular label but green and white rather than red and white. Now here are the results: Just as many people bought the 'Gongdotte' cans as bought the regular Campbells cans. The difference in the two cans was not noticed. But what happened to the green and white cans? People left them strictly alone.

Pirelli is another example of a logo which is more than a name. The distinctive representation of the name becomes a thing itself. You can slice off the top of the logo and it still 'reads'.

Try putting the name in the headline

Do something really old-fashioned. Put the name of the product in the headline or failing that in the slogan, or failing that make sure that the name comes out of the advertisement. Who knows you may end up selling somebody something. And the next time somebody asks you what you work on and you say X she might even complete the headline for you.

'Just wear a smile and a Jantzen.'
'That's Shell that was.'
'I'd walk a mile for a Camel.'
'Don't forget the fruit gums mum.'
'Did you Maclean your teeth today?'
'Things happen after a Badedas bath.'

---

[1] *Communications of an Advertising Man.* 1st edition 1961.

Use a mnemonic

A mnemonic may be visual. For example, the floating 'woolmark' mentioned earlier, or the famous 'white tornado' used by Ajax liquid cleanser some years ago. The trouble with the latter is that (as in the case of a symbol) you have to make sure that people associate the mnemonic with the brand name. However, when Lifeguard disinfectant used a lifeguard, bathing shorts and all, they overcame that problem.

A mnemonic may be verbal. For example PAL for dogs – *P*rolongs *A*ctive *L*ife. Award yourself the CDM (Cadbury's Dairy Milk).

Use a pun

These range from the sublime to the excruciating. 'Player's Please.' 'Avant Guardian.' 'Tide's in dirt's out.' 'Does Powe tend to corrupt?' 'Join the Truman beings' (probably my own pet hate). And for a miniature TV set – 'Climb upon my knee Sony boy.' They all forge the brand name into the promise.

I always wanted to do one for the Egg Marketing Board 'Un oeuf is as good as a feast.'

Use a rhyme

Here again teeth may be set on edge.

'Crunchie makes exciting biting.'

'Whenever you cross the road use the Green Cross code.'

Nevertheless even the more serious advertising agencies aren't averse to rhyme. They are not up for the job of poet laureate – merely strengthening by every means available the link between promise and product.

McCann-Erickson were once employed by a manufacturer of car batteries. One of the team, Joan Bakewell (whatever happened to her?) produced a four word slogan 'I told 'em Oldham'.

Awareness shot up instantly. People were quoting the line eight years after the campaign had finished.

Use assonance

Examine words whose sound resembles that of the brand. For example: 'My Goodness. My Guinness.'; 'Beanz Meanz Heinz.' The subsequent alteration of the s to z helps visually further to identify the brand. Incidentally, the slogan is a triple rhyme in parts of the north-east and Scotland where Heinz is pronounced Heenz.

There is also *visual* assonance. 'Say yes to SAYE.'

Use alliteration

Alliteration is as old as Beowulf and as old hat as Spiro Agnew. Nevertheless it can help. Ask Phyllosan:

'Phyllosan fortifies the over forties.'

'Brook Street Bureau got big by bothering.'

Maybe it ought to scan?

Sometimes a line scans because it is meant to be sung. But not always. In the war there was the exhortation 'Lend to defend the right to be free' (also containing an in-rhyme). Undoubtedly rhythmic lines are easier to recall.

'Set it and forget it with Twice as Lasting hair set' (another in-rhyme).

'Soak yourself soft like this Johnson's baby.'

'Fabergé made love and called it Kiku.'

Music helps

Somebody once said 'If you've got nothing to say sing it', and certainly some of the lyrics of advertising songs look pretty thin plain on the page. Nevertheless music does help you give a distinctive character to your commercial. And if you use the same words on a poster or in a press ad they strike a chord. The poster sings! Music can make even the most difficult and unmemorable brand name come to life. If Johnny Johnson, the doyen of commercial music writers, can put a beat to the 'Co-operative Permanent Building Society' there's nothing music can't do.

But make sure it's distinctive. In music as with everything else advertising follows trends rather than starts them. First of all someone hears a particular sound of, say, a group or a singer and appropriates it for a commercial. Then someone else uses that sound. Possibly the very same agency for a very different client and before you know it once more yesterday's idea has become today's technique and tomorrow's cliché. Or an agency has developed a housestyle.

Sound helps

The range of sound is almost as wide as the range of visual devices. A single voice or a combination of voices can add distinction to the sound of the product name, concocting an aural trade mark. Accent, delivery, emphasis, pronunciation, all can be employed in an attempt to brand. Whether it's an echo chamber or a sound effect ('Setlers bring express relief' uttered as if a train were doing the talking).

It's never too late to identify

Although you should never plan to add identity as if it were icing on a cake, it is better to do that than let something through which may sell the competition when a little ingenuity could possibly prevent it.

I was on a TV commercial award judging panel. First we shortlisted. Then we saw the short list. Then we made our final selection on the basis of points. A clear winner in one category was a paint commercial. We all applauded our joint choice. The idea was simple, relevant and original. It came out of the product. It demonstrated. It had pace. What more could one want? It

was for a polyurethane paint. To show its strength the pins of a
bowling alley had been coated with the product. Then all hell
broke loose as a succession of balls hit the pins. The pins were
examined in close-up. Not a mark! The jury was just about to
ratify the ballot's numerical decision when one member said:
'What was the name of the paint?' Of the eleven jury members
five said one name, three said another, three couldn't remember.
They were all wrong. And they had seen the commercial three
times in the past hour! And paid far greater attention to it than
any normal person! Yet the solution was simple. All that it needed
was to write the name of the brand one letter at a time on the
individual pins. That way it would have remained on screen
throughout the thirty seconds without in any way detracting
from the dramatic effect of the demonstration. That way it would
have won its award. More to the point, it would have been a
more effective commercial. Not for paint – but for a *specific brand
of paint*.

It is worth stating that the majority of the jury who mentioned
a paint named the brand leader. This was telling evidence of
the advertising law on identity. If an advertisement does not
identify the name of the product the consumer will probably
assume that the product being advertised is the brand leader.
Therefore no matter how good the idea, how original and distinctive in itself, you still need to forge the brand name indelibly
into the idea. Otherwise the brand leader will benefit. Indeed
the more powerful the unidentified ad the more the brand leader
benefits!

24

Doctor Johnson, Glenn Miller and

the seven deadly sins

Doctor Johnson (I forget which agency he was at) said two hundred years ago: 'The soul of an advertisement is promise, large promise.' Doctor Johnson also said in 1759: 'The trade of advertising is now so near to perfection that it is not easy to propose any improvement.' Which proves he wasn't right all the time. But the doc was right about promise. It's just as true today and nobody has said it better.

I remember the first time I met Glenn Miller. I was waiting outside the Corn Exchange, Bedford. Our paths happened to cross. He was doing a broadcast and I was collecting autographs. I had waited an hour. He came out of his staff car and rushed up the steps. 'After the show,' he said. I kicked my heels for two hours, one of which was spent listening to the live broadcast on his car radio with his sergeant. There was a crowd by the steps. I was in front. At last Glenn Miller came down with a British major. I went forward. The major brushed me aside. Glenn Miller tapped the major on the shoulder and said, 'I promised the kid'. And that was the second time I met Glenn Miller.

An advertisement may be the first meeting of consumer and product. The second meeting may be purchase. The advertising man makes promises on behalf of his client but it is the client who has to keep them. If the advertiser allows a promise to be made which he knows he cannot keep he deserves whatever ignominy or legal action results. (There are authorities who regulate this from within the industry. There are government departments who are vigilant without.) But the toughest reaction and the best safeguard to the consumer is lack of sales. An unkept promise loses repeat purchase. As the adage goes – advertising can sell a bad product once. Thankfully today the percentage of deceitful promises is very low. There are borderline cases where the authorities permit the 'acceptable puff' ('the finest X in the world') or the fantasy statement or hyperbole. The attitude of the CAP or ITCA is more adult today. It recognises that in certain areas advertising is something of a game where literal truth is not the only truth and the consumer is not an idiot who believes everything, a game in which the consumer knows the conventions. Nevertheless the underlying truth of the fantasy must be veri-fiable. Evidence must be forthcoming of any claim made on television for example. Today then it is not simply a question of promise them anything – but which promise?

Every ad must have a promise. Examine all the advertisements in today's paper, on the box tonight or on your way to work. Virtually all of them will be stating or implying a promise. Sometimes you have to work at it before realising what is being implied. Sometimes an advertiser asks you to provide the promise.[1] Sometimes the advertiser has assumed that mere mention of his name is enough. Sometimes a brand is so well known that name-reminder advertising is adequate. When a name does not immediately conjure up a product or, more particularly, a product advantage, then such arrogance is counterproductive. Sometimes an advertiser appears merely to be giving you news – he is moving shop, putting up prices, apologising for a mistake, 'wishing this function every success' – announcements which seem to promise nothing and often to act as a disincentive. Nevertheless the long-term effect of any public announcement by an advertiser to a consumer is to move that consumer towards purchase and though, say, an announcement of a price increase may seem to be doing the reverse, the fact that the advertiser

---

[1]The Australian Labour Party's compaign had a slogan : 'It's time'.

is doing it not surreptitiously but publicly is contributing to his image or corporate identity and such advertising is, as we have seen from the chapters on the continuum, different from other forms of advertising not in kind but in degree.

The promise begins at the latest with a proposition. As we saw the proposition must be related to a consumer desire. Thus it is folly to begin defining the product promise without defining the consumer and getting to know her. The need to get beneath the what to the why of consumer purchase led to the vogue in the late 1950s for motivation research. Some of the heat and hot air has abated but the original reason for enquiry is as valid now as it ever was. It is fashionable to make fun of the earnest middle European psychologist-cum-sociologist-cum-witch-doctor who sees symbols in everything and hidden motivations in every normal human function or problem. And, frankly, some of their practitioners brought the odium on themselves. Nevertheless the very people who knock Ernest Dichter are the people who use his ideas, albeit in a modified form. The language suffered a change: 'consumers buy the sizzle rather than the steak' or 'appetite appeal' or the one word 'motivate', are witnesses to the adman's acceptance of the postwar researchers' effect upon the trade. 'Imitation is the sincerest form of flattery', as the omnipresent Doctor put it.

Dichter's magnum opus is the *Handbook of Consumer Motivations*, subtitled *The psychology of the world of objects*. It is required reading if only to rid you of any lingering doubts you may have of the viability of a strictly logical, factual (100 per cent Reason 0 per cent Tickle) approach to advertising; to remind you of the paramount importance of the consumer ('It would be fair to say I am consumer orientated', Dichter) and the differences between them (see for example Dichter's comparison of furniture buyers in the USA and Japan).

If you hope to make a mark on a trade or industry you have to bang very hard. Overstatement and overclaim may bring a counter-attack but at least it makes you visible and gets you remembered. If you modestly present a modest thesis nobody takes notice. Ask McLuhan.

People buy products for a baffling mixture of 'reasons'. Pinpointing the actual motivator is difficult and, having done so, don't yet shout Eureka: you still have to communicate, in a credible and yet often disguised way, that the motivating factor is actually part of the product. The deeper you probe into the motivational field the more delicate your communication task (e.g. product fields such as cigarettes, cosmetics, fashion wear). The bald statement of promise is adequate for most product categories on most occasions but for some products the real motivator is to be inferred from the advertisement: perhaps it is hidden in the body copy, perhaps it is actually denied in the advertisement, perhaps the picture while seeming to illustrate a subsidiary promise is in fact acting as the prime motivator. For example, the marketers of books through mail order know that people buy imitation tooled leather volumes as much for their impressive looks and titles as for their literary or educational content. But it is the latter two appeals which get the top billing since the direct appeal would provoke a negative reaction (cf. It's smart to drink Campari) and the route to the primary motivation has to be oblique by way of the body copy or the illustration suggesting what the text does not say.

Often the bald statement of the main promise is unnecessary since it is taken for granted and/or is generic to several brands. A supermarket, for example, may decide not to talk price cuts since supermarkets and bargains are generally synonymous. It therefore concentrates its main approach upon freshness or choice or trading stamps, though ever watchful by means of consumer research that the customer does believe that its name presents good value.

To ask why a consumer buys a product may seem unnecessary. It seems obvious to the manufacturer and to the consumer when she is interviewed. But both of them could be wrong, the first in what he thinks and the second in what she thinks she thinks. The subject is far more complex and is affected, of course, by the nature of the product. Ask yourself why you buy a loaf of bread or why you buy a car. Even the first answer is not straightforward. Bread is a staple. Yet if the need for nourishment is the prime motivator why not buy flour and yeast and make it yourself? 'Because bread is more convenient.' But there is probably more goodness in home-baked bread. 'The bread I buy has vitamins.' But home-baked bread is cheaper. 'I buy a family loaf which is cheaper than the small loaf.' But if you want to save money why do you buy a sliced loaf? 'It saves time.' That's why you buy it wrapped? 'Not only that. Wrapped bread stays fresher longer.' How thick are the slices? 'Thin. That way I get more.' Do you ever buy thick sliced bread? 'Occasionally. My husband likes toast.' And so on. But notice all this discussion has been about a staple product – bread baked by a single bakery. It has not begun to deal with the choice of bread between bakeries (or between white and brown, or crusty and farmhouse, or bread and crispbread). The complexities are numerous. With a car they multiply.

Perhaps you were tempted to equate bread with need and a car with desire. This is a useful rough divider of appeals. But once you examine any product you begin to realise that the number of basic needs are very few. Self-preservation, food, shelter . . . that about sums it up. Advertising does utilise appeals to all three. Yet having satisfied each of these basic needs a man soon entertains individual desires. As we have seen the need to satisfy hunger soon blurs into individual preferences for type of bread. The need for a roof over your head gradually becomes a desire for a type of roof and so on. The need/desire dichotomy does not take us very far. I believe we have to substitute a check-list of our own, and that all advertising's promises can be classified under one or more of the following nine basic drives. They consist of a mixture of needs and instincts.

- Self-preservation
- Love for others
- Self-expression
- Envy
- Sloth
- Lechery
- Gluttony
- Pride
- Covetousness

I don't apologise for using six of the deadly seven (I've omitted anger – it's used very rarely). They represent the extreme form of human instincts. As a checklist it is easy to remember.

There is no product which can't make an appeal to the majority of those nine drives. (Not of course in the same advertisement.) Try it yourself with as mundane a product as a box of matches.

Self-preservation	Safety matches – none safer
Love for others	Light the candles on her cake . . .
Self-expression	Different colours for different occasions 'Matches your every mood'
Envy	The matches of the stars
Sloth	Easier to strike
Lechery	You never know who'll ask you for a light
Gluttony	You can never have too many matches in the house
Pride	British made
Covetousness	More matches per box

Now take a daily paper and see how many of the categories are covered in one issue. I tried it and found:

Self-preservation	Dry air can be harmful to health
Love for others	Should you die your family would . . .
Self-expression	Imagine! Your home almost covered with giant roses
Sloth	Stop weeding!
Lechery/Envy	Join the latest free-bosom look . . .
Gluttony	Pick real strawberries for up to 9 months of the year
Pride	Would you spend £1·50 to look years younger?
Covetousness	100 toys £1

All this in a Saturday issue of (surprise) the *Guardian* of 28 October 1972.

One other instinct might be included to judge from the large number of headlines which included the word new – love of novelty. Yet though advertisers would seem to promote novelty for its own sake there is generally a secondary promise (often admittedly only implicit). 'New' is an excellent motivator. Novelty will stimulate purchase but the purchaser is looking for a better way of satisfying an existing desire. And even if she purchases something new for novelty's sake then she is in fact being motivated rather by self expression or pride of ownership.

The product name itself is often a promise. It used to be easier to christen a product with a claim but legislation has made it far more difficult. Noxzema skin cream means No Excema. Platignum suggests a precious metal. (Neither of these neologisms would be permitted today.)

Comfort is a fabric softener. This is perfectly valid. It is not so specific a claim, nor is it deceitful. The advertising began with a sung slogan, 'Softness is a thing called Comfort.' Subsequently the integrated campaign was superseded by a new promise of clothes-care: 'beats fibre fatigue'. This interesting development suggests that comfort/softness is not the main motivator for consumers or that it is no longer an exclusive property or that since it is already taken for granted in the brand name, another claim can also be assimilated by the consumer.

Signal toothpaste is striped. It's called Stripe in the US. The American promise when the product was launched was that it cleaned teeth effectively as well as being fun to use. The same approach was used in the UK. It was an attempt to justify the purchase of a seemingly flippant product for the serious business of cleaning teeth. But apparently it was not justification enough. It was replaced soon after by emphasis on the fact that the stripes contained mouthwash. The purchaser is given a justification for purchase. She knows it's got stripes, that it looks like fun. But she didn't know about the mouthwash and there's a real benefit. Whether that's also the real reason she buys it is another matter. Perhaps she buys it because she thinks the kids will use it more if it's fun. So the mouthwash story serves as buttressing reassurance.

The motivating promise of Signal existed already in the product. (It was found, incidentally, by the J. Walter Thompson creative team who invented the product after 'brainstorming' on toothpaste generally and finding an obscure chemist who had perfected a method of tube manufacture which could lay a stripe on the toothpaste.) Other examples of promise in the product: a pre-buttered waffle (Pops up buttery); a shampoo that doesn't tangle hair; a stocking which supports the leg and also looks expensive ('Pretty Polly – sheer support' – a good pun). Advertisements promise people things they want and things they never knew they wanted. The public wasn't crying out for a waffle which popped up buttery or a cracker that 'tastes as if it's buttered already'. Or a cure for 'night starvation'.

Advertising sometimes has to remind people how much they like things they have forgotten about. Appeals have to be aimed at the lapsed user. It's a large market. For example, Cadbury's Dairy Milk Chocolates must have more lapsed users than never-users. Their television campaign is as anxious to win back old custom as retain existing and stimulate new custom.

This chapter began by stressing the need to make promises which can be kept. This is not a plea for believability: it is a plea for truth. An advertisement which is true may not be believed; yet purchase may take place. People are willing to suspend disbelief to try a product, particularly if it is new. There is much confused thinking about believability (especially, as we saw, in the case of fantasy). Consumers show a healthy degree of scepticism about product promises. Although you should not let this scepticism tempt you to say *anything* about a product you should not necessarily try to find a promise which is universally believed. Any distinctive expression of your product benefit will arouse indifference, suspicion or even disbelief in some quarters. You must accept this. The only alternative is to state the product ingredient and show it. But that is not advertising. Advertising is advocacy. And not everybody believes an advocate. If an advertiser wants to be loved by everybody he should stop advertising. How, asks the consumer can all those competing products be best for me, which is what all of them seem to imply? They can't. Face the fact that a lot of the public don't like you and disbelieve what you say. Furthermore, that some of the people who try your product do so with the intention of proving you're a liar. Some of them change their mind. But not all. If what you say is honest then you have nothing to worry about – save the fact that you haven't the monopoly either of sales or people's affections.

Your troubles start when you promise something you can't deliver. Perhaps because the product isn't available. Perhaps because the advertising overclaimed. The *Sun* newspaper when it first came out as a revamped *Daily Herald* oversold itself. A totally new paper was promised. Initial sales were good. The public picked up at the news-stand . . . a *Daily Herald* with a new name. The vast majority of new readers did not repurchase. When Rupert Murdoch bought the *Sun* and out-mirrored the *Daily Mirror* the advertising made even more strident claims but the paper lived up to them. The circulation zoomed. Who knows what might have happened if the first *Sun* launch had played its strengths (essentially that of the old *Herald* with a little re-burnishing) and not gone in for promises the product could not keep?

Today's *Sun* advertising is about the best in Fleet Street. Because it comes out of the product. It is a sample of the paper. I will go further. I maintain that every advertiser should attempt to make his *advertising as near as possible a sample of the product*. It is easier, of course, in the case of newspapers. You list what is in the issue, include extracts, put the ad together in the style of the paper itself. Nevertheless each advertisement can deliver something of the actual product. Even if it is only a feel, a tone of voice.

This 'theory' is no more than an extension of the earlier belief that any advertisement may be made more effective by moving it along the continuum. Samples – actual samples or 'pieces' of the product are given out at the sharp end of the continuum. The salesman can give the consumer a piece of product to hold or feel or eat. Direct mail can encompass a sample or a free gift. A newspaper or magazine can include a piece of the actual product (e.g. Band-aid, J-cloth, perfume sachet, Nescafé slipped into the magazine or attached to a page). Or the ad can give information about the product in such a way that the consumer is vicariously tasting, feeling or eating. The copy and the illustration (or the audio and video on TV) are a substitute for the real thing. The individual taste of Cinzano is represented by optical and sound effects together with the phrase 'the bright lights taste'. The refreshing quality of a drink can be tasted by showing thirst-making images – a dry, dusty desert, a searing sun, etc. A foreign language school can give you a few phrases to practise with. An American candy, Life Savers, showed the product realistically and captioned the illustration: 'Don't lick this page.' A copying machine took a full page ad, drew a dotted line inside the page and thus demonstrated the machine's breadth and depth. A ride in a car. The feel of a flour. The tingle of a toothpaste. These are not simply demonstrations – they are samples of the product. They are more effective commercials because they exploit television's limitations to the point where those limitations seemingly cease to exist. The viewer is trying the product. As Harry Wayne McMahan has said more than once in *Advertising Age*, 'Demonstration is television's long suit.' Yet how little is it used.

McMahan insists that an advertisement should reward the consumer. I concur. The consumer should take something away from the ad. Perhaps it is information about the product or advice on some aspect of cooking or life. But the best and most potent reward is a piece of the product itself. Clearly it can't always be done. But equally clearly it is not being done as often as it could. Promise is the soul of an advertisement and therefore though we have reached the end of this chapter we shall inevitably refer to it again.

25

Simplicity – and other complex thoughts

VIPS.

Of all these Simplicity is the most difficult to write about. Though most people in advertising would agree with the dictionary definition of simple – 'consisting of one thing or element . . . not complex' – they would disagree about its interpretation.

Some would be very simplistic. The product equals X (a product feature, for example). Research has proved that X satisfies consumer desire Y. Therefore all the advertising has to do is present X to those consumers and they will buy it. Others, while admiring such resolute single-mindedness would disagree. To them advertising is not as 'simple' as that. The how is as important as the why: the route is never that direct. Others would believe in pursuing a basic promise throughout all the advertising campaign but adapting it according to the target audience. They would in fact divide their audience into 'sub-targets' and suitably adjust their approach varying it according to age or class or according to the media in which the advertising appeared. Others yet would have no basic promise but a *series* of promises for a series of audiences. Certainly if the product is sold in different countries the nature of the promise may change dramatically for a variety of reasons, e.g. competition has pre-empted the claim, there are local peculiarities, local legislation forbids certain appeals, the product is in fact used for totally different reasons (particularly in underdeveloped countries) etc. But even in the UK the same product may successfully be promoted across a broad spectrum of appeals.

Again, an advertiser may say that there is no one appeal for his product, no single promise which will attract the total potential audience. The truth is that some products have a variety of promises each of which could work on a substantial section of the potential audience. Why should a manufacturer confine his approach to a single unified promise? Why should he deny the full potential of his product? You can understand such a manufacturer's impatience with an agency which tries to sell him a slogan. 'No slogan can sum up what we are.' Now often this attitude may simply be another example of greed. He tries to be all things to all people.

The scene is the client's office. Facing him are an account executive and a writer. They are looking at the script of a proposed television commercial. The client reads it a second time. There is a hush. You can hear the pile settle in the Wilton. The executive scrutinises the client's inscrutable features. The writer is reading the in-tray. Suddenly an explosion! 'You've left out water-repellent.'

The client pudges the script. The executive reacts with disbelief, follows the client's gaze, reads. He thinks for a moment. This is the test, the moment six months of arduous discipline in the graduate trainee scheme have fitted him for. He clears his throat, turns to the writer and says: 'You've left out water-repellent.'

The writer, who was thinking of joining CDP anyway, is about to say something constructive like 'Get stuffed' when the client amplifies his objections.

'The competition is saying water-repellent but we've been repellent for years.'

The writer shrugs. 'We're tight for time. If that goes in something else will have to come out.'

Now this far from fanciful episode illustrates a common human condition. Client and agency agree on a unified proposition but the idea is rejected for not being comprehensive. Possibly the chosen medium is wrong. In our illustration clearly the choice of television for what appears to be a complex technical story is questionable. However, the wish to include all manner of selling points occurs in package-goods clients advertising in media other than television. But if they hope to attract attention and arouse interest (visibility) they have to resign themselves to concentrating their attack and this means inevitably a lopping off of minor claims. By trying to say too much they will end up not saying anything.

Often the people they are trying to please are not the consumers but members of their own organisations. The result of the joint labours of an agency-client team may bear little resemblance to the objectives they jointly agreed. Strategy is too often given the nod by the same client management who subsequently muddy the water by raising objections which have to be accommodated. The result is advertising by committee. If the reservation is a serious one then it should have been considered at the outset. Therefore the agency needs to go back to the beginning and reconsider in the light of new facts. If it is not serious it can easily be dismissed. Which is easier said than done. Fear of the boss, a pulling of rank, a pressing deadline . . . all contribute to a situation of make-do-and-mend.

Committee advertising is easy to plan. Start with a mutually agreed promise. Add a committee. And you get committee promise. Or com-promise for short.

A trained eye can detect committee advertising any day of the week. The commercial which ruins a single-minded story by adding a subsidiary related product at the very end. An end shot of the pack which incorporates a flash giving details of a special offer not mentioned in the rest of the commercial. A slogan which seems out of place in the advertisement since it does not encapsulate the argument of the ad: it is a hangover from a previous campaign and lives on perhaps in a subsidiary position, though its *raison d'etre* has gone. An ad which crowds in so much detail that comprehension is minimal and eyesight strained – always supposing it can attract attention in the first place.

And yet there would appear to be no simple answer to the

question of simplicity. What would you do were you an advertiser with a complex story to tell who is informed by his agency that the best medium for his potential audience is television? Do you attempt to tell all in the time available? Do you cut frequency and increase the length of each of the reduced number of spots? Do you leave out what you believe to be powerful arguments? Do you change to another medium despite its seeming unsuitability? Do you divide your budget among different media, believing as many people do, that each medium has a different job to do? This perhaps could allow you to tell your whole story in press, the barebones on television and run the company slogan on posters. Some advertisers seem to regard their multi-media advertising campaign as a book. The poster is the frontispiece; the television advertisement the preface; and the press campaign the text. Or possibly each chapter is a different advertisement.

For example, Tampax has an advertising plan which has changed little in the past twenty years. A Tampax ad is easy to spot (visibility) and easy to recognise (identity); it is also simple in layout and the promise is singleminded. Nevertheless one ad is slightly different from the next. The advertiser rings the changes. He appreciates that the Tampax story cannot be told in one advertisement, that a slogan cannot adequately encapsulate the total promise or the number of interrelated promises. All an advertisement can do is represent exactly a particular consumer satisfaction to a particular group of consumers. A roster of such advertisements will cover the whole potential market.

Then suppose you had to promote tomorrow's edition of a newspaper in a sixty-second commercial. No reader buys the paper for all its items. Your television audience is even wider than your existing readership. You could attract non-readers with one item, lapsed readers with another and reassure existing readers with a third. Can you do this in one commercial?

Though this may sound a negation of all that has gone before there are two reasons for an affirmative answer. One general: one specific. The general point we shall deal with at length. The specific point concerns the nature of the product. The newspaper, since it appeals to several different types of reader, can afford to offer different types of bait. The effect upon a viewer of a commercial of many parts is almost invariably confusion. However, in the case of a newspaper or publication or indeed a television company screening a trailer of forthcoming programmes, the individual viewer selects from the hodge-podge those items which interest him. This is very different from the normal packaged goods advertisement which crowds into a short space several compartmentalised themes which may seem mutually exclusive and contradictory in turn. In the latter case confusion is understandable. The consumer is not sure what he is being offered. In the former, however, though indigestion may occur, the consumer knows that he is being offered a variety of things, one or two of which he may be interested in and may motivate him to buy irrespective of the other items which he will receive as a result of that purchase.

Occasionally a multiple claim can work for packaged goods. But the public is sceptical of the all-purpose product even if it uses that product for a variety of purposes. Would the woman who washed her hair in Fairy Liquid (as many do) be attracted to the product if the advertising portrayed this secondary use? More to the point how many other consumers would be dissuaded from purchase? How would you promote a product which performed all of the following functions:

1. Promoted a sun-tan without burn.

2. Repelled flies and insects.

3. Removed tar and grease from the body.

There is such a product – I've used it. It has not yet appeared on the market. What would it look like if it did? Where would it be sold? And as what?

Many products have other uses some of which the manu-facturer knows about only after consumer research. Deciding what to do about them is a delicate operation. Should the sales situation remain buoyant he will probably decide to do nothing. Or perhaps run an isolated test. A downturn may tempt him into advertising a new use. But that use will have to be related to the existing use otherwise confusion and rejection will result. Furthermore, the British public is somewhat sceptical of versatility in product or personality. There is an intuitive national distrust of the complete man, a sad decline from the glorious Elizabethan ideal. Versatile products are thus Jacks-of-all-trades. (Unless, of course, they fall within a special versatile category – for example, Sellotape, Uhu glue, Vaseline.)

Even when the product has only one use there remains the problem of which way to present that use (i.e. which promise to concentrate upon). Yet there are ways of promoting several promises within the same campaign and within the same single advertisement. It will depend, of course, on product type, available budget, media choice and how the advertising is handled.

If this gives the impression that the answer begs the question by prefixing it with an all-excluding qualification (that all I am saying is 'horses for courses') I hope what follows will correct it.

The second and general point I wish to make is this: the most important aspect of simplicity is single-mindedness of tone. The Tampax campaign, for example, runs a gamut of reasons for purchase but maintains an identical sameness throughout. Each advertisement is unmistakably Tampax. Similarly though the composite newspaper commercial may deal with several items each item is treated only as that newspaper would treat it. You will observe from this that identity and simplicity are inter-related. Guinness currently advertise on every possible medium. There is no slogan and yet the campaign has a unity far stronger than a mere unifying slogan – a unity of tone. Every Guinness advertisement projects the identical persona. Whether it be a poster in the summer JUST THE WEATHER FOR DARK GLASSES or a poster in the winter TALL DARK AND HAVE SOME; whether it be a women's magazine ad NICE GIRLS DON'T DRINK GUINNESS or a television commercial (a non-Guinness drinker drinks a glass with his eyes shut, enjoys it and then opens his eyes and says: 'But I don't like Guinness') or a cinema commercial (where two drinkers stare out of the screen, the one believing he is in a pub, the other telling him he is in a cinema).

The variety of approach is matched by a variety of promise. Guinness is satisfying, can be served cool; is worth overcoming your prejudices for; is part of women's liberation; is a 'sociable' drink, etc. Though none of my flat-footed statements is in fact a copy-line. Nor are they all included in any single advertisement.

Guinness advertising is recognisably Guinness because it treats each of its many promises in each of its several media with exactly the same sensibility. Guinness satisfies a complex pattern of needs and requirements. So for that matter do many products. To concentrate on one promise and then pursue it relentlessly to the exclusion of all others may be the correct policy for the majority of advertisers but it is clearly not a universal law. 'Simple' we know means 'consisting of one thing or element'. The advertiser must decide what that one thing is: is it a single promise unswervingly projected or is it a single personality whose makeup is complex but whose every manifestation is consistent?

The first policy is more common than the second. It is the traditional approach. But economics is on its side as well as history. There simply may not be enough money to vary the individual components of a campaign in one medium let alone allow the advertising the luxury of a second medium or a support campaign. Sometimes production costs prevent an advertiser from changing his advertisement according to the particular publication he appears in. If newspapers and magazines differ from each other as much as their owners claim then it would seem sensible to adjust one's message or the direction of the appeal to accord with each particular publication. But the commissioning of new artwork and 'mechanicals' eats into the production budget. Even to decide on four advertisements instead of three in a campaign will add to expenditure. Whether the increase in flexibility is worth the extra expense or, alternatively, whether it is better using media money for production and thus increase flexibility at the expense of frequency . . . such questions are advertising's equivalent of the one about angels on a pin head.

The first policy states with commendable logic 'We want to be one thing to all people. We don't expect all people to respond in exactly the same way. We expect some people to reject us for the very reason that others accept us. We shall concentrate our efforts on the area of most potential. Greed dissipates those efforts.' The second policy states: 'We want to be different things to different people in what we say: but one thing to all people in the way we say it. We believe that the consumer is a complex being, that he or she may buy our product for different reasons at different times. Indeed, though he may read two separate publications he is somehow different reading one than he is reading the other. If this is so with one consumer how much more complex must it be when we consider consumers *en masse*. Accordingly we attempt to provide the consumer with a lot of information and several promises and let him get to know us and all of our attributes so that he may choose those which accord with his needs and requirements. We shall not be greedy by attempting to do everything in one advertisement. On the other hand we shall not pretend that a single ad can do justice or a single phrase contain our essence. But we shall be ruthless in maintaining a unity of mood.'

Attempts are frequently made to sum up a variety of promises in a composite slogan. Though for what purpose other than to satisfy an atavistic desire for a slogan I cannot discern. For example, 'X gives you more to choose from'. 'It's all at the X now', 'X gives you more of what you buy a so and so for.'

A critic once said of Caliban in *The Tempest* that no such creature could exist but if one did he would behave exactly as Shakespeare depicted him. If a product were to live a life of its own it too must behave exactly as its creators decree. This means that the product performance must be consistent with the product character and that each manifestation of the character must be of a piece with every other. I am not advocating a brand image philosophy, asserting that brand image is more important than product claim or whatever. Brand image is a fact of life. It may not be the prime reason for purchase but every brand has an image and it is better that this fact be recognised by the advertiser and that he defines that image at the outset rather than let successive brand managers and agencies and creative groups decide for him 'what character it should have today'.

David Ogilvy is clear what he wants his products (all of them apparently) to have – 'a firstclass ticket through life'. The advocates of USP are clear, too, though they would probably use less fanciful language to express it.

I remember attending a large meeting at Procter and Gamble

to discuss research into synthetic detergents and soap powders. We had been reviewing attempts at eliciting consumer reaction to the various competing brands. The conclusions were less than revealing. After about an hour of seemingly profitless discussion I suggested that we ought to ask consumers: 'If you were going to a fancy dress ball would you go as Fairy Snow or Persil and why?' The silence was a mile long. And yet not long afterwards Stephen King, in charge of creative research at JWT was asking not very dissimilar questions of a group of housewives and filming their responses. What sort of person did they think Persil was or Daz or Fairy Snow? The housewives' replies were fascinating. They spoke of products as people they knew, piecing together a complex but consistent pattern of characteristics induced from their own experience and the behaviour of the product through its advertising. To be fair to P & G they themselves soon adopted a freer attitude towards their strategies. They experimented with their 'tone paragraph', that third section of the quintessential strategy document on which all creative work is based. They invited the agency to draw up 'character studies' of each brand.

It should be observed (and I have never seen the point made before) that this desire to build up character profile composed of several contributing traits has grown in parallel with a desire to get beneath the simple statistical classification of consumers according to age, sex or social economic groupings (A, B, C1, C2, D, E). As Francis Harmar Brown says:

> One has to ask what sort of people they are . . . how they see themselves, what sort of relationship they have to the product field we are dealing with. We also need to know something about the whole pattern of attitudes and behaviour which underlie the purchase and use of the product and the choice of a particular brand.

The vogue word for all this is *psychographics*.

It is perfectly understandable that an interest in consumer psychographics has grown in tandem with an interest in product psychographics since what one is trying to achieve is a marriage of consumer and product, and, just as one does not choose one's mate for one particular characteristic but an amalgam of many, so one chooses a product for a mixture of qualities (real and imaginary) which cohere into a recognisable whole and with which one identifies: in certain categories it is relatively unimportant but in others, such as cigarettes, it is paramount. Furthermore, qualitative research not only provides an insight into consumer behaviour and motivation, it also directs the advertiser to attributes which can provide the key to a product's image. Therefore it should precede all creative work on the brand and ideally should precede the initial launch of the product. Cigarette campaigns realised this before the others. The Piccadilly No. 1 incident is a case in point. The fact that the advertisement virtually stated the proposition is not to deny the validity of the preliminary thinking. The key to that strategy was the fact that people upgraded themselves when they smoked Piccadilly No. 1. The market was segmented accordingly.

Market segmentation is a vast and intricate subject. One of the best analyses was written by Alan Hedges[1] who puts the case for concentrating 'on a clear and definite appeal to one class of needs even if this means neglecting the requirements of other groups of consumers'. Note that he talks about class of needs rather than class of people because, as he goes on to show, the dividing line may cut across other more normal dividing lines.

Any market can be broken down in a vast number of different ways – for practical purposes the total number of possible ways can be regarded as infinite. Each of the following categories, for example, could give rise to a host of different kinds of categorisations and the list is not by any means exhaustive.

A. *The Product*
  1. its characteristics
  2. its price
  3. its performance
  4. its purpose
  5. the satisfaction of using it

---

[1] *Market Segmentation.*

B. *The User*

   1. demographic characteristics (sex, age, class, religion)
   2. product usage pattern
   3. product attitudes
   4. life-style
   5. self-image
   6. psychological or sociological typology
   7. media exposure or shopping patterns
   8. geographic region

C. *The Usage Occasion*

   1. circumstances of consumption
   2. time of consumption
   3. mood of consumption
   4. purpose of consumption

These categories are loose and overlapping and the list could be extended indefinitely but they serve to illustrate the variety of ways in which segmentation can be approached.[1]

One way of describing such segmentation is to say what Bloggo users have in common is the fact that they use Bloggo. Don't let the cynicism fool you. Despite the circular nature of its argument it utters a truth and waves a flag warning you of the dangers of superficial targetting.

We seem to have departed somewhat from our theme of simplicity, but in emphasising the need for defining the character of the brand and that of the audience I am in fact emphasising also the need for singlemindedness of approach. The 'one thing or element' which simplicity is about is not a single promise or a single visual style, though these are important, but a unity of tone. Every manifestation of the product must be consistent with the defined image.

There is another aspect of simplicity which we ought to deal with, though it should not detain us long – *simplicity of execution*. All the efforts to achieve single-mindedness, from initial research to approval of the basic idea, can be sabotaged by sloppy craftsmanship. Approval of the idea means approval of the disciplines

---

[1] *Market Segmentation.*

inherent in that idea and inherent in the proposition which brought it about. Approval is not a signal to go wild. Douglas Haines[1] says: 'A good art director must have a strong finishing burst ... he must be as unbending and particular when he scrutinises finished artwork as he was with the first rough scribbles. It is endlessly surprising to see how art directors will relax their grip when it comes to such details as retouching or masking.' And photography, one might add, or lettering, or typography, or (including the writer in the general criticism) the copy and the subheads and (now the agency producer) the choice of artistes and what is in frame during the shoot and what music accompanies the film, etc.

All this is detail. But none the less important for that. A product profile is made up of such detail. One jarring element, one wrong word, one ill-chosen model, one 'clever' shot or expression can detract significantly from the total effect of the advertisement. Of course obsessive attention to detail can be laughed out of court ('I stopped buying the product when they changed the typeface to Bodoni Condensed') but *details matter*. A complicated layout which frustrates readership may undo an otherwise very simple advertisement. A choice of the wrong typeface (or the inclusion of exclamation marks) may give the product an alien tone of voice. The choice of the wrong voice in the commercial will do the same. The question to ask is simple: '*Is every detail consistent?*' If not change it or remove it.

People don't look at advertisements very often, and rarely because they want to. They are dissuaded from approaching too closely by a complicated layout. At home they often have no option but to watch the commercial but they can easily be distracted. The use of a well known actor can lead to a domestic argument over who he is or what play they last saw him in. The naturalistic interview in the street can be made totally meaningless by the naturalistic actions of passing small boys or buses or (in one particular commercial, for what I do not remember) a bouncing ball in the play area of a block of flats.

We once wrote a commercial for a disinfectant. The theme was

---

[1] *What Advertising Is.*

the danger of unseen germs. A baby was playing on the floor. We needed to stress *three* areas of danger. We hit on the idea of reinforcing this by showing building bricks with numerals on their faces. It was done for the best of reasons – to integrate the commercial. However, in order that the bricks could be seen in the foreground the camera would have to zoom in and out three times. This we thought would detract from the simple format of the commercial, essentially one shot. We would need to dispense with the bricks or find bigger ones which could be seen. None could be found. So we had some made. Each side was nine inches long. They worked perfectly except that they dominated the scene and viewers wrote in to the television station to ask where they could buy the bricks!

Consistency and integration of execution and idea are not easy to achieve. The creative man must continually ask himself 'can I make this simpler, easier to read?' and 'does each element contribute to the single effect I want to achieve or does it lead the reader or viewer away from the advertisement?'

I know of no great idea which is complicated. (That is not to say that all simple ideas are great!) But many advertisements are complex in the sense that they comprise several thoughts. An advertisement may need to incorporate many paragraphs of text (even if nobody reads them the fact of their being there may contribute to the overall image of the product). As we have seen, the arrangement of these elements does not have to be unduly tidy – but there does have to be an underlying order. There is no universal law of advertisement design except fitness for purpose. The purpose is to communicate to the target audience a promise about the product. Each constituent element of the advertisement must contribute to a totality of design which is consistent with the defined image of the product. If the product were a person would he behave like this?

Simplicity isn't all that simple.

26

Research . . . or perhaps, to
three places of decimals

This chapter will not attempt to survey the whole area of research in advertising. Instead it will concentrate on that type of research with which the creative man comes in contact. And it will do so from a subjective creative view point.

Had those words been written ten years ago, the reader would have expected much hostile criticism of research. Before that writers and artists had accepted research: it supplied essential market information on which decisions could be based. Creative people began to get uneasy when the researchers seemed to be telling them why people bought and what therefore would be the best approaches to adopt to reach consumers. Hostility grew when the researcher entered that particular area which the creative man regarded as his own, the journey from proposition to idea. He was also sensitive to the researcher's insistence upon gauging reaction to the finished advertisement. Here, of course, he was on less firm ground. Whereas he could reasonably argue that the creation of advertisements was something of a mystery, the end result of his activities was meant to be action of some sort, something which could be measured.

In the days when advertising effectiveness was equated with sales the roughness of the measurement was always a handy defence in case of failure. If sales went up it was due to the ad. If they didn't it was due to any of a dozen ingredients in the marketing mix. But when measurements became more selective and sensitive, when shifts of attitude directly attributable to advertising were put under the research gaze, some creative men realised that mystique was no longer a defence and, probably for the first time, that their job was capable of analysis and their performance capable of improvement through such an analysis *of their mistakes*. If attitudes did not shift according to plan the creative man was to blame. If the consumer did not understand what was plain to everyone in the agency, again it was the creative man's fault. Naturally he felt vulnerable. When the advertising achieved its sales target he shared the limelight with the rest of the team. When it didn't he was alone in the spotlight. (Success has a thousand fathers. Failure is an orphan.) So it is understandable that the creative man hit out and the researcher was the obvious target.

Often he didn't deserve it. Sometimes the manner of a researcher would try the patience of Job let alone a sensitive creative man whose brainchild was either being dissected or replaced with a new model. The truly objective and dispassionate researcher who said that if X happens Y also happens, often gave the impression that X ought to be the headline or the whole campaign idea and that the creative man was, if not redundant, no more than an artisan.

It was the methods which the researcher sometimes adopted which provoked the creative man to wrath and earned the scorn also of other members of the agency. Some methods attempted to approximate a normal viewing situation, and invariably failed. Respondents were asked to view a commercial in a theatre with a hundred others. A colleague, Dennis Mutter, described theatre testing as follows: 'At best the results can give an indication of how a commercial will fare when viewed in the wrong conditions by an audience in the wrong frame of mind.' Some methods were supposedly 'direct' measures of response. You turned the switch if you were interested in the commercial. Or looking at a magazine you marked what you read. Others were indirect measures of response; for example what happened to the pupils of your eyes or your sweat glands when you read an ad? You were observed as in a laboratory. Many of the assumptions on which the research was based were not shared by the creative man. His major battle was conducted against the concept of recall. This is an apparently reasonable hypothesis: namely that for an advertising message to have any effect it must first of all register on the consumer's mind; in order to ascertain whether it has in fact registered one needs to ask her if she can recall it. First one asks if she can recall any advertisements within a specific period of time (e.g. the previous night's television). This is *spontaneous* recall. Then one gives the respondent a hint (e.g. 'Do you remember seeing any commercials for such and such a product category?'). This is *prompted* recall.

Creative people were naturally pleased if consumers could recall their commercials but they were angry if their work was rejected in test because it didn't get a sufficiently high recall score. Many advertisers would not run a commercial unless it achieved the minimum acceptable score. Yet during this heyday of recall – and it lasted some ten years – not one advertiser to my knowledge (certainly none with whom I worked) could show positive correlation between recall and sales.

What was worse was the *creation of advertising in order to be researched*. This disease, though thankfully no longer an epidemic, is still with us. Research instead of helping the creative man towards a goal became a goal in itself. If the name of the game was numbers . . . well creative men could play the numbers game as well as anyone else. Commercials were written which could get a high recall score. If high attention was important at the beginning of a commercial then commercials would be written with intriguing openings. Press advertisements were laid out to get a high reading and noting score. Research departments of leading American agencies compiled statistics of successful and unsuccessful advertisements (i.e. those ads which scored well or badly on some defined measure). The agency would then conduct a 'factor analysis'. This was the inexact science at its most scientific (and its most inexact). Advertisements were divided into three equal sections: high, medium and low scoring. The middle section was discarded. The high and low scoring ads were then examined in considerable detail. Were there any factors common to the highs which were absent from the lows? And vice versa? As far as I can remember there were no zero scores at all, i.e. all factors appeared in both sections. Nevertheless certain factors appeared more often in the highs and certain others more often in the lows.

The mountain laboured and the creative man looked at the mouse. Rather as he had looked at 'rules' of copywriting or design. The major points of all factor analysis were commonsense nostrums concerning simplicity and directness and unity. Not too many words in a headline. Make sure the vision and sound relate. Split-screen is confusing. Photographs are better than art for food advertisements. People are interested in people, etc.

At best factor analysis confirmed some of advertising's basic lore (and to do it justice that was a useful service). At worst factor analysis was used by 'scientific' agency people to institute laws of advertisement construction which could not be departed from. Responsible creative men who respected the spirit of such laws rejected their unthinking imposition and commented, reasonably, 'if every advertisement follows the same principles what chance has any single advertisement of standing out?' Furthermore, although a study of factor analysis would lead the creative man to do nothing wrong it didn't encourage him to do something different. If everything were done by the book what about the writer who wanted to write, if not a book, then at least a page of his own?

Though the assembly of scores is potentially dangerous in the hands of an agency it is dynamite in the hands of an advertisement testing organisation. Because whereas for the agency research is but one aspect of its operation and it can be reasonably detached, for the testing company research is everything (i.e. a particular method of research predicated upon certain assumptions). If, for example, the XYZ research organisation peddles a system of measuring advertisements, let's say by weight, then it has to rely on two factors: (1) weight is related to advertising effectiveness, (2) their method of measuring weight is valid. The organisation therefore has to get sufficient numbers of advertisers and agencies to agree to both (1) and (2).

You may indeed wonder how anyone who by definition is meant to be a disinterested seeker after truth can bring himself to start a company which claims to have the truth already within its grasp. But let us consider not ethics but business. Surely those two factors are a very shaky foundation upon which to build a commercial enterprise?

Package deal research (and there's still plenty of it about) stands or falls on the trade's acceptance of both its assumptions, philosophy and method. Yet neither has been proved. Moreover, the research company has a vested interest in maintaining the status quo. It has amassed a great deal of scores and uses them as a yardstick against which to measure succeeding advertisements. Once either the philosophy or method is questioned then the whole superstructure crumbles. But advertisements are still rejected because they appeared in the 'wrong' quartile or because they didn't get a high enough score. It's all very well for researchers to say that the difference between 54 and 51 is 'not statistically significant', but the figures are there and an order of merit is imposed.

But I am wholly in favour of research. And so are the majority of creative directors. The creative research situation is no longer one of entrenched positions and rigid attitudes. Researchers work within creative departments. At Garland-Compton, for instance, some 50 per cent of one year's research was commissioned by the creative department. What brought about this change? On both sides patience, understanding, a willingness to admit mistakes, and, above all, a mutual admission of ignorance. Once creative man and researcher admitted to each other that they did not know how advertising worked but were anxious to find out they began to help each other across no-man's-land.

This essentially is what I want of a researcher. Not a prejudiced answer or a prepacked method, but help. Help maybe in defining what questions I want to ask in the first place. Once the researcher had proved he wasn't acting as an examiner he was called upon to help in the journey from P to I. And the motivating force which drives all activity in the narrow part of the funnel is the desire to find not simply a solution but a *new* solution. In that the creative man and the researcher are as one. The very reasons which lead the creative man to reject the packaged deal researcher are those which lead him to accept the seeker-out of truth.

What I want from my researcher is a partnership, a working relationship, an understanding of my problems and, above all, an ability to tackle each research task pragmatically. I realise that the partnership demands my contribution – a frankness, a willingness to give up preconceived ideas, an appreciation that something isn't necessarily wrong because that isn't the way I would have done it. And if my pet idea gets killed I shall not try to revive it. An Australian creative director once said that the sight which infuriated him most was that of creative people holding dead babies to their breasts.

Now exactly how can the researcher help the creative man? Before we can answer that it may be useful to ask 'where?'

I had the pleasure and privilege of working very closely with Ann Burdus (currently in charge of research at McCann-Erickson) when both of us were at Garland-Compton. I am indebted to her for teaching me much about research and for allowing me to quote from a lecture she gave to a weekend course of the Market Research Society:

There are four main stages at which a research man can contribute in the advertising process:

Strategic research
Development research
Evaluative research
Campaign assessment.

Strategic research is aimed at positioning the product correctly in the market by identifying target purchasers and their needs. It is believed that the sensitive use of research at an early stage of the thinking about a product should produce both positioning and claims for the brand.

Development research is a term used to cover all research carried out by the agency between the drawing up of the advertising brief and the formal presentation of work to the client. The role of research at this stage is to assess creative ideas against the advertising brief in the context of consumer reactions and to explore all problems which might arise and which can be resolved by the application of research techniques.

Evaluative research is carried out on finished or almost finished advertising to ascertain that the work meets pre-set standards and to act as a feedback of information about reactions to the finished advertisements.

Campaign assessment is carried out after the campaign has been running over a measureable period of time (the length of time being dependent on the nature of the product and the campaign), to ascertain the advertising is working in the intended way and to establish how it should be modified in the future.

Let us examine each of these against the funnel. Strategic research clearly happens up to and including *P*. Campaign assessment equally obviously happens post *I*. Development and evaluative research are harder to pinpoint. The former definitely occurs in between *P* and *I* if by *I* we mean the final idea which eventually becomes a finished advertisement. If, on the other hand, we think of several small *I*s happening which need evaluating prior to the approval of one *I* then evaluative research can be said to take place not only post *I* but also between *P* and *I*.

I do not propose to deal with strategic research and campaign assessment. They have been taken for granted throughout this book. Their role has not been in contention. We shall concentrate upon development and evaluative research, looking whenever possible at actual examples of that research in action and drawing whatever general conclusions we may.

Strategic research may help you arrive at *P*. *P* may then be researched (i.e. before the creative man has done anything to it). This is known as concept research. Here again we could enter into an argument over what constitutes *P*. If in fact sufficient strategic research has been undertaken the very fact that *P* has been defined should also tell us that *P* represents a concept which consumers understand and appreciate the need for. If in fact the proposition is related to a consumer desire there is no need to research it at *I*, it will already have been researched at *P*.

For the sake of clarity I now have to qualify the rather simplistic schema which the funnel represents. The journey from manufacturer to consumer is in fact a journey of several false starts. In the first section the facts may lead you to many *p*s before you arrive at the *P* which actually goes through the narrow part of the funnel. If *p* is rejected you start again. Similarly several *i*s can be rejected before *I* is arrived at. Each time this happens you get back to *P*. Sometimes you have to go back to the *very* beginning. I labour this point simply to make you realise that the procedure is not cut and dried nor is it a single progression but probably a series of progressions, a linear snakes and ladders. To revert to our original unqualified model, each example represents merely one journey through the funnel.

Concept research would appear to be straightforward. After all it is simply a question of finding out if such and such a proposition is meaningful to the consumer in terms of her actual needs and wants. This is all very fine provided the advertiser appreciates that research which concentrates on the proposition is not only limited but potentially misleading, since it discounts what the idea can do to the proposition and what the execution can do to the idea. One danger is that research may throw out a proposition which when transmuted into an idea could well have succeeded. Respondents, for example, could well reject a proposition not because the promise is irrelevant but because another product is already satisfying that particular need or want. Thus the differentiating intensifying alchemy of the idea upon that parity proposition is not given the chance to work. Concepts can be tested in isolation but they are not finished advertisements and accordingly not only is the full potential of the proposition not realised but, since the respondent is put in a difficult position sometimes of imagining a product which does not yet exist, not to flesh out the skeleton with illustration and text is to make this difficulty even greater.

Concept research is a step on the way. Too often it is regarded as providing a definitive answer, notably by the researcher whose scientific mind prefers to deal with finite things. A proposition is clearer, the meaning is exact. Whereas an idea is ambiguous, complex: many meanings may co-exist, perhaps on different levels. A proposition is not the idea, let alone the advertisement. To return to poetry, the American critic Stauffer says: 'The intellectual content, the argument of a poem is no more the whole poem than the tag line of La Fontaine is his fables.'

Accordingly the research I want to concentrate upon here is in fact what I have tended to concentrate upon during the last ten years, research into advertisements at the early stages of their preparation. The 'thing' being researched is recognisably an advertisement. The sooner in fact the researcher has in his hand something approaching the end product of our labours the better. It can be summed up as workshop research or 'copy clinic' as it used to be called. One essential characteristic is informality. It must be almost instantly on call. It should welcome participation of the creative man. It should be top of the mind. It should occur to him to use it as soon as he has a problem. He is, let us assume, designing a pack. He wants to use red. No other product in that field is red. Blue is the accepted colour. Maybe red therefore is wrong . . . ? Rather than answer his own question with a rejection he should talk to his research man: 'Is there a way of finding out?' The workshop is pragmatic. There is no set procedure. Often a new advertisement demands a new technique but the objects are the same: communication and comprehension, with any added insights a welcome bonus.

What then do I ask research to do?

1. Put me in touch with the audience

Research documents can have a frightening effect on the creative man, particularly if he has no claim to numeracy. They have a serious mien, a forbidding format, a strange language – and figures! The average family consists of 2.4 people. But the same department which turned flesh and blood into these lifeless statistics can make them real again by putting the creative man face to face with the consumer. By having him watch a depth interview or listen to the taped playback or watch the video-taped playback or even join in a group discussion. He must be trained before he can participate, for the hasty word or the anxious desire to get to the point of the interview may invalidate the whole session.

Once he appreciates that the researcher is on his side the creative man generally finds there are more questions than the respondent has time for. There is none so devout as your late convert. The creative man may well start asking questions to which he ought to know the answer himself. He may use research to check out too many inessentials or to filter out the inferior from the superior approach. And thus ask the researcher to do the job his own judgment should perform. But if he gets to the consumer and doesn't ask too much he will learn. He may be reassured when he doubts. He may be confirmed when he knows. It may support him in his arrogance, throw light upon his ignorance (and often a custard pie in his face). But he is afforded the rare insight of seeing a consumer in relationship with an advertisement. Or a product.

However, though it is profitable to communicate with consumers about products before advertisements have been sketched out (or even in the strategic research stage), the creative man is probably fooling himself if he thinks that research will provide the idea. Key phrases do occur in such situations, leads are subsequently developed and often an idea can be traced back to a moment of truth in an interview. But, unless I have been unlucky or myopic, in my experience no advertising idea has sprung fresh out of a research session like Venus out of a shell fully grown and beautiful. More likely than not the interview has been one of two or three factors which came together at a later moment to create an idea.

Hearing the words consumers use can be very revealing. It is a useful corrective to copy clichés. Often a consumer's turn of phrase can be incorporated in an advertisement. But generally it provides raw material to be fed into the funnel and a useful check on one's ideas. It rarely provides its own (or a headline even). Because we aim to talk the consumer's language, we also assume that the consumer talks it. She may well do so, but rarely is it worth listening to in an advertisement. Even the best consumer interview commercials owe as much to the brilliance of the editing and the assembly of fore-and-aft material as the actual interview. What the creative man creates is not reality but the *illusion of reality*. And that is hard work.

I once worked on a cake mix. The research asked respondents to try these mixes and comment upon them. Vanilla, ginger-bread and chocolate. The words they used to describe the tastes were meant to be vital to the success of the enterprise. One particularly enthusiastic researcher culled the list of answers and, overreaching himself, earnestly begged the creative department to follow a certain route. 'Note,' he said, 'how a statistically significant number of respondents refer to the taste of the chocolate mix. I'm sure we ought to feature this word in the advertising.' We weren't proud or offended. As I've said, a great idea doesn't mind who has it. You're probably wondering what this word was. I'll tell you. The significant number of housewives referred to the taste of the chocolate cake as . . . wait for it . . . 'chocolatey'. We were too choked to cheer. But – and this is the point of the fore-going rigmarole – we often go to research for the wrong things. Instead of being reassured that the product was living up to its claim, instead of hearing firsthand what consumers thought of the product, we were asking the research to do things for what it wasn't intended. We were asking it to do our job.

As I said, occasionally something of this sort happens. A respondent says something truly original, expresses a concept in a striking, novel way. And always supposing it is novel and not just novel to the creative man (who may be so out of touch with reality that 'mind the doors please' may strike him as pure poetry). What the respondent is doing is *creating* (turning *P* into *I* maybe) and we just can't bank on this happening or plan our activities on the premise that the consumer shall usurp our creative role.

A year or two after the launch of Ritz crackers some graduate trainees were asked to make a presentation on the history of the brand. It was very well documented and presented. They came to the slogan 'Taste as if they're buttered already'. This they said was not a copywriter's phrase. It was how an actual housewife had actually described the biscuit after actually eating it. Now I know the writer who sweated a day over writing that slogan. I watched him shave this morning. But I didn't put them wise – you don't want to knock folklore.

It's the creative man's job to create the ad. If the consumer does it for him that's a bonus. But it's not what I expect from research. I just want research to put me in touch.

2. 'Tell me – am I communicating?'

Put these words on a piece of card and frame them over your desk:

● We know what it means – do they?

When communications research shows that a significant proportion of respondents don't understand what the ad is meant to communicate, the creative man gets good and angry. It's human nature. He has spent all that time and energy. His colleagues not only understand it they like it, so does the client. But when a man gets that angry the person he's really angry with is himself!

The creative man's job is a lonely one. He needs to communicate, particularly if the idea he gets is truly original. Is it any good? Or is he the only one out of step? But the person he normally communicates with (his colleague) is likely to give him the answer he wants rather than the answer he needs. And both of them know the background, the strategy, the objective which that message is meant to achieve. When it hits a respondent ignorant of the context and, let's face it, often ignorant of the world which the educated writer and artist inhabit, the reaction could be very, very different. Or a dull nothing.

Here is an example of communications research which took place before the campaign had started. Evaluative research. In other words had the research proved negative we would have had to start from scratch.

Long John Whisky had a low awareness level. It was essential to give it an identity, to differentiate it by means of the advertising. The ad showed a tall man and carried the line: 'Drink Tall Drink Long John. The Scotch with that 10 Foot Feeling'. Drink tall? Literally it means nothing. We thought people would infer a feeling of strength and superiority (cf. ride tall, walk tall) which the second part of the line backs up.

We conducted a national sample recognition test using an

omnibus survey to find out if something we understood was comprehended by the public. Also to find out if there were any unsuspected negatives. In fact what we found out was a largely unsuspected positive. The main interpretation was that Long John was meant to be drunk as a long drink with plenty of water or ginger or soda. I regard this as positive because, although it wasn't what we primarily intended the public should take away from the ad, it nevertheless contributed to the idea of Long John being a strong whisky (one that would stand up to being mixed with water or whatever). The subsidiary interpretation was in fact the one we had bargained for – Long John gives you an uplift. And this was reinforced by the interpretation of the ten foot feeling that 'it makes you feel taller, bigger, more confident, makes you feel good or better, makes you feel out of this world', etc.

Subsequently campaign research was undertaken, not to check comprehension (since our sample had adequately given us that information), but awareness of Long John as a brand of whisky. In this market, as in many other, a brand needs to be seen as a *candidate*. The acid test is this: 'If the brand you normally buy is out of stock which other brands are candidates for your substitute choice?' Obviously to qualify as a candidate a brand must have awareness. The awareness figure of Long John rose appreciably as a result of this campaign – and, needless to say, it was important that we had checked out previously what it was that the public was aware *of*. The comprehension research revealed an unsuspected positive.

Often though you have to ask:

---

3. Are there any unsuspected negatives?

Some creative people will tell you that this is the only justification for research, to make sure there are no hidden problems. Never mind about comprehension, do they see anything wrong with it that we can't? However, though this is a valid question, it is not put that way. Thank heavens. Instead the advertisement is researched for comprehension and a special watch kept for negatives.

I tell the following story against myself. You may as well learn from my mistakes. We were working on a campaign for New Zealand Cheddar cheese. We had agreed a proposition. 'It is a mild cheese: therefore it can be used for many dishes.' The astute reader will scent a problem straight away. A Dual Strategy (see chapter 25 on Simplicity). Now dual strategies, dual promises, can work. We were sure that this one would and when we researched the ad this was not the point we were checking. We were checking the headline. The illustration showed a variety of dishes and the headline read: 'Bite into the Cheddar that doesn't bite back.' We wanted to know if that clever phrase said mildness. But communication research isn't that straightforward. Our simple folder test checked correctly comprehension of the total advertisement. There were three interpretations of the ad. In order of frequency:

1. The cheese is versatile
2. It is good for you
and a long way behind
3. It is mild.

It shouldn't have needed research to find out that the visual did not support the message. In fact it detracted from it. The copy line is clever and a lot of people simply ignored it. Mainly because of the dominance of the visual. You can imagine, however, that if this phrase were treated singlemindedly, perhaps with a picture of someone eating the cheese or the cheese shown against other, stronger cheeses, it could work, and work well. It was different and could have given a memorable identity to the brand. But in an attempt to get over versatility as a sort of visual bonus we were in fact detracting completely from the message of the headline. It taught me not to use research as a substitute for thinking. It wastes time and money.

The ad never ran. And, despite the fact that the research probed the respondents and reported that 'the majority of the informants expected the cheese in it to be mild rather than strong . . . [and] that this is the sort of cheese they would prefer', the client had every reason not to run it.

A more surprising negative was revealed in a simple folder test for a drink called Underberg. It's a German alcoholic herbal concoction much used for the settling of German tummies. Middle-aged *Hausfraus* drink it in the middle of the day, probably for medicinal purposes, possibly because they enjoy its effect. However, it really is excellent for hangovers. We were launching it in this country. The purpose of the test was to discover if people understood what Underberg was all about. We prepared a simple ad with a simple headline and easy explanatory copy. We showed the bottle and put the name large in the baseline.

Just before the research went into the street (so much cosier than the field) a member of the research department added a question to the questionnaire. 'What is the size of the bottle?' Now it wasn't a point the creative department had any doubts about. It was a three inch bottle but we had photographed it held by a human hand over a glass. Everything was in scale. What we were interested in was not size but comprehension of the product idea.

When asked the size of the three inch bottle approximately half the respondents said between half a pint and a pint. This was due to the 'assimilation effect'. *People see meanings they expect to see.* Three inch bottles are not part of the normal person's everyday experience.

Maybe there was another reason as well. We in the advertising business have mucked about so much with sizes and proportions (cheated with angles, exaggerated, called small packs 'large' and medium packs 'giant') that the consumer is understandably confused and has no star by which to steer. We altered the ad. We showed the bottle actual size, captioned it 'Actual size of bottle'. We put it next to the price, a picture of a half-crown and wrote underneath that 'Actual size of money'.

4. Are there any suspected negatives?

This is similar to the previous question except that the atmosphere is far more tense. And the agency camp is clearly divided. The research is undertaken with a more defined purpose. Instead of saying to the researcher, 'see what people make of this', you say 'look I think we've got a problem with this element – before we go ahead we'd better satisfy so-and-so that it's OK.'

We did an ad for a sweet. There was fruit juice in the sweet. The commercial showed the fruit, the juice going into the sweet, the pack. We then wanted some words to act as an injunction to the consumer, to tell her that when she tasted the product she would be tasting the juice of real fruit. The line we all liked was 'let loose the juice of the fruit'. Well not all of us. Actually a couple were very worried about a possible *double entendre* in that phrase. And as one of the two was the client we had to research it.

I have already made a plea for research to be pragmatic, to come up with new methods as creative people come up with new ideas. They came up with one. How *do* you find out if people have dirty minds? Well . . . you ask them what something means and time the pause before they tell you. If the pause is much longer than the normal (and obviously you ask a lot of questions, including the phrase under observation) then clearly they are having difficulty. The results were clear enough. People paused and paused. And the endline was altered.

Here again a warning word. Too often (though not in the above case) a suspected negative is researched when commonsense tells you it should not be there in the first place. With research readily on tap there is a temptation to use it too much. The creative man is tempted to check a tired idea. The account executive, desiring a quiet life, placates him by testing. 'And, of course, you never *know*.' This is research run riot. It's top of the mind all right – and leaking out at the sides. Commonsense is not to be trusted. A foot is put in it rather than down. People fear to do anything on judgement. They pussyfoot and become neurotic.

It's what I call the secondary problem syndrome. Instead of tackling the primary problem (will the ad motivate people towards purchase by changing or reinforcing an attitude or whatever primary goal we set up?), we get bogged down in all sorts of secondary problems, *which don't relate to the primary one*. This obsession with what might go wrong is in danger of inhibiting us from finding out what might go right. Research can aid us to try the truly different. Instead it is being used increasingly to commit us to doing the opposite – the ordinary, the safe, the trite. This attitude is what David Ogilvy so brilliantly attacked when he described the man who uses research 'as a drunk uses a lamp-post . . . not for illumination but for support'.

5. Can I do the original?

Research, as I say, can allow us to test all sorts of new and outlandish approaches. The realisation of this fact only began to dawn in the mid-1960s (and in some places the sky is still dark). The fact is that research can actually release the creative man from the ordinary by allowing him to test the unknown! As Marion Harper said 'we want research to tell us what's new that works'. By 'works' he doesn't necessarily mean 'produces sales' but communicates what we want to communicate. In the film *Risk and Responsibility* Jeremy Bullmore says: 'In research risk and responsibility go hand in hand.' Once this was realised the creative man and the research executive did more than sign an armistice, they formed an alliance. For not only did research release the creative man from the ordinary, it *released him also from the creative contribution of other people*. Account executives, marketing men, brand managers, have a vital role in defining *P* and assessing the results of *I* but the journey from *P* to *I* belongs to the creative man. A lot of people had tried to muscle in. He fought them off with varying degrees of success. However, once he let in the sympathetic researcher, he realised that he could become immune from further incursions. The time previously spent examining half-formed ideas, rejecting, revising, compromising, could be spent on sensitive development research.

I've chosen just one example. In 1967 Murphy decided to introduce painted television sets. A range of colours. We recommended one launch advertisement. There was a large illustration of one set, the red set. Above it a headline: 'The new Murphy is revolutionary. That's why we painted it red.' And lines of copy describing the inside of the set and the quality of the picture. The copy mentioned the rest of the range. At the bottom in a coupon was a small colour chart indicating the rest of the range. The account team were dubious. So were agency management. Why show only one set? How many people wanted a red set? Wouldn't it be safer to show the whole range?

The creative team were adamant. They felt that by showing only one set greater impact would be achieved and nothing said you had painted sets quite as much as the colour red. But the set was shown against a limbo background. Shouldn't it be put into a harmonious room setting so that people would see that the colour would blend in with their colour scheme? No, said the creative team. The sort of people who would buy these sets are adventurous anyway, can probably imagine what the set will look like in their rooms and probably have individual ideas about furnishing.

But why do the headline and the copy talk so much about technicalities and so little about colour? Because the colour speaks for itself. It's better for Murphy to reassure them about the inside. This isn't any old set that's been painted. It is an improved version of a model introduced only the year before. But isn't the word 'painted' somewhat downgrading? No, it describes what has been done to the set exactly. Furthermore, with colour television coming soon it would be confusing to say 'that's why we coloured it red' and besides revolutionaries don't colour, they paint!

À propos of account executives, was it Voltaire who said, 'I disagree with what you say but I'll defend to the death your right to show it to the client'? The client too had doubts. We, on the other hand, had research. Which we would have to pay for. We did a folder test with three matched samples to discover if the main points of the advertising strategy came home in the recommended *single set* ad or in one of two alternative ads, one showing *some of the range*, the other showing *all*. We discovered that of the three samples the one which was shown the recommended ad had a greater comprehension of the main points, i.e. (1) they understood the sets were in coloured cabinets; (2) they thought these were good quality sets; (3) they knew that a range of colours was available. Red did in fact say colour. And the impact of the single set meant that more people *got into the copy*.

The client ran the ad. He set a target of 10,000 sets for the first year and sold 27,000. Normally one hesitates before attributing sales to advertising, particularly in the area of consumer durables but, in this case, the ad contained a coupon which pulled handsomely and this clearly had a direct influence on the result. The set was still on the market in 1973 and the most recent campaign still featured one set per advertisement.

6. Which is better?

This is the question I ask most frequently because research which can never give finite answers about an advertisement's effectiveness can tell you which of two is better – always provided there is a generally accepted definition of the word 'better'.

If there is a genuine division of opinion in the camp (or in myself) concerning two advertisements, research can arbitrate. It will probably throw added light in other areas which may also help.

One postulates that if an ad is to work at all it must initially communicate. If one ad communicates twice as meaningfully as another this does not mean that it will sell twice as much product. However, it is reasonable to suggest that it will be more successful. Moreover since we have probably agreed a certain communication goal for the campaign and such is the state of our science, this is the quantifiable task we have agreed with our client, it is apparent from such research that one of our ads will cost the client twice as much money to communicate as the other!

Given the choice of two headlines the best account director, the most creative directors, might find it difficult to choose. There may appear to be only a stylistic difference between them. They may seem no more than two interchangeable interpretations of the same thought, two barely different ways of saying the same thing. What research does is to quantify these differences and reveal them in a new dimension.

We were working on a jelly. We did a rough ad showing a plate of strawberries and the jelly pack. We did two alternative captions.

(a) 'If you like the taste of fruit you'll love the flavour of X jelly.'

(b) 'The flavour of real strawberries.'

We did a small-scale folder test and then some depth interviews to find out if we were communicating the idea of fruit content and generally to explore the subject of fruit in jellies.

Ad (*a*) communicated it far better. Ad (*b*) made the more challenging claim and was rejected as incredible. Despite the fact that the illustration was identical, the (*b*) caption roused blatant suspicions about the fruit content in the jellies.

You will have gathered that the solution which was of use to us was somewhat divorced from what we thought the problem was. What we intended testing was the communication effectiveness of the two phrases, one emotional (*a*), the other direct (*b*). Because the nature of the research allowed the respondents to dilate at length, there was introduced into the research the dimension of *believability*. The people, instead of answering simply 'yes, I understand', would say for example 'Yes, I understand but I don't believe'. And as a result ad (*a*) was to them far more credible. So much so that despite one's reservation about the importance of believability it had to be run. The research therefore took two virtually identical advertisements and differentiated them quantitatively.

These are some of the questions I ask of research. I don't ask it to do my job. I do ask it to help. To help me gain an insight of the consumer, to find guidelines, to confirm or deny opinions, to settle doubts, correct illusions. I ask the researcher to be sympathetic, humble, pragmatic, inventive, not tied to any technique. I ask him to be fast, cheap and articulate.

I believe in research. I believe the purpose of research is not to fill important looking but dusty reports. Nor is its purpose further research (though sometimes this may be inevitable). But action. In research not only risk and responsibility go hand in hand. So, too, do the bastard artist and the inexact scientist.

27

Media ... whims ancient and modern

I like the word media. It means we get our priorities right. A medium is a means by which messages get transmitted. It is at the service of the message. It is not more important than the message. Marshall McLuhan overstates when he says it *is* the message but his basic premise is true: the medium seriously affects the nature of the message.

This chapter looks at media from a creative viewpoint. It observes the way media are selected; compares print and television; runs past posters and ends with a few asides. Despite the subjective bias and superficiality of the 'survey', one thing should emerge: the challenge and opportunity afforded by each medium should make the choice more difficult.

Media choice is made too soon. Often by the wrong people and for the wrong reasons. I shall be told that there is only one reason for media choice – cost effectiveness. I propose to omit discussion of cost effectiveness. Not because I deny its position as a major factor but because I believe other considerations should enter into it and very rarely do. These other considerations are important: is it fair to ignore them for the single reason that we don't know how to measure them?

Another reason I like the word media is that it's plural.

'Well,' says the account supervisor, having returned from the client, 'it's very much the same as last time except for one thing, they've increased the size of the tea bag without increasing the amount of tea. Price remains the same and there's a new one pound pack. That's about it.'

The creative man sums up the situation: 'Thirty seconds?'

'I think so, don't you? I'll have a word with Neil.'

Neil is the media man. He deals with media which is plural for medium. Only you would never think so to look at his desk or his diary or the charts on the wall. To Fleet Street Neil is a medium man – and the medium is television. For the product under discussion it is from Neil's point of view understandably cost effective. From the creative man's point of view it makes sense too – product in action, demonstration. From the account supervisor's point of view it is equally obvious: it was television last year and sales are good.

What I want you to note in this little episode (imagined but based on fact) is the speed at which the media choice is made. Or to be exact, the *generic* media choice. The media man spends most of his time on the specific media choice (i.e. which publication if it's press, which contractor if it's television and how big the spaces, how long the spots). The choice of *which medium* to use occupies him and the agency a disproportionately shorter time. Occasionally the agency will review its media policy on an account: or, in the case of a new product, look at all media: or, in the case of a test market, look at media available in that region. Sometimes indeed the subject of the test could be the media themselves (e.g. posters and TV in one area: posters alone in another). But these are the exceptions. On a going brand nearly always and on a new brand more often than not, the generic media choice is a matter for little or no discussion.

There are two comments worth making at this point. First, since there is no delay in deciding between media it follows that the decision *to use media at all* is quickly taken. The agency has been employed by the advertiser to help him sell his product. One may respond by correcting 'sell' to 'advertise' but the distinction in this context is not meaningful and certainly would not be welcomed by the advertiser. The agency perhaps should consider other courses of action, other ways to invest the money allocated to advertising. Employ a commando sales force maybe, or do a direct mail campaign or put at least half the appropriation below the line (see next chapter) or get widespread use of the product by influential popular figures (PR)?

There are several possible answers to the question 'how best can I use the sum of X to help sell Y?' But the agency, remember, is paid by the media. It is employed by one man and paid by another. (One of these days we'll all look back at this quaint practice rather as today footballers recall the £20 maximum wage.) This is not to suggest that any reputable agency is influenced by where their money is coming from before making a recommendation which gets rid of that money! Besides they can always recommend below-the-line with a clear conscience and the knowledge that they own a merchandising subsidiary. No, push the thought of commissionable media bias from your mind. The pressures, you see, are there irrespective of considerations of commission. If an agency has thought nothing but commissionable media for several years then it will go on doing so, and automatically.

The second comment concerns the agency's reasons for media choice – both generic and specific. Strictly speaking each medium pays the same commisison – 15 per cent. But the work involved by the agency in each of them and opportunities for making money on production invoices vary substantially. Moreover, the size and number of insertions or screenings, the number of different advertisements required, the amount of checking of material . . . all these affect the profit picture of an account and can't be far from the surface in any deliberations within an agency on which medium to choose and which section of that medium and at what size and at what frequency.

One advantage of the fee system, which more and more agencies are adopting, is that agency representatives no longer feel divided loyalties. They can make a recommendation to their client without feeling that the client's interests are being pursued at the expense of the agency or (perish the thought) the agency's at the expense of the client. No longer need he examine an advertising philosophy to detect the hand of the accountant: 'a few large spaces', 'dominate the page', 'one commercial which will run until research tells us it's tired', 'you can't afford to look unimportant.' (*Who* can't afford?)

Generally, though not invariably, television has benefited when the accountant has written the advertising philosophy. The amount of work per pound spent is usually less, the opportunities for mark-up greater. But television has another ally, the creative man. Or so some members of all non-electronic media will tell you. 'TV is fashionable. It's showbiz. The writer and the art director want to make movies.' There is a lot of truth in this. After all the journalists themselves turn to television to make themselves known. It is a fashionable medium, it does have excitement, it does provide all manner of advantages (movement, sound, demonstration, music, mood, etc.). It seems to work.

The media are so concerned with the creative man's love affair with television that they suspect – wrongly in my opinion – that he has the major say in media choice in his agency. Accordingly some of the other media with less than an outstanding cost-effectiveness story to tell are seeking a 'dialogue' with creative people (group heads, senior art directors) and bypassing the agency's media man to do so. They are picking up the gauntlet thrown down by many top agency media men in the industry – What is the nature of your readership? How do people read your publication? What is the quality rather than the quantity which you deliver? – but instead of returning it to the owner are taking it to the creative people and saying: 'Look, you and I know that all that cost per thousand stuff isn't what advertising is all about – it's creativity, we know that.' Nothing is more calculated to turn the least numerate creative man into an avid reader of *BRAD* than the spurious suggestion of a rapport between him and the media based upon a shared distrust of the computer!

Far better for each medium to sell itself for what it can do, to play its strengths. And the strengths of each medium are considerable. The diversity of strength of the several media offers the agency a vast range of options, endless possible combinations. It is for this reason that I decry the speed with which initial media choice is made and why I believe it is a more difficult job than it is generally assumed to be. For the media man *and the creative man*.

The creative men haven't always had this fancy for television.

Once upon a time there was no television. And even after four or five years, when the medium had taken hold, many writers and artists were avoiding it. I had the job about then of introducing the rest of the creative department to the wonders of the new medium and tried to teach print writers to write and art directors to visualise, commercials. The more experienced the man the less adaptable he was. And many a copywriter understandably resented being taught advertising by someone much less experienced. He would accept that there were one or two techniques but to him it was basically just another form of advertising. Which it was – except that there were more than one or two techniques and an inability to master them would negate all experience in advertising which the copywriter brought to the job.

One or two of the exercises I used then (1959) are worth dusting down and using again since they demonstrate the differences between the two major media (and therefore illustrate their strengths) and since any reader who has grown up with television may be amused by the thought that television's language needed to be taught (don't you just know . . . get it through the pores like osmosis whatever that is?).

What are the differences between press and television?

1. Press is static. TV moves. (You look at one you watch the other.)
2. Press is silent. TV has sound, music, effects.
3. Press can be read. TV is heard – but can also be read (e.g. supers).
4. Press imposes no time limit on reading. TV imposes limits. If a point is missed the viewer can't go back.
5. Press can adjust the size of type to incorporate a long copy story or a text which may be read by the really interested. TV can usually afford no more than 65 words within 30 seconds. (Rushing the audio is TV's equivalent of reducing type size – and it rarely works.)
6. Press allows the reader to come back to the advertisement when he so desires. TV does not.

7. Press can't make the reader read. TV has a greater chance of making the viewer view.

8. Press allows the reader to cut out a coupon and send it away. TV can simply super an address (subsequently, of course, it introduced Ansafone).

9. Press allows the reader to use the advertisement. It is tangible and can become the reader's property. TV is ephemeral.

10. Press can have topicality. It can benefit from its surrounding medium (i.e. news). TV has immediacy. The advertiser can talk *live* to the viewer.

11. Press is not read simultaneously by all members of its total audience. TV is seen simultaneously by all members of its total audience. (By total I mean all the people who see the one ad.)

12. Press can illustrate the product and by using several illustrations can simulate movement. TV has real movement and can show products in action, can demonstrate advantages.

13. Press can underline, use bold type, print a variety of type faces and type sizes to vary emphasis. TV can employ degrees of vocal emphasis, different voices, musical underlining.

14. Press can indicate pronunciation. TV can pronounce.

15. Press has no control over the order in which an advertisement is looked at. TV controls the order and can thus tell a story the way it wants it told.

16. Press advertisements can be reproduced, photographed, run-on for merchandising purposes. TV cannot easily do this.

17. Press roughs bear a close resemblance to the finished advertisements. TV scripts and storyboards are indications only. Preliminary work is done in one medium for eventual execution in another. (A 'finished storyboard' is a contradiction in terms. Storyboards are far less frequent today. In the beginning were these pictures . . . a comic strip version of the script. The main trouble with storyboards was that they were used at three different stages of a commercial's life by people with different degrees of sophistication in the medium for different purposes:

(*a*) the writer and artist in writing the commercial,

(*b*) the agency team in presenting the commercial,

(*c*) the production team in shooting the commercial.
Another problem was the *rigor mortis* which could set in once a piece of planned movement was fixed in a frame. A detailed storyboard was counterproductive. If the script called for a tree in a garden, an artist might show a larch in the garden of a suburban semi and that was what the client would expect to see! Storyboards were tails wagging dogs. As Dennis Abey said, 'The nearest thing to a finished commercial is one man acting it'.)

18. Press is relatively cheap to produce. TV is usually expensive.

19. Press is relatively quick to produce. TV is usually slow.

20. Press allows you flexibility within the generic medium – you can choose which paper to go in. TV allows you no flexibility – there is only one commercial channel.

21. Press offers limited regional facilities. TV is both national and regional.

22. Press can be strictly regional. TV is regional but to the viewer appears national.

23. Press is read by one person at a time. TV is often seen in the home by two or more people who can discuss the advertising.

24. Press offers several sizes. TV offers several time segments but since there is no other material butting up against it, every commercial is in a sense a full page.

25. Press advertisements do not intrude – people need not read them. TV commercials intrude into an entertainment medium.

26. Press advertisements are spaced irregularly throughout the paper. TV commercials are shown in slots of two minutes' duration.

27. Press need have few intermediaries between rough and publication. TV must have several between script and transmission.

28. Press can deliver a complicated sales argument. TV has to concentrate on few points (preferably one).

29. Press is black and white, fact and news. TV is black and white and colour, news and entertainment.

This analysis, in covering the major points of difference, has revealed many of the strengths of the two media and the opportunities which each of them presents to the creative man who uses one or other – or better still in conjunction. The decision which to use should depend on many factors, e.g. type of product, stage of product's development, target audience, cost of media, complexity of story, need for trade support, competitive media activity, etc. Somehow, however, the secondary problem syndrome takes over. 'We can't be in press because the client is a television company and Head Office view all the branches' commercials together.' 'We can't be on television because we have to keep a folder of advertisements for the Chairman.'

What is television's essence?

Of the many attributes of television one above all characterises its essential difference.

● Time

Time is the discipline and driving force of the medium. It imposes the toughest limitation and offers the greatest potential. The limit on the number of words and the number of scenes; the ordering of material; the arrangement of elements to fight the transient nature of the medium . . . these are some of the challenges. The artist's job as we have seen is to exploit his limitations. The TV creative man is fighting against time. Ironically the more he tries to do in the time available the shorter that time will seem. Whereas an art director can fill his eight-inch double with twice as much text as that found in another eight-inch double, the TV man does that at his peril and risks total non-communication. On the other hand, when an art director designs a simple uncluttered layout it may admittedly stand out on the page but it won't seem bigger than it is. Whereas a TV man can make fifteen seconds seem like thirty. Consequently the client who is concerned lest the company look unimportant has less to fear with a short time segment than with a small space.

What is the difference between copy and audio?

Incidentally the use of the two Latin words 'video' and 'audio' always struck me as an American affectation until I realised that they had one great advantage over vision and sound. The use of the first person puts the emphasis on the consumer. Sound is manufacturer-orientated, 'I hear' is what the consumer does.

I set myself the task of answering this question (subsequently I asked it of trainees): What is the difference between copy and audio? We all know the superficial answer – copy is meant to be read and audio is meant to be heard. But what does *that* mean?

Suppose, I asked myself, I were to pick up in the street a scrap of paper on which were some thirty words of text and no indication (in terms of video instructions or sound effects or music, etc.) of the medium for which this text was meant? How could I tell if it were copy or audio? If one is supposed to be read and the other heard then surely internal evidence of the text should indicate the medium as clearly as any formal arrangement into paragraphs and scenes? It was reminiscent of practical criticism at college when all you had to go on was the poem – no poet's name, no notes in the margin, no date of composition. The fundamental characteristic I discovered is fragmentation. Good audio follows (though not slavishly) normal speech patterns. Copy obviously does not: it follows normal literary patterns. Copy can afford the shaping and internal arrangements of relative clauses within sentences. Television can do the same but only at the expense of meaning.

Audio has to fight against time. Transience is its guiding spirit. A second gone is a second lost. If a thought or word even is not taken in then the following thought or word may have no meaning. Long sentences, it would seem, are out. But within reason it is not a question of length but complexity. The structure has to be simplified. One can convert copy into audio without too much difficulty – always provided the number of ideas it has to communicate is not great, but one has first to break down the elements and then reassemble them. And reassemble them in a certain order (through time as it were).

Try this now!

Here is a test which will demonstrate the differences between copy and audio (i.e. between the written and the spoken word). Since what you are asked to do involves speech it would be useful to record your answer so that you can check your progress and check your version against mine. It is essential that you speak the answer – *do not write it down.* The next paragraph consists of one sentence of information. I want you to relay that information to an imaginary third party. Both of you (for reasons which will become obvious) are standing by a window overlooking a car park. Ready?

The bicycle next to the green car in the car park belongs to the housekeeper's brother-in-law.

Now tell the other person at the window everything you have just read. (You can read it once more if you need.) And you can point out of the window.

OK? How many elements in your spoken version? Three? Have another go.

Right. Here's how I would tell that story. We are standing by the window. I point.

See that car in the car park?
The green one?
See the bicycle next to it?
Well you know the housekeeper?
That bicycle belongs to her brother-in-law.

What have we done? We have broken the original sentence into five elements (or short sentences). We have reassembled them in a certain order and have attempted to make comprehension easier by building the story up block by block. In doing so we have inevitably used more words (over 50 per cent more in fact) since the compression which press can get away with confuses the ear and, consequently, each element needs to have space for itself (hence such additional words as 'one' and 'it', repetitions of car; two mentions of bicycle; 'well you know'). Each element makes a point and acts as a link with the preceding and following element.

Finally examine the five elements as shots in a film.

See that car in the car park?	Long shot
The green one?	Closing in to mid-shot
See the bicycle next to it?	Pan right still closing in
Well, you know the housekeeper?	Cut to housekeeper
That bicycle belongs to her brother-in-law	Pull back to two-shot

Not very long after I started using this device the standard of television writing improved. (*Post hoc non propter hoc.*) Kids who had grown up with the medium were writing for it as a matter of course. The first inkling I had that the art was intuitive occurred when I gave a young girl a test to ascertain whether she had potential as a trainee television writer. I asked her to write a script for a fifteen second commercial for an up-the-market brand of cigarette. She described the action as follows:

1. A 707 is taking off.
2. We see the 'Fasten seat belts. No smoking' sign alight then off.
3. We look along a row of seats at two men. The first is removing his seat belt. The second has already removed his and is taking out a packet of Benson and Hedges.
4. Close-up of hand holding pack and first man's hand taking a cigarette.

The girl had never written a television or film script before yet she understood the medium, the montage of scenes. In filmic parlance we call the first shot an establishing shot. Note how the next shot picks up from the first and how the third picks up from the second (the sign is immediately followed by both elements of that sign taking effect: a belt is unfastened, a man is about to smoke). Note, too, the simple way it's cut together, the transition from the take-off to the sign going out concertina time. Note finally that the order of those four shots is *right* (shuffle them and they make no sense). All this untaught.

However, though young writers were taking to television and the spoken word as if by instinct, their copywriting ability was less pronounced. Television's first effect on copy was to remove much of the phony 'advertese'. Advertising's special language was

more embarrassing out loud. Copy fell into line. But the colloquial style of television, though it brought some fresh air to copy,
also left it flabby. Copy can afford to be tight and elliptical. It
has to draw pictures with its prose. It proceeds less as a castle on a
chessboard than a combination of knight and queen. Copy has
headlines and one day we all woke and wondered where they
had gone. The headlines and the copywriters. Today there are
about a dozen top flight copywriters in London (there are very
many more TV writers) just when press advertising could do
with them.

But fashion is cyclical and I detect a movement back to press
among the creative demi-monde. It may lack the prizes and the
acclaim but the task is harder and the rewards (for the client
that is) more immediate and satisfying. In TV fads are fast in,
fast out. There is an over-preoccupation with entertainment, with
the minidrama, with the song (heaven forbid one use the word
jingle today!), with the presentation and trappings of showbiz.
But at the heart I detect a sense of ennui. This could work to the
advantage of press, as may the consumerist's demand for facts
about products rather than fancies, since press allows you to tell
a long information story.

Magazines offer the creative man a whole spectrum of
opportunities and the chance to communicate with segmented
audiences. Agencies are widening their media schedules to include
the 'underground press'. The 'sophisticated male' is now well
catered for. And the girl can trip across the river of life from one
stepping stone to the next, from *Valentine* to, say, *Vogue*, by way of
Honey, Nineteen, She, Look Now, Over 21, Woman, Nova, Cosmo. The
specialist press (trade, technical, sport, hobbies) offers another
spectrum. Local dailies, particularly the new evening papers
printed web offset, regional weeklies, the freesheets (controlled
circulation newspapers which are given away, with two thirds of
their pages devoted to advertising) . . . all these offer attractive
choices for the client's budget. Yet how often they are regarded as
support media at best and minority interest media at worst. The
great god cost-effectiveness (which I promised not to mention)
decrees that the cheapest way to reach do-it-yourself enthusiasts
is not in the DIY magazines but television. Or people reject a

medium for reasons based on information which is out of date. Creative people are notoriously ill-informed about media. They do not read enough newspapers or magazines, let alone publications outside their own special interests. They miss the stimulus which an outside encounter can bring. They miss the opportunity to adapt (preferably, rethink) an idea from one medium to another. Of course they are busy people (though the gaining of knowledge would seem to be part of the job) and the media themselves and agency media men must take the trouble to keep creative departments informed. But the media are, as a whole, slow to inform the creative people. Free copies of magazines, for example, reach media men and account executives, but seldom the creative department.

One medium which is stirring itself is outdoor. Posters have a place in popular affection. People recall them – their first encounters, not only with advertising but also with the written word. Posters are personal, they represent landmarks along a route. They invite participation and offer a joke or an exciting picture or simple information. They are seen by real people from bus tops. And by company chairmen who never go by tube from the backs of limousines. They say goodbye at airports and welcome you home. They have a place in people's affections but not that many schedules.

However, the outdoor people have refurbished their selling techniques and got rid of their cloth cap image. They are researching the effectiveness of the medium. They are offering a wide range of sites and a greater degree of flexibility. Here again, the creative man is often rooted in past prejudices. Here are some of the comments which I have heard put forward to take outdoor off the candidate list: outdoor is expensive, inefficient, under-researched, under-serviced, 'wrong for our product', inflexible, 'full of nothing but cigarette advertising'. And yet this medium today offers a single crown, double crown, 16 and 48 sheets, supersite, Adshel (illuminated bus shelters), transport advertising (in trains and on buses). How all this can be dismissed with one precooked comment baffles me. The differences between, for example, a 48 sheet and a bus shelter can be quite profound: the one is high up above the traffic and glanced at, the other is on the pavement at eye level and can be read at comparative leisure by people waiting for a bus. And yet how are they used? Nine times out of ten in the identical manner.

This is probably the chief indictment of the creative man's attitude towards media. He gets his idea and then adapts it across all media. The colour supplement ad is blown up for the poster and shown in black and white in the national daily. The end shot of the commercial becomes the bus side. There are exceptions. And I don't mean to knock a desire for uniformity. But I bristle when double crown notice board type advertisements turn up on bus fronts, when the copy for a bargain space press ad is belted out on television, *when the creative man fails to appreciate the essential strengths of each medium.* If instead of simply cutting an idea to fit a shape he would each time return to the idea and say to himself, 'How best can I take that idea and using the strengths of this other medium make it work?' Even if this means starting absolutely from scratch. There is a significant difference between this and merely shoving one form of the idea into ill-fitting shapes.

Every advertisement can be made less remote. Each ad can be pushed along the continuum. Simply to adapt rather than think through each ad for a different medium is first to deny that the medium has specific strengths (or that it has an effect upon the message which makes the message in some way different from the same message in other media) and second, to deprive the advertisement and therefore the client of its full potential as a motivator of consumers towards purchase.

The interrelation of a specific medium and the message is a greatly under-researched subject. Is the same advertisement in *The Times* and the *Sun* actually the same advertisement? Even to the man who happens to read both papers? Could he not, for example, prefer to be treated as a *Times* reader in the one and a *Sun* reader in the other? What mood is he in when he sees your advertisement? This may seem impossible to discover and yet in some cases you can be pretty sure. Going to work the commuter may be tense. Returning he may be relaxed. Could you not therefore put different versions of the same idea on the up-platforms and down-platforms of commuter stations? Posters on fixed sites offer a tremendous advantage. You know *exactly* where people will be when they see your message. A Supersite along an intersection means that the ad is read during traffic jams. Therefore the number of words on that particular poster can be increased. Better still, why not follow the example of British Rail and address the fuming driver by telling him how quickly the journey to London could take him by Inter-City? Radio similarly offers you the captive motorist though you can't be certain of the jam or the location. And the tyre manufacturer who wants to speak to him can also have a space like the back of a bus. And an ad in a theatre programme is read by a man in a theatre ('think on't'). On television you can fix a spot in a break in, before or after certain programmes. You can't, of course, tie in with that programme but you can gauge the mood of the audience midway through *Aquarius*, say, or before the News. In the press you can take a special position next to the crossword in *The Times*, for example (there you may get your scanner *en passant* and your intelligent reader with time to read); or beneath the *Guardian*'s leader column (a solus site this for about £50). If given these spaces shouldn't you realise their full potential rather than do a bastard version of, say, your thirty second spot? Play the strengths of the media. Magazines have been carrying free samples for years; why not newspapers? Why not, indeed, thought KMPH who launched J-cloth in a test market by incorporating a 'page' of the stuff in the local press. Sachets of perfume can be stuck to the page of a woman's magazine.

- Radio isn't press copy read out loud.
- Television isn't radio with moving pictures.
- 48-sheet posters aren't press ads blown up.
- And double crowns aren't 48-sheets 'blown down'.
- *The Times* is not the *Sun*.
- *Nova* isn't *Nineteen*.
- Nor is a mailing shot a classified . . . or a sandwich board, a back of a ticket, a painted bus . . . or an ad in a London taxi on the back of an upturned seat.

The media department booked some taxi cards for BOAC. The requisition came to the creative group: 'adapt the current poster'.

I put my oar in, got the team together, told them to rethink the current poster idea in terms of the medium. We were talking VC10-derness. The VC10 seat gives a passenger more leg room. The man looking at the taxi card was also seated wasn't he? . . . The team came up with a simple message 'Even if your feet can reach this you'll still have room in our VC10 – BOAC'.

● Advertising is getting people to do things. By means of media.

● And media is *plural*. Which means there's more than one.

28

Blow the line!

I stopped my car at the Texaco Station. To get my tea bags. The petrol attendant picked up the nozzle and said 'Shall I be mother?'

A line exists in advertising. Above it agencies make money; below it they don't. Or, to put it another way, advertising expenditure through commissionable media is 'above the line'. Expenditure on *sales promotion* is 'below the line'. Like all divisions it is a mixed blessing. It facilitates allocation of responsibility. It also acts as a barrier. The advertising agency man tends to regard the promotions man as an inferior version of himself (below the salt). It irks him to see an advertising budget cut to provide funds for promotional activity, particularly when he regards it as a bribe to keep the trade happy or a defensive marketing posture in a tough competitive situation. It irks him, too, to see advertising money spent on 'scheme' rather than 'theme' (i.e. on the promotional activity rather than the main campaign for the product itself), since this to him seems to reverse the natural order of things and makes advertising play a support role. It irks him, too, to see the promotions man in the gravy.

The line between advertising and sales promotions is the subject of this chapter and much agonising in the business. For the growth in below the line is evidence of power going out of the manufacturer's hands and into those of the retailer, particularly the larger retail chains who can force him to support a brand with heavy discounts and promotional activity. This growth has concerned advertiser, agency and consumerist alike. Though advertising people ought not to rejoice at the prospect of having the consumer lobby as an ally: the attack on promotions is by no means as unmitigated as that on advertising; consumerists who decry plastic daffodils and such trivia and ask why don't manufacturers instead cut the price, welcome the genuine savings and extra value which certain promotions offer.

So substantial has been the encroachment of below the line on the budget that advertising agencies have countered by setting up their own sales promotion subsidiaries or associates. In the good old days they had merchandising departments and promotions were devised by the agency as part of the service or for little fee. Now the agencies find it difficult and embarrassing to charge the true market rate for this work and have to set up a wholly-owned company. But with this compartmentalisation the separation gets wider. The line thicker and more impenetrable. Enlightened companies regard advertising and sales promotion as two aspects of fundamentally the same activity (BP never speaks of advertising managers but ASP managers) and agencies, belatedly admitting that this is so, regret either that they did little about making the client pay for it when the agency did it or that the agency has spent the last ten years offloading it.

Meanwhile, below the line, the practitioners have been attempting to put their house in order. They have formed associations (Sales Promotion Executives Association, British Premium Manufacturers Association) and hold exhibitions (Incentive Marketing Exhibition, run by the magazine of that name) and they are busy trying to rub out the image of the market trader with a load of dubious merchandise.

Promotions is an area which has become crucially important to the advertising man and which he has often regarded with indifference, if not disdain, passing it aside to the specialist. The specialist, for his part, has been just as happy to act independently of the adman. And it is this relationship of their two functions which is the theme of this chapter. It falls into three parts:

1. Definition of sales promotion.
2. Examination of the differences between sales promotion and advertising.
3. Examination of the relationship between them.

Part one: Definition

When an advertising man talks to a promotions man he finds one word cropping up: 'creative'. 'Creative' is taken to mean aesthetic. When, for example, a promotions company executive says, as one did to me, 'It was a very good promotion. Very successful. But it wasn't very creative', he means, presumably, that it didn't satisfy some criterion other than effectiveness.

A marketing executive in an agency said: 'You've got two promotions. One of them's creative. You research one against the other and you can bet it will be the humdrum one that will win.' There is a general impression that below the line is less 'creative' than above the line. But creativity in the aesthetic sense is just as invalid in advertising as it is in promotions: and in the practical sense just as valid.

Let us first take our definition of advertising:

● 'The origination and/or communication of ideas about products in order to motivate consumers towards purchase.'

That is practical and all-embracing. Maybe it will do also for below the line?

But first how do the practitioners themselves define their subject? *Incentive Marketing* says that it 'embraces the process by which a secondary product or service is offered in order to promote a consumer article for which there is a steady demand.' It's the best definition I met: the key word is secondary. It's easy enough to list what we mean by promotions:

Money-off
Free premiums at point-of-sale
Free mail-ins

Coupons
Sampling
Self-liquidating offers
Bonus packs
Personality promotions
Competitions
Sponsorship

But how does all this differ from advertising? A marketing executive in a promotions company advised me to think of it this way: 'Advertising is strategic. Promotion is tactical.' This appears to make sense. Below the line does have a tactical support role; it helps a manufacturer to get his product sampled or be visible at point-of-sale, it allows him to get out of short-term trouble, etc.

Here is the definition of sales promotion afforded by the Articles of Association of the Sales Promotion Executives Association:

●   *The stimulation of sales in complement with advertising and merchandising within the conduct of sound business practice.*

'Within the conduct of sound business practice' in no way *defines* sales promotion. It merely qualifies it as far as the organisation is concerned. It's probably in the Articles to keep certain people *out*. Maybe the backstreet operator with four thousand teddy bears to flog and looking for a likely company. And what about 'in complement with advertising and merchandising'? (Incidentally, isn't sales promotion the same as merchandising?) What about those cases of 'stimulus of sales' which take place *without* complementary merchandising or advertising? There must surely be many examples of companies using sales promotion as the sole means of stimulating sales of their products. Right. So if we delete that and the reference to 'sound business conduct' we are left with this: *'Sales promotion is the stimulation of sales.'* Which doesn't take us very far. It falls considerably short of our definition of advertising which we shall bear in mind as we examine a few promotions in order to arrive at a definition.

First a quick stroll round the paddock to look at the runners.

Money-off: '2p off' flash on a packet of Ritz.

Free premium at point-of-sale: Plastic bowl with Daz.

Free mailings: Coupon, form or other 'proof of purchase' on a packet, say, of a new product which the consumer then mails to the manufacturer in exchange for a free second packet. (Buy one get one free!)

Coupons: Either included in the product (e.g. cigarettes) or in magazines or delivered through letter-boxes redeemable at stores.

Sampling: Samples of product can be given away at stores, attached to other products of the same company, delivered through doors or included in magazines.

Self-liquidating offer: If the consumer saves three packet tops she can then purchase an item at less than the retail price (e.g. football game with Sugar Smacks). The manufacturer buys the item in bulk and sells more of his product so the extra costs are covered. (Hence self-liquidation.)

Bonus packs: More of the same product is sold for the same price – 'Extra 20 per cent free'.

Personality promotion: e.g. girls dressed as the product visit an area and either give away samples or knock at doors and give money to housewives who can show they use the product.

Competitions: Entry forms are on the product or in the press. 'Proof of purchase' accompanies entry. They must by law demand an act of skill. They can't be lotteries.

Sponsorship: e.g. Gillette Cup (cricket), Texaco Cup (soccer), Piccadilly world match play championship (golf), etc.

The *Sun* newspaper promotes all the time. They will in the fortnight before the start of the football season promote a book. Inexpensive, covering all the fixtures, lots of pictures and this is the point – spaces for other pictures *to be collected from the paper itself*. They promoted an anorak in various colours adorned with badges of soccer teams. They called them Socceraks. The promotion had flair, allowed the purchaser to identify with the club. It used Bobby Charlton to endorse it. But above all it was practical. It was reversible – club colour one side, serviceable dark shade the other. So that a mother would be tempted to buy one for her son. Only she would first have to buy the paper and more than once to get the necessary coupons. It was a very appropriate promotion. It reflects the policy of the paper. The *Sun* is good on sport, young and full of ideas. Thus the promotion is not simply a straightforward incentive to buy the paper. It is also saying something about the paper.

One would imagine that this promotion, in common with many, had two objectives:

1. *To stimulate purchase by non-readers and irregular readers* and thus pick up extra sales hoping to keep them via the paper itself.

2. *To reinforce the image of the paper.* The sparky promotion must be seen in the context of others plus that of the sparky paper itself.

You will see that the tactical strategic distinction has fallen at the first fence. The *Sun* promotion is both tactical and strategic.

Whitbread's Chandy is a soft drink looking harder than it is. A non-alcoholic man's drink sold in pubs. Advertising and merchandising support the product concept, summed up in the slogan 'Drink and Drive on Chandy'. Whitbread's supported this idea by promoting tough masculine sporting events – motor racing, free-fall parachute jumping and an 80-mile cycle road race grand prix. The route of the race passed, would you believe, several pubs all of which stocked Chandy. And the race reached its climax between 12 and two o'clock, Sunday opening hours. Each pub contributed, ran a book on the result and gave a special prize for the cyclist who reached *his* pub first. In all these events Chandy got tremendous support from local bottlers in local pubs. The winner got a medal. Each competitor got a pennant. The competition, like Alice, gave prizes for all; awareness of Chandy, like Topsy, just growed. *And the product has become more important as a result of the promotion.*

Andrex has managed to increase brand share against very strong competition by distinctive advertising and closely relating scheme to theme. Here's an extract from an article in the IPC magazine, *Women's Market.* '*Consumer promotions emphasise quality.* Another contributing factor has been the use of consumer promotions, designed to encourage continuity of purchase and strengthen the image of the brand. The 'Dream bathroom' offer, for example, offered the consumer a selection of high quality products at a reduced price, thus laying emphasis on the quality and value of Andrex and successfully linking it with a modern bathroom setting.'

'Strengthen the image of the brand.' How often does a product come out of a promotion as strong, let alone stronger, than when it went in? It happened, I think, with the *Sun* and Chandy, with Esso's World Cup; Brooke Bond PG Tips Happy Reunion competition (uniting families scattered across the world); Birds Eye Lifeboat scheme (where instead of the customer receiving a price-cut she and the advertiser made a joint contribution to a lifeboat fund) ; and in Robinson's Baby Foods 'Baby of the Year'. In all these the product became more important as a result of the promotion.

Part two: Differences

On the evidence of the promotions mentioned so far can we draw a distinction between advertising and sales promotion? Clearly 'stimulus for sales' doesn't go far enough and the strategic tactical distinction clouds the issue. Sales promotion can also be said to 'move towards purchase'. Advertising also 'promotes'. BUT. Advertising promotes a product *via* the product, by means of its actual or built-in characteristics.

Sales promotion, on the other hand, promotes the product by means of something *outside* the product. What has already been referred to as a secondary product or service. A promotion could succeed *despite* the product. In other words, even if you already know and dislike the product, the promotion may induce you to buy it. Whereas in the case of advertising if you already know and dislike the product advertising will *not* induce you to buy it.

● *Advertising uses the product to sell the product.*

● *Sales promotion uses something outside the product to sell the product (or to be strictly accurate – something outside the regular product).*

That something else can be a plastic daffodil, a trip to Spain, a

doll, a bike, a model plane . . . or the Lancashire Captain holding
aloft the Gillette Cup at Lord's. Or, of course, it can be money.
Actual or disguised. A bonus pack is not the product – certainly
not the regular product – it's money. Just as money-off . . . or a
coupon.

Sampling could be said to be the only example of sales promotion which uses the product to sell the product. Again it isn't
the regular product. No. The distinction I submit still holds
water. Advertising from *within* the product. Sales promotion from
without. Via something else.

Now – the crucial point. What about the relationship between
the product and that 'something else'? Or does it matter? I
maintain it does. Certainly long term.

There are brilliant exceptions. The link between Esso and the
World Cup could be said, by a stretch of the imagination, to be
. . . what? . . . international leadership. But there's none at all
between Shell and Make-Money. If it's a truly great idea – and
you happen to be first – fine! But even then, what about the long-
term effect?

There was a promotion for Fairy Snow. A jungle safari. A
nice idea but relevant? A jungle is the last place I'd expect to
find fairies, let alone snow. Does it matter? Obviously not, say
Fairy Snow. Obviously not, say Crosse and Blackwell who
simultaneously also ran a jungle safari promotion for their baked
beans.

On the other hand, P & G's Camay ran a competition which
was beautifully relevant and image-enhancing. 100 Pifco Beauty
Aids. Sun lamps, hairdryers, rollers and a vibratory massager
with 5 applicators. Lyons' Coffee gave away place mats.

Esso Blue offered pillow cases. Esso Blue? Reckitts Blue I could
understand. Robin Starch I could understand. And Robin Starch
offered sheets. Cadbury's Drinking Chocolate ran a housewarming competition. 'List 15 points which contribute to making
a housewarming party a real success'. The prizes? Furnishing for
the house, of course.

Shredded Wheat featured an on-pack give-away. 'Soccer
greats selector disc'. And that is relevant to the sporting image of
the product and a franchise at least a decade old. (And Cubs –

a spoon size shredded wheat – were offering, free inside, 'Football Stamps'. The promotion enhances the image to the appropriate market and the major brand is able to support the otherwise relatively unsupported minor brand.)

Sometimes the link between advertising and promotion is so firm it's tangible . . . Findus are totally integrated. Their Good Food World ad campaign spawns their promotion: 'Free gifts from the Good Food World'. The *Larousse Gastronomique* for instance. And in *The Grocer* appeared an advertisement to the trade:

> If you've got the mousse
> They get the Larousse.

Promotion and advertising helping each other. And the product more important as a result of the promotion. As with new Soft Blue Band whose promotion, like its advertising campaign, was concerned with the New World.

Product and promotion should be related. Brilliant exceptions are few. Remember – everything you do in the product's name affects the product's image. And the promotion should be appropriate to the product image and, if possible, enhance it.

We can detect four types (or degrees) of relationship between promotion and product.

1. The first – and most common – is the total *absence* of any relationship at all. The plastic daffodil, the Paris weekend competition, Shell's famous Make-Money, Mazda's Mickey Mouse offer. They are often very successful but I question the longterm effects of over-use of unrelated promotions.

2. The second category is what I might call the *link tenuous*. Cow and Gate giving away *cream* coloured Capris or possibly the Esso World Cup promotion where the link is between an event of international importance and a company with a similar stature.

3. The third category is the *appropriate relationship*. Here the offer, prize or scheme is relevant to the product. It seems right and proper that the brand should run that promotion – and it is quite probable that the one will be identified with the other. Sugar Smacks, whose whole pack is, in a sense, a personality

promotion (Star Trek characters – space energy, etc.), offer Star Trek pyjamas. This integrated activity clearly enhances the image of the brand. Dulite similarly promote a brush holder. Andrex run a Dream Bathroom competition and Efferdent run one on 'Winning smiles'. Robin Starch run a SLP on sheets and Scotties paper towels offer a vanity mirror.

4. The fourth and final category differs from the previous types in degree. Whereas in category 3 the promotion is *appropriate* to the product, here the promotion is *integrated* with the brand or the brand's advertising. Only Heinz could run a Heinz Bean Bard contest. Only Findus could offer Gifts from the Good Food World.

Or to look at those four categories another way . . . A promotion in category 1 could be run by any product, in any product group. The same virtually applies to promotions in category 2. In category 3, however, there is a strong generic relationship. The promotion may not be uniquely identified with the brand – other products in the product group could be associated with the promotion. Though by pre-emption they are probably excluded. But in category 4 the relationship is *specific* rather than generic. The promotion is integrated. There was a phrase for this at Benson's. It's not above the line or below the line – it's *on the line*.

A product has an image. Advertising helped to create it; product performance, in keeping the promise of the advertising, reinforced it. Long-term advertising helped to win new users and retain brand loyalty, increase brand share. It makes no sense to allow the promotion to ignore or, worse, undermine that image for the sake of immediate short-term gains when it could, whilst still getting those short-term gains, *enhance* that image and thus strengthen the advertising, leaving it in a better position when the promotion is over to *continue* to hold new and existing consumers.

If you are asked to evaluate a future promotion you'll have to ask a lot of questions:

Is it practicable?
Can we afford it?
Has the premium popular appeal?

Better still is it – or can it be – personalised?

Has the promotion flair?

Is the competition easy to enter – fun to do, not impossible to judge and what element of skill is required?

Is it possible to give all competition entrants a prize?

Will the promotion engender favourable free publicity for itself and the product?

Is it sufficiently different?

etc., etc.

But the most important question of all is: Is the promotion appropriate for the brand, related to it, if possible integrated with it and will the image of the brand be strengthened as a result of the promotion?

The advertising man and the promotions man are both in the business of having ideas about products which motivate people towards purchase. But whereas the former uses the product to sell the product, the latter uses *something other* than the product. The choice of that something other should be made with care. Don't lose identity. Don't debase the brand. Don't reduce the potency of the advertising and, above all, remember everything you do in the product's name affects the product's image.

29

Aristotle and Fairy Snow

The inexact scientist shares with the scientist a belief in progress. The bastard artist has no such belief. He endeavours to become more proficient at his trade but he does not subscribe to the concept of increasing excellence. Science by definition builds on its past. Each discovery adds to the corpus of knowledge and in solving one problem may offer the key to another or suggest yet another problem. Science is linear. Art 'progresses' in quite a different way. Though the artist may not be as obsessed as the scientist with the need to discover, he is, nevertheless, attracted by the idea of innovation. But whether what he produces is 'better' than what was formerly produced is for history to judge. Certain periods or movements can be said to stand out as peaks on a landscape. Except that the landscape has a habit of shifting, of assuming new shapes as one looks at it, rather in the manner of an image seen in a distorting mirror. Science, too, offers these changes of emphasis or attitude – but they are concerned with science itself, its purpose and role in society rather than the products of science. Theories of 'science' may be as wayward as those of art, but it is undeniable that the theories and subsequent proofs of each succeeding major scientist must represent an advance on the situation which he inherited, a pushing back of the frontiers: and thus a linear progress. The artist may succeed in breaking with all convention but his 'new art' is as much a reaction to his context as a striving for some abstraction called progress. Indeed, he may consciously or unconsciously employ techniques of past centuries in the service of his 'new art'. He may strike out on his own and then to his wonder and disappointment discover that someone has got there before him. This happens also in science. But whereas identical scientific discoveries occur in different places more or less simultaneously, the artist may find that his 'competitor' pre-dates him by five thousand years.

He may deliberately rethink the present in terms of the past regarding, say, a Grecian attitude to life as an ideal, and produce a work of relevant modernity which yet owes its structure to a model some two thousand years old. He may alternatively merely copy the past, ape a style, construct a façade or pastiche. He may bring about a renewal of interest in a past period, a Gothic revival or, as recently, a nouveau Art Nouveau. But the interest manifests itself in works. A renewal of interest in the science of a past period would not so manifest itself. Apart from the possible participation of a few cranks a flat-earth revival, say, would hardly get off the ground. Art takes the horizontal line of science, holds it vertically and lets it swing like a pendulum.

These attitudes coexist in advertising. When I first entered advertising I remember an art director decrying a particular typeface – Cheltenham Bold. It was oldfashioned. I pocketed the information vowing that no ad of mine should ever show such a face to the public. Ten years later Cheltenham came into vogue. Cooper Black had a revival in the early 1960s.

These swings of the pendulum are not simply arbitrary whims of fashion (though they are often mainly that). The bastard artist – if he is genuine – is acting responsibly within an immediate context. The specific problem shall produce a specific answer. If he borrows – from whatever source – he must know or feel that the borrowing helps him towards a solution. Unfortunately he often borrows for other reasons. To be seen to be knowledgeable and *au courant*. For fear of not conforming. (It is OK for an ad to stand out from the crowd – but not for an art director to stand out from the in crowd.) But the responsible advertising man (writer or art director) will call into service whatever suits his task – and the context and environment of the advertisement. If he chooses a scraperboard illustration in preference to a photograph what moves him is not a stray fancy for the technique (he may personally hate it) but a consideration of its suitability for the product image, its ability to portray accurately the important details of the product, the complexities of fast run reproduction on 65-screen newsprint, the competition's choice of illustration technique.

He will be guided by the same criterion of fitness for purpose and exercise the same catholic taste in his choice of advertising theory. Though he has a personal 'liking' for undersell he will choose a tough USP approach if the situation demands, despite the comments of his colleagues who tell him it's old hat, or the more serious strictures of his own agency's 'house style'. If long copy is called for he will shut his ears to the siren call of 'long copy is out'. If he is working on a retirement pension advertisement he will not set the copy in sans serif six point reversed out of black: that would certainly stand out but if older eyes can't read it . . .

He will, of course, be interested in mechanical improvements. The fisheye lens which captures virtually everything within its gaze; electronic flash and fast film which allow him to take a whole spectrum of shots within a short space of time and capture several facets of a model's mood before that mood evaporates; a zoom lens which lets him go from infinity to a pinhead in a couple of seconds; rigid cameras strapped to helicopters to give him new scenes and new angles and hand held cameras to give him mobility: all these will help his art. But he does not choose a technique to solve a problem, since a technique is not an idea. He chooses a technique the better to express his idea. All new techniques, science servicing art, represent initially a step backwards. Just as you can't have an omelette without breaking eggs, it would appear that you can't have a breakthrough without breaking something up.

Every 'advance' in art, the introduction of a new art form or mechanical improvement, begins with a period of adjustment. The artist has to learn to handle the new tool; the audience has to learn to appreciate the new 'language' and not to hanker after the old. One can imagine a couple of disgruntled Athenians trudging home after the first night of a play by Aeschylus and complaining that theatre would never catch on; 'It hasn't got the action. Give me a good epic every time.'

When printing was invented illustrations had to be cut in wood. Thus accompanying the advance in communication was a retreat in the standards of illustration.

The earliest 'movies' were anything but. The stories were filmed plays – with the added disadvantage of silence. The camera was in a fixed position – about the middle of the sixth row of the stalls. Characters made their entrances and exits stage right and stage left. The camera operator cranked until there was no film left on the reel. Then the film makers learnt to cut, to assemble sections of the story (or film) in such a fashion as to make the story more meaningful. Instead of sitting in the sixth row of the stalls, the watcher could be in the front row or by the actor's right shoulder or at the back of the gallery. Then he found he could be in two places at once: he could be with the hunter and the hunted, going from one to the other and back again at an increasing rate. And the camera which at the beginning was stationary, learned to swing left and right (pan) and up and down (tilt). It could be attached to a moving car or train. By this time the movies were moving. They had learned to tell their stories in their own way, to rely less on captions of dialogue and more on acting, expression, arrangement of material. They had not only learned to do without sound, the absence of sound had provided a discipline which played a major part (probably *the* major part) in the development of the new art form.

And then what happened? The talkies. Imagine, thought the public – all that adventure, romance, comedy, *plus* hearing the actors speak. But it wasn't going to be like that. Not at first. As Hollywood was soon to appreciate. The freedom of the studio floor was severely curtailed. The microphone picked up every sound. The director could no longer shout instructions while the camera rolled. Noises off cost money on a sound stage. And, unfortunately, the noisiest thing of all was the camera itself. Some means had to be found of blanketing camera noise: this was the blimp, a large metal casing which completely covered the whirring machinery. But it made the camera much heavier and considerably restricted its movement.

Therefore at that precise moment when the cinema had learned to fly it was back in the confined space of the theatre set with the camera taking long scenes in one position. Admittedly it had the benefit of sound (so film makers could dispense with all those captions, most of which they had dispensed with already). And therefore they could attract stage actors and could film plays (exactly as the earliest movies had done). The established movie stars had to learn to speak. The 'legitimate' actors had to learn to act in close-up. The cinema audiences gawked at the wonder of it all and two latterday Athenians could be heard grumbling on their way home 'give me a silent movie any day'.

Another limitation, of course, was language. The silent cinema was international. Language brought barriers and methods had to be found of crossing them. Early talkies also sang. In fact all the films of that period seemed to consist of was talk and song. The pessimists predicted a short life. 'Once the novelty wears off . . .'

But the *very first* movies had been side-show entertainments. Patrons ran screaming from one hall as a train rushed at them. In the hands of artists the novelty developed into an art form. Some later innovations never graduated from the sideshow. Three-dimensional film meant little more than a 'lion in your lap'. Cinerama was a travelogue writ large or a ride down a roller-coaster. The same fate almost befell Cinemascope. Early Cinemascope films were very wooden. The vast narrow screen meant initially less flexibility of movement and much concentration on landscape: action going on at stage right and stage left. But directors and cameramen overcame the problem.

Another advance which was initially a step backwards was television. It was cinema only much smaller. The difficulties of live transmission in a confined space without a break meant a cramping of style and expression. At home, whereas radio sets (once they had shed their earphones) could be placed anywhere, television sets could be placed only where people could see them and thus became a focal point and had to compete with the traditional focal point, the hearth. Early television news broadcasts were simply that – filmed radio broadcasts. When the BBC announced plans to extend its news coverage and illustrate what it was reporting the comments of some critics were scathing. It would trivialise the news. What pictures could be shown? Since news was immediate and newsfilm (then)was not, the illustrations would be at best of the news of the day before.

Returning to our subject – but retaining this theme – when commercial television happened in 1955 the earliest commercials went through the identical process we have been examining. Their initial form was, in effect, a bastardised version of another. Just as early movies were photographed stage plays so early commercials were smaller versions of cinema commercials. The only experience this country had enjoyed of a similar medium was the cinema and therefore it provided both the model and the practitioners. Consequently those early commercials were not fitted for the medium. There were too many mid-shots, and long shots, too many crowd scenes, too many night shots. The cinema might be cosy but it wasn't intimate. The cinema was also – with justice – considered an entertainment medium : commercials in order not to intrude had to remember that and many were little films, pretending to be anything but a commercial, telling stories which revealed embarrassingly at the end the name of the product to a universal groan from the audience. With a few notable exceptions the commercials of the first year of independent television were not television but cramped cinema.

In the USA, which had had a different model, the earliest commercials aped radio. The seated presenter would deliver a pitch rather in the manner of the radio commercials discussed earlier, employing the same repetition of the brand name, despite the fact that it could *show* the product, whereas radio had to overcome in whatever way it could the absence of vision. It will be interesting to see (or rather hear) how commercial radio develops in the UK, with television as a model; whether in fact we shall hear TV commercials without pictures or whether the medium will find its feet, its form, without much trouble. The latter, I expect, since the experience of other countries, Luxembourg and the pirates, will help. Nevertheless, for a lot of the new boys there will be a hiccup or two.

So far this chapter has made two points. One, advances in an art, through the introduction either of a new form or new mechanical development, are accompanied initially by a period of adjustment which is often retrograde in nature. Two, a theme we have met repeatedly, the artist's job is to exploit the limitations of a medium, to regard those limitations as potential strengths and play them for all they are worth.

And now, back to Ancient Greece. What our two Athenians were upset about was the rigidity of the new medium, drama. The epic, orally handed down, employed a wide canvas, a series of incidents in many locations, and *action*. The drama concentrated upon a short period of time and all action seemed to take place offstage.

Another Athenian, Aristotle, watched the development of drama and, from observation, drew up a set of rules. Drama had, of course, existed before the rules, just as the making of press and television advertisements was to precede the codification of 'rules' by which to do it. Some of the limitations were imposed by the nature of the medium; its origin as a semireligious activity; the amount of information which had to be assumed by an audience which shared the history and/or had it explained to them by a commentator or chorus; the vast size of the auditorium which demanded that the actors wear masks in order to be seen by the back row. Other limitations, the division into scenes, the relationship between actors, chorus and audience and, above all, the internal dramatic development – these were a result of working within the medium, trial and error and adoption of those things which appeared to work. Limitations, therefore, were either imposed from without or self-imposed by the dramatist.

In the *Poetics* Aristotle examined those limitations. A play, he found, has to obey three unities. The unity of *place*: the action happened entirely in one location. The unity of *mood or theme*: in other words, don't mix moods or introduce sub-plots. The unity of *time*: all the action took place in the time the play took to be performed. (There were no conventions such as a falling curtain or a slow fade to denote passage of time. *Oedipus Rex*, therefore, takes place in the last hour of Oedipus' sighted life.)

Aristotle said that two other elements were essential. Anagnorisis, discovery, recognition by the central character of a key fact which leads to the denouement of the play. Peripetia, a reversal of fortune. Thus, in *Oedipus Rex*, Oedipus finds out about his dad (Anagnorisis) and, unable to live with the fact of his own incest, blinds himself (Peripetia).

These laws are not unbreakable. They would appear to have no relevance outside classical and neo-classical drama (e.g. Corneille and Racine or Milton). Shakespeare discarded them. The cinema doesn't need them. Nevertheless, many dramatists return to them (as we observed earlier when considering the visual arts), not to ape a bygone style but in order to utilise a discipline which may allow them to flex their creative muscles and rethink a contemporary problem. Indeed, the unities impose a very tight discipline which is of benefit to a contemporary dramatist. No matter that the initial rationale may have gone. Indeed, there may be very telling economic arguments for obeying the unities. One set, one time period, no sub-plot (and therefore not too many actors): these could be the result of a tight budget imposed by a hard-pressed theatrical management.

The television commercial as it developed also grew its own rules. And they bear a striking resemblance to those of Aristotle! Consider first the limitation of time. One minute allows the writer very little opportunity to tell a complex story. Moreover, unity of mood or theme is dictated by not only the time limit but the 'laws' of good advertising. As we have seen an advertisement has to be single-minded. The shorter the commercial the more pressing the need for *unity of theme*. By the same token the action needs to happen in one location: therefore *unity of place*. And probably within the duration of the commercial itself: therefore *unity of time*.

It may surprise you to discover the number of commercials which any one night obey two, if not all three, of the unities: plus the Greek tradition of limiting the persons on stage at any one time to a maximum of three. Yet the reasons for it are plain and owe more to advertising than Greece. The purpose of drama, said Aristotle, was catharsis, the purging of pity and terror. The purpose of a commercial is also movement, though of another sort, towards purchase, but it too utilises the emotions.

Remember those commercials for Fairy Snow which featured Joan and Leslie Randall? There was unity of theme (the simple one of proving to an antagonist the superiority of Fairy Snow to her current washing powder). There was unity of place (the 'dramas' happened in a tea-shop, a classroom, or over a garden wall). The unity of time was broken but once to allow the product to be experienced. There was discovery (the antagonist discovered that her washing powder was not as good as she had always imagined). There was reversal of fortune (from scepticism to belief, from envy to acquisition, from discomfiture to victory). These, of course, were minidramas, more product-based than most, but minidramas nevertheless. To find them obeying laws, no matter how ancient, of drama is therefore not so surprising. But other commercials which do not seem to be dramas at all also pay their respects to Aristotle.

The demands of the medium and the demands of advertising enforce an observance of the unities. As McLuhan observed, commercials 'reflect a truer understanding of the medium. There is simply no time for the narrative form, borrowed from earlier print technology.' Note, too, the number of 'non-drama' commercials which involve discovery (a 'taste sensation', a new way of doing something, a low price). Indeed, discovery is as germane to advertising as the idea itself. Discovery presupposes that the information imparted is not already appreciated by either the viewer or the character in the commercial (or both). Obviously, for if such knowledge already exists there can be no surprise. Since every advertisement should (as we have already seen) attempt to surprise and discovery is a concomitant of surprise, then discovery is a basic requirement of a commercial.

Whereas discovery is related to the *idea* of the commercial, reversal of fortune is related to the *execution*. It is an execution device, one of many and therefore it occurs with less frequency.

The real limitations of a medium are not to be broken or ignored. It achieves nothing to treat one medium as if it were another. For example, to crowd a press advertisement's copy into a thirty-second spot or reproduce a storyboard in a press ad or show a paragraph of text on a supersite. The limitations must be explored – and exploited – and each communication task must represent a new exploration, a new exploitation. Because the limitations of the medium are not exactly the same for each communication task. What may be forbidding in one situation may provide an opportunity at another. Generic discipline of the medium must be re-examined in the light of *specific disciplines of the communications task*.

Pirelli took a bus side. The narrow thin band is a restrictive form. Most advertisers regard the shape as a restriction on movement to which they acquiesce. Pirelli, on the other hand, regarded it as a challenge which in their instance could be overcome. They were advertising slippers. Unless they showed one person supine the product could hardly be shown in use. But a bus is *full* of people ... They showed the bottom halves of seated people all wearing Pirelli slippers. The top halves were occupied by the actual passengers in the top deck. The generic discipline of the medium was re-examined in the light of the specific discipline of the communications task. In a sense Pirelli enlarged the area of the advertisement. Just as a cunning use of fifteen seconds can make it appear thirty. A poster featuring a well-known logo can show merely a fraction of it. The viewer 'completes' it in the surrounding space. Thus the whole poster, as seen by the viewer, can be three times as large as the paid for poster site! Similarly in television, to end a commercial on an unresolved melody line invites the viewer to participate in resolving it in the succeeding seconds of 'free' time.

Here is another example of exploitation of limitation, from an alien medium – the peculiarly Italian form of commercial, the 'carosello'. Each lasts two and a half minutes but only thirty-five seconds are the 'commercial', five seconds at the beginning and thirty seconds at the end. The rest must be entertainment. In the early days advertisers would surrender the rest of their time to popular entertainment of any sort and insert their self-contained sell. They linked the two rather obviously and awkwardly. Then the bright boys began to see that the non-commercial segment could in fact support the commercial. Not simply by providing entertainment appropriate to the product's target audience, but by enhancing the image of that product.

I watched in my hotel room – some ten years ago – a carosello for Alemagna, a big bakery and confectionery company. It consisted of a *fin-de-siècle* comic playlet in rhyming couplets. What that had to do with cakes and sweets I had no idea. Until I discussed it with an Italian adman. He explained that Alemagna's chief competitor was Motta who dominated the market. They were old-fashioned and respected. Alemagna, on the other hand, were new to the market and, according to research, not experienced enough in the public mind to have the know-how to make traditional Italian sweetmeats. And that, of course, explained why Alemagna chose to present turn of the century drama. The limitation had proved an opportunity.

Two final examples. We have discussed the danger of trying to do two things at once, the dual strategy, the dual promise. Occasionally, however, a medium can facilitate it, the two aspects instead of existing side by side may fuse into a whole.

Shredded Wheat had been presented for some three years as the Sportsman's Breakfast, featuring footballers and cricketers on the field and endorsing the product. It was then decided to widen the appeal to mothers and daughters. But it was important to retain the sporting image and not to 'give up the existing franchise'. Several solutions suggested themselves. For example, to show girls' sports – which would have made the product sissy. To show the sons and daughters of famous sportsmen – being trained by their famous fathers – which seemed ordinary and less exciting. The best solution came when the art director on the account realised that the sound and the picture, whilst complementing each other, *need not duplicate* each other and, further, that a commentary consisted fundamentally of two elements – what is said *and* the manner in which it is said.

The agency shot a live-action commercial showing a family at breakfast. They pass the pack, help themselves to the product, add sugar, add milk. They eat. A fairly straightforward food commercial situation. However, the audio was delivered *in the manner of a sports commentary*, with the same sort of excitement and accompanied by crowd noises.

Here we are at the table. It's young Brian first off the mark with Shredded Wheat (*whistle*). There it goes into the bowl.

Mum's got the milk now – she's passing it to Brian and yes (*crowd roar*) she's *pouring* it on! Now it's Shredded Wheat to Dad. He's taken one – he's trying for another (*crowd roar*). He's done it. Two in the bowl first time ... And now it's Shredded Wheat back to Mum at the serving end.

When *The Times* decided to build its circulation in 1966 it considered, correctly, that there were thousands of potential readers who had not been told how good the paper was, who had not been given a chance to sample the paper, who had in fact been frustrated by the unchanging front page. The appearance of the news on the front page was a signal to potential readers that perhaps things had changed: moreover, it opened the door and appeared less forbidding. Yet the best method of convincing these people was denied *The Times*: the Newspaper Publishers' Association forbids a newspaper to give away copies. The task facing the agency, Garland-Compton, was to make the advertisement as near as possible a sample of the paper. *The Times* negotiated spaces in evening papers across the country and each night assembled a half page and full page microcosm of the following morning's paper for inclusion the same evening. Thus a reader would turn the page of, say, his *Evening Standard* and discover that he was reading *The Times*. Thus the limitation imposed by the NPA was overcome and the paper was made 'accessible'. Of course, it meant a lot of work. A different 'advertisement' each day and different advertisements for each evening paper incorporating wherever possible news of local interest.

The examples in this chapter reiterate the theme: the artist's job is to react actively to limitations. Ideas often happen as a result of the interplay of discipline and imagination.

30

Reverse gear

We have spent twenty-nine chapters assuming that the creation of advertising happens, if not in an orderly fashion, at least in a linear fashion and that the direction of motion is one way. This chapter throws the switch. It does not deny or refute all that has gone before but it does suggest that there are other ways in which advertising can be produced, ways which are diametrically opposed to normal methodology. There is a reverse gear if only we know how and when to use it. There are three aspects of advertising where the best way to proceed may be back-to-front.

1. Company and agency procedure.
2. Creative planning.
3. New product development.

1. Company and agency procedure

Company hierarchies as we have seen are mirrored in the agency structure. Relatively junior agency executives communicate with their opposite numbers. As a result they are usually entrusted with the initial presentation of the agency creative work. Only if both sets of junior executives agree will the material ascend the hierarchical pyramid. Material which has taken the agency considerable time and is the result of the labours of senior creative people is thus put at risk at a meeting of essentially inexperienced people. Material is sometimes rejected at this stage and often it is modified and possibly further modified up the pyramid. Thus by the time it reaches the man who has the ultimate responsibility the work may partially please everybody but entirely please no one.

What if the procedure were reversed? What if the decision-maker were shown the work first instead of last? This is not a plea for the removal of intermediaries but for the saving of time and especially the saving of ideas, the potential of which may be recognised only by the top man who presumably possesses the sort of insight and experience which enables him to recognise an idea. What if he were shown the material in rough form and asked to give a go/no-go decision coupled with general guidance? This would save time. For it is better that he says no then than later. It would ensure that a professional voice is heard at a crucially important stage. It could save a potentially good idea from premature oblivion. Better surely to involve him when he can do most good than treat him as a rubber stamp?

2. Creative planning

One victim of advertising's postwar preoccupation with its professional image was the scant regard it held for hunch. It had no place, seemingly, in the marketing and research orientated world of the 1950s. Anyone who flew by the seat of his pants couldn't expect letters after his name. Those pre-war advertising men who wrote successful ads without benefit of marketing or research had been lucky or things had been easier.

You can't base a business on hunch. On the other hand serendipity, by definition, must produce results which are different from one's competititors, some of which may be profitable. The question is: how can chance discoveries be catered for within a business organisation? The usual answer within industry is R and D. But research and development departments are hermetically sealed away from the main body of the company. In advertising agencies today the nearest equivalent to R and D is a 'new product workshop' but serendipity is hardly the order of the day. The workshop is fed a brief in the same way that the parent agency is fed a brief. The process is linear sequential. Accidents happen but are not main-stream or planned for. In fact, more often than not, they are an embarrassment.

The agency review board procedure is an attempt to systematise creativity within a business environment and to subject it to the sort of criteria which the agency applies to other aspects of its activities and which the agency's clients similarly apply internally to their own activities and will therefore understand.

There are two key meetings. At the first the strategy is reviewed by a board. The product group (i.e. account, marketing and creative people) present their strategy and it is approved, rejected or amended by the board prior to submission to the client. Once approved by client the strategy is fed into the creative machine. An advertising campaign emerges at the other end (*P* has become *I*). This, too, is reviewed by the same people this time sitting as a 'plans review board' or some such. Strictly speaking the role of this board is to review the creative work and auxiliary plans against the previously agreed strategy.

Sometimes the agency dispenses with the first meeting. Indeed, many agencies don't run a plans board system at all. Nevertheless, they do hold meetings at which creative work is reviewed and these meetings begin with a recapitulation, a statement about the objectives of the advertising, a reading out of the strategy. After all it would be unprofessional to approve or reject something for the wrong reason.

Once the strategy is firmly fixed in the board's mind the work is revealed. And this is the trouble! Everyone in that room knows what the ad is supposed to be saying. They are in no position properly to gauge either impact or comprehension. The consumer, on the other hand, armed with neither strategy document nor extra-sensory perception, sees the thing for what it is – a simple advertisement. In fact the last people to *judge* the effect of the work are the people in that room. Not that the people are wrong, the situation is. It's rooted in the past. It presupposes knowledge. *It goes the wrong way*. The board are committing the same mistake for which they criticise some of their clients: manufacturers who make a product and then look for a consumer. They are being manufacturer- rather than consumer-orientated.

Too many meetings are concerned with what has happened rather than what will happen, with backlog rather than 'frontlog'.[1] The committee looks at an advertisement and *recognises the strategy* (backlog) instead of *discovering something new about the product* (frontlog).

Too many meetings are concerned with secondary problems. Perhaps the previous meeting had sent the creative group away with the task of reconciling two opposing points of view or two conflicting objectives. The group's success will be measured by its ability to solve this problem (e.g. how to say 'different' while retaining the franchise of existing satisfied users or, less praise-worthy, how to keep Joe happy while pleasing Bob): how it answers secondary questions rather than the primary question: will this ad motivate potential consumers towards purchase?

Wouldn't it be better if the meeting *began with the ad*? And the experienced board were then asked: 'What do you think the strategy is?' At least this way the agency would get some idea of what reaction the ad would elicit from an audience ignorant of what went before.

An advertisement must attempt to surprise, in thought or execution or language, if it is to stand a chance of standing out in today's overcrowded media market place and of involving the consumer. Committees as at present structured can knock the surprise out of advertisements. Yet it should not be difficult to devise a system (e.g. co-opting at Stage Two a couple of members experienced in advertising but fresh to the problem) which would ensure that the ad produced the reaction 'Mmm? . . . aah!' and not simply, 'Mmm . . . that's what I was expecting.'

3. New product development

So far in suggesting that ideas should be looked at before the strategy is revealed, I have assumed that the strategy has, so to

---

[1] I am indebted to Jean Roe who coined this word.

speak, 'happened'. I would now like to push the back-to-front thesis a significant step further.

Why shouldn't the idea precede the strategy? Particularly in the area of new product development and line-extension (when new products are built upon an existing brand).

Advertising agencies are becoming more and more concerned with new products and racking their brains for methods of being paid for it! No longer can it be included as an extra bonus within the commission. But it is difficult suddenly to charge for something which the client hitherto received for nothing. Hence the establishment of separate 'workshops' or, failing that, separate development groups *within* the agency. The reason is thus financial, a consequence of the commission system. But innovation surely should be part of an agency's *raison d'être* and not hived off to a specialist cadre (who incidentally may be relatively out of touch with current client requirements, problems, resources and even longterm thinking). If a manufacturer goes to an agency for ideas about its products why should it not also expect to get ideas which *become* products? Why not indeed, says the agency, provided some way can be found for charging for it. And since no satisfactory method has been evolved and clients either regard such development work as part of the overall service or as an additional service which, since it costs them little or nothing, is therefore worth little or nothing, new product thinking remains a secondary activity.

And yet the very people who create advertising ideas are capable of creating new product ideas. They are not often encouraged to since the agency wishes them to concentrate on work which brings a return. Furthermore, they themselves are so conditioned to thinking in advertising terms and along a linear sequential path that stray thoughts are generally stifled at birth. Not only ideas which could become products, but advertising ideas even for products already in existence, which may necessitate a change in composition, marketing, packaging, or name. It could be as simple (and as heretical) as 'I've got a great idea for an ad. Pity we haven't got a product to fit it.' To which the standard answer is 'Why don't you concentrate on what you've been paid to do?' But to which the answer should be 'What is it? If it's good we'll change the product or repackage it or extend the line or make a product to fit.'

Imagine a scene in a creative office. The writer and the art director are working on a car account. The writer asks for a cigarette. The art director throws him his packet. The writer says:

'Danke schön.'
'What?'
'Danke schön.'
'Dunk a what?'
'Schön.'
'What a great name for a doughnut.'
'What?'
'Schön. Then we could say "Dunk a schön".'
'Stop messing about. Now this front wheel drive – what's it mean to the average family motorist?'

Now imagine another scene. The client's office. He is a major producer of cakes and biscuits. The account supervisor flanked by two assistants stands by a chart board.

'Well, sir, we have thoroughly explored the cake and biscuit market in the search for a hitherto unseen opportunity and I am pleased to tell you that we have discovered a sector which has been considerably underexploited. The doughnut.'

The clients look at each other. Shoulders shrug. Eyebrows rise. The supervisor continues.

'The market has been static but hardly unprofitable. Meanwhile, as your own experience shows, considerable activity in the form of diversification and segmentation and promotional support has gone on in the area of biscuits and cakes. We believe there is a hole in the market and . . . er . . . the doughnut.'

Polite laughter.

'The question is – how to rejuvenate the doughnut? Our marketing intelligence department have conducted some desk research and have looked at the growth of delicatessen outlets in the UK. Our recommendation in a nutshell, gentlemen, is that your company launch a continental doughnut. Not a "me-too" product but a new type of doughnut. The exact nature of the

K

innovation we have not yet decided on since clearly this must be a matter for considerable research with yourselves. We do, however, see them individually wrapped and branded.'

The proposal is discussed. The agency is given a provisional go-ahead. The account supervisor leaves a green document containing background figures and facts and a red document prepared by the agency's research department 'detailing the incidence of foreign travel among the C1's'. A date is fixed for a second meeting to look at creative proposals.

Four weeks later they reassemble. The account supervisor begins:

'Gentlemen, good morning. As you you know, when we last met we recommended that your company explore the possibility of launching an entirely new form of doughnut, a *continental* doughnut. You have subsequently agreed with the findings of our initial investigation and have assured us that such a course is viable from both a marketing and a production point of view. Today we propose to show you our initial creative thinking against the agreed strategy. Our first task was, of course, to give the product an identity – a name. Here it is.'

He reveals a chart. There is a photograph of a wrapped doughnut named Shern.

'And here, gentlemen, is our continuing slogan "Dunk A Shern". An ... er ... Austrian expression which you are all aware means "thank you". This allows us to utilise the brand name centrally in memorable advertising. We envisage situations where a character says "like a doughnut?" and another replies "Dunk a Shern".'

The campaign is presented. The clients smile. One of them compliments the agency on its exact and brilliant interpretation of the agreed strategy. The supervisor says 'thank you'. The brand manager says 'don't you mean dunk a shern?' Everybody laughs except the product manager. He has a query.

'That's all very well but what happens in year two? Always assuming the launch is successful, how do you follow up?'

'I'm glad you asked that, sir. We would, of course, strongly recommend a range. In year two we suggest you bring out an almond-flavoured doughnut – a Bitter Shern.'

Here then are two methods of arriving at the same solution. I am suggesting not that one is better than the other but that both methods are viable. And that the reverse gear may, in fact, produce ideas which the standard procedure will not throw up. If as agency manager you accept that the reverse method is viable you immediately unlock a store of ideas which frustrated creative people have put away in the face of the relentless logic of account executives and the equally relentless pressure of normal agency priorities. Tell creative people that there may instead be a market, literally, for their mad thoughts and you have not only made a friend you may even have provided your own meal ticket for the next few years. What was previously regarded as waste material could in fact be a profitable byproduct.

There is, alas, no way to programme such activity. To structure serendipity is to destroy it. Chance discoveries happen when they will and though, as we have seen, there are methods of stimulating random associations within the normal framework of agency procedure, in the case of totally new product ideas since there is, by definition, no brief, indeed no product, such a structure cannot, except in the widest of terms, exist. Instead management must instil an attitude of mind throughout the agency which welcomes and encourages the unplanned, off-brief, back-to-front stray thought.

The book of advertising can afford at least one chapter of accidents.

K*

31

Where do we go from here?

This book began with a rapid survey of advertising's immediate past. It ends with a hesitant peer through the mists of the immediate future. Part guess, part wish, part projection of the existing trends . . . and (the largest part) incomplete.

1. The end of the commission system

The fact that the commission system has withstood prognostication of demise for half a century is no guarantee of its eternal survival. Moreover, the acceleration and growth of other forces (outlined in this chapter) will so substantially alter the status quo that previous arguments for its retention will no longer carry the weight they once did.

2. The birth of the eclectic manufacturer

When a client chooses an advertising agency it is presumed by both that the end product of the allegiance is advertising. Whereas before a manufacturer chooses an advertising agency he really ought to ask himself two questions. The first is – 'Am I in need

of advertising?' He is certainly in need of help. If he is a sophisticated marketer he may know what he wants and enlist the
assistance of an agency to provide media advertising. Even so
there may be other areas where part of his advertising/sales
promotion budget could be better spent. Who is likely to tell
him? Hardly – for a variety of reasons – the advertising agency.
The less sophisticated manufacturer may need more fundamental
help – in marketing, the setting up of a sales force, product
design, packaging and so forth. What he needs is the type of full-
service agency which today he probably cannot afford. Ironically
the full-service agency can now be afforded only by the very
clients who have outgrown the need for it. Ask a major manufacturer what he needs from an agency today and he will tell
you brilliant creative work and efficient media buying – the rest
he can do himself. Thus the answer to the first question is: 'Yes
– I need advertising and possibly something else.'

The second question therefore is: 'Do I need an advertising
agency?' Or 'Shall I get the breadth of the service or indeed the
depth of thinking in a specialist area from an advertising agency?'

Eclectic means 'choosing the best out of everything'
(Chambers). Future manufacturers will continue to assume more
and more control of their marketing communication function.
They will demand to know what 'everything' consists of. To
choose themselves from among it rather than delegate that choice
to an agency whose viewpoint may of necessity be restricted, if
not prejudiced. What will be the agency's response to this
assumption of greater sovereignty on the part of the manufacturer?

3. Accelerated polarisation and fragmentation

In the past decade the total number of agencies has only slightly
declined but the *pattern* has changed rapidly. The big agencies
have got bigger through a combination of growth and acquisition.
Small agencies have specialised (classified, recruitment, technical,
creative hot-shops, financial, etc.). In between, medium-sized
agencies have been taken over or have sought amalgamation in
order to get out of the dangerous middle ground. Some of the

largest agencies have spun off satellite small agencies or self-contained specialist companies to offer a personal service in particular fields.

This trend will continue. What will distinguish the large agency from the small will be the number of different specialist skills it can provide. Large agencies will eventually provide an *à la carte* service. Clients will choose those services it needs and pay for them only. It is possible that a client will choose widely – creative work from three different agencies, media from the fourth, below-the-line from an independent company. He may entrust the coordination of this activity to one of his chosen agencies or even employ a specialist company to do just that. Perhaps if he selects the major agency that agency may own other satellite companies which the client also employs. Thus it may suit the client to have the agency coordinate everything. On the other hand, he may elect to do the coordination himself.

Tomorrow's eclectic client will know as much, if not more, than the agency about the whole spectrum of services. Thus I see a return of the old advertising manager, refurbished and surveying a wider terrain, who will make it his job to know all the various companies (their people and their work) which he will feel free to use whenever the occasion demands. He will operate as a film producer operates – selecting for his next picture the director because he has worked with him before, the lighting camera man whom he has not but whose *work* he knows, the actor who is right for the part and the actress whom he reckons has been miscast in previous roles, etc. What prevents this from happening today? First, the commission system which ties an agency to a client (an unbillable cord); second, especially in the case of the large advertisers, the complexity of the agency client relationship from which it is difficult to extricate oneself. Indeed, a large advertiser recently assured me that it took his company all of two years to move its account (i.e. from the day it decided to leave X till the day Y started work).

4. Extension of media choice

The loosing of the commission tie will bring about a greater flexibility of attitude on the part of media planners. I expect to see a growth in controlled circulation publications and a much more selective use of standard media. If agencies are paid by the client and not the media they will probably devote more time to suiting the advertisement to its environment. I expect to see far less blanket advertising (the identical ad in far-from-identical media) and much greater use of small spaces. I expect the media will have to work harder to sell space. They will have to provide greater details of their readership, qualitative as well as quantitative. Advertisers will want to know how readers read and how viewers view.

5. Advertising will have to work harder

I expect to see much more direct response advertising, not merely because retailers will advertise more (see later), but because advertisements which invite response are a means to check the efficacy of the advertising and the media. Advertising, in other words, will endeavour to become more 'scientific'.

6. The increasing power of the retail chain

Self-service, supermarkets, hypermarkets . . . the growth of all is undeniable and the effect has only just begun to be felt. A major agency which does not handle a retail chain is vulnerable. They will increasingly call the tune. They will dictate to manufacturers, determine how and where their budgets will be spent. Already some supermarkets stock only one or two brands in a product field – plus their own label variety. They in their turn have become large advertisers and no longer is their advertising restricted to presenting price saving. Instead, supermarket chains are promoting their own image, using advertising to give an added value to their products. Indeed, many own label brands are no cheaper – in some cases more expensive – than competitive branded products.

Self-service, the use of the store as a prompt for the housewife (a sort of massive shopping list) means that manufacturers must regard the store itself as a medium, the shelves as columns of advertisements. This will throw the onus on the pack designer.

He will have to grab attention and make the pack radiate quality reassurance, value for money. He will have to study the store as he studies the magazine or newspaper, he will have to see what the competition is doing and especially how his product is positioned. For example, is it displayed at eye level or beneath or above? Should he consider treating the back of the pack as the equivalent of body-copy? and so on.

And the growth of own label will demand that a packaged goods advertiser make strenuous attempts to maintain an identity for his brand which enhances its intrinsic value in the mind of the consumer. Never easy at the best of times and made more difficult by the pressures from below the line and the need to secure short-term success, the maintenance of identity must remain paramount because, as Alan Hedges says, 'it gives him his only direct leverage on the trade . . . it represents his only tool of effective longterm demand management' (see also 9).

7. Advertising will grow up

Prodded from without by consumerists, by legislation and new government departments, and within by the more dutiful members of its own fraternity, advertising will act more responsibly. It will cease to treat consumers as gullible morons. Nor will it treat them as a grey mass. Though it will enact the latter reform largely for economic rather than social reasons. It will be far more profitable to segment the market according to psychographic demarcations, matching products to people and eschewing greed to settle for a section of the community who will identify with a particular brand for a complexity of reasons.

Exaggeration will largely disappear. Advertising will polarise: fact, information, under-statement, at one end; fantasy, hyperbole and tongue-in-cheekery at the other.

I do not expect advertising to consist solely of product information – the name of the brand plus a list of ingredients and the price. I believe that advertisers will be allowed to continue to act as advocates for their products rather than weights and measures inspectors. However, I expect that advertisers will need to furnish proof of every statement if called upon to do so and that this atmosphere of consumer protection will stimulate many advertisers to tell longer product stories than heretofore. Therefore I expect them to use press increasingly. Press allows an advertiser to spread himself and it is less of an entertainment medium than television. A by-product of this will be a greater diversity of approach between media within the same company.

8. New methods of distribution

It is becoming easier[1] to make a new product and more difficult to distribute it. If a handful of key buyers refuse to stock it – except on prohibitive terms – the rest of the market may be insufficient to afford the manufacturer the opportunity of satisfactory trial. Whereas a supermarket can introduce a new line or test at will, the high cost of entry precludes all but major manufacturers from attempting it. Thus new distribution channels will be sought. Not least of which will be direct selling via the established media – and new media set up for the purpose. I expect to see a growth in personal selling door-to-door, increased use of the milkman and the newsagent, more catalogues, diversified use of large stores. I expect sampling to grow – dropped through letter boxes or given away in 'gift pax' schemes to new mums or newly-weds or couples on moving into a neighbourhood, in an attempt to create a demand and then force outlets to stock. I expect to see agency skills released from the bondage imposed by the commission system, being applied to this problem of distribution. The boss of Coca Cola made it his business to make the product available virtually anywhere and everywhere or, as he put it, 'within an arm's length of desire'. Whereas today's advertising creative men are concerned with the origination and communication of ideas about products which motivate people towards purchase, I expect tomorrow's to be equally concerned with *moving purchase towards consumers*.

9. New types of products

The high cost of entry referred to above may force manufacturers

---

[1]Always provided that raw materials (and packaging) are available!

to concentrate on genuine innovations rather than me-too products. Retail chains already stocking one or two brands plus their own label variety, will hardly welcome a new entrant unless it provides a genuine improvement or difference or, better still, breaks new ground. The failure rate of really new products is high: allegedly only one in seven succeeds. Nevertheless it may for some companies represent their only chance of shelf-space. And should they win volume their success will attract imitators, not least of which will be the retail chains themselves. Furthermore, since, as we saw, for the chain the cost of entry is relatively negligible, they themselves may begin to innovate. Currently, of course, they let the manufacturers lead the way. Their role is somewhat parasitical. Other bodies invest in research and development, test markets and educating the public. Once the product looks like repaying its investment, the chain duplicates the product and undercuts its price. The consumer benefits but what consumerists generally fail to appreciate is that much of that benefit is due to advertising!

Another way for manufacturers to gain shelf-space is by means of minority products. At any one moment the country's leading advertisers of packaged goods are examining areas which a decade before they may never have considered because they were too small or static or represented activities which they knew little about. Economic pressures have forced them to change their attitude. Though advertising can rarely start a trend it can give an existing trend considerable impetus. Witness the development in diet foods, muesli health foods, herbal toiletry products. Today they are big business, yet ten years ago they were minority areas. Delicatessen and wine are similarly beginning to take off. And who is going to mass distribute Britain's first indigenous mineral water?

Large companies, of course, are better placed to enter minor leagues. For one thing they have the resources. And should a small independent company achieve a breakthrough in a minority area they also have the power either to buy it out or swamp it with heavy competitive activity. Furthermore, they are already repre-sented in store. Their salesmen need merely add one item to their list when they call on buyers. Diversification is such a fact of life that it is no longer a surprise to find a pharmaceutical company making soft drinks or a shoe polish company making intimate deodorants. I wish I could offer more hope for the independent small manufacturer. Unless he can control or, better still, invent his means of distribution, he is unlikely to be able to resist the power of the big batallions.

Another 'new product' trend which will accelerate is the division of the market according to consumer type. I expect to see existing product categories being extended or replaced by new ones. For example, shampoos were once divided by purpose into beauty and medicinal (and in one or two cases beauty/medicinal); then the categories were determined by their type – for dry, greasy and normal hair and, latterly, 'fly-away' hair. Then manufacturers sliced the cake according to ingredients – lemon, herb, balsam. Thus not the pressure of consumerism (see 7) but the pressure of competition and the need to establish identity and shelf-space will accelerate growth in consumer type differentiations, matching the 'psychographics' of products to those of consumers. The emphasis will switch from 'X is best' to 'X is most suitable for some people'.

10. Growth of new types of service

The word 'consultancy' has unfortunate connotations in UK advertising. Consultants are often fired executives who cannot find employment. The majority of creative consultants work anonymously for agencies and thus cannot claim credit for the work (often excellent) which they create. And if recognition is difficult to come by so, too, is reward.

However, the trend to consultancy service has grown both here and overseas in the past two years. What distinguishes the new consultants from the old is the fact that they work not for agencies but for clients – direct. They are thus in competition with agencies. Independent media broking services, have begun to gain recognition. An advertiser may go to such a service to place his appropriation. The broker places it for considerably less than 15 per cent. The remainder is returned to the client to use to buy creative talent. This is particularly prevalent among international advertisers in international media who often even dispense with the services of a broker and deal with the media direct.

One of the largest press advertisers in the UK does not have an agency. In the United States an exciting new team – the Project Group – works direct for clients on a fee basis. The Creative Business, my own company, services large international business with creativity, supplementing that provided by their existing (mainly large) agencies and also provides small companies with a total service, only a small part of which is advertising. In Germany, France, Australia and Canada also, consultants are working directly with clients, competing with agencies and, if appropriate, channeling the client's budget into areas other than normal advertising.

It will not be long before advertising people themselves will apply their skills to developing and even operating new methods of distribution which may totally avoid normal media advertising. One large agency group has put all its media planning and buying resources together in a separate building and called it the Media Department, ostensibly to service its own member agencies but also to attract work from other clients who may never use its other services. It is also smart enough to realise the increasing range of services these clients may need. Within the group is a small fashion agency, a below-the-line company and a range of small personal service agencies.

To this could be added new product development, financial advertising, direct response, sponsorship promotion companies. The media function makes the agency a centripetal force. Once it is removed the agency becomes a centrifugal force. Acting independently the hitherto internal departments find other non-advertising uses for their skills. Accordingly I expect advertising people increasingly to take on assignments in politics, charity, education, publishing, etc. When the commission system goes, anything goes.

The central core of an advertising agency is – as I hope this book has shown – its creative department. What differentiates agencies from manufacturers can only be those functions which

the manufacturer cannot himself perform directly or get performed indirectly by going elsewhere (i.e. by types of organisations other than advertising agencies). Thus, at the time of writing
manufacturers look to agencies to provide media and creative
services. But the media facility is already being provided independently by other types of organisations and even by manufacturers themselves. Attempts have been made by manufacturers
also to incorporate the creative function but house agencies will
never really succeed since two vital components for creativity are
missing: variety and independence. Creative people prosper in
an atmosphere which allows them frequently to change gear (not
to mention car) and to act not as paid employees of advertisers
but as their advisers.

Creativity differentiates an agency from a manufacturer and
its standard or type of creativity differentiates it from other
agencies. Other services which it has accumulated will either
remain in a subsidiary form or probably be spun off into self-
contained satellite companies. The business of running an agency
will, except for the few enormous organisations, change radically.
Agency heads will be chosen according to different criteria.
Fundamentally they will need to be able to construct and maintain the correct environment for creativity to flourish. Many will
themselves be practising creative people. As managing directors
of client organisations they would, without exception, be
inadequate. But they will not be judged by their client on their
knowledge of discounted cash flow, but by their ability to provide
ideas about their products and ideas for new products which the
clients themselves cannot provide. Of course such agencies will
need to be financially managed but the business of business will
be either delegated to appropriate and sympathetic managers or
entrusted to holding companies who will be responsible largely for
all non-advertising matters in the agency. KMPH, for example,
run an extensive group of agencies and specialist companies. They
share what David Kingsley calls 'common financial plumbing'
allowing the advertising men and other specialists to get on with
what they know best. With such a framework they can con-
fidently appoint a creative director to the position of managing
director of their major agency.

This redefinition of the role of the chief executive (replacing the 'business of business' by the 'business of creative') coupled with the shedding or elimination of services, leads naturally to a reordering of internal structures. Agencies need no longer structure their organisations to correspond with those of their clients or devise operating procedures which are more suited to the manufacture of toothpaste than the creation of ideas. This redefinition of an agency's role, realignment of priorities, re-arrangement of internal structures and, above all, the fragmentation of services, will in turn significantly affect the structure and attitude of the clients who are being serviced. It will throw a far heavier onus upon the client, the eclectic manufacturer.

It is no accident, for example, that the manufacturers who are already employing independent services are staffed in key positions by executives of an entrepreneurial spirit. The conformist organisation man who seeks the security of the large full-service agency and delegates his birthright, hedges his bets and spreads thin the blame, sees the emergence of independent services as an uncomfortable challenge and will hope to defer the moment of truth. The entrepreneur, on the other hand, will regard it as an opportunity to express his individuality. He will act prag-matically. He will be offered a broader spectrum of talent, a wider choice of action, an infinite number of variables. But if ideas happen when thoughts come into collision, then the chances of innovation, of *real* innovation, will be increased. So, of course, will be the difficulty of his job since probably he alone will be responsible for the coordination of the services he employs. Responsible, too, for the mistakes. But this should not worry him since unless he regards his title (brand manager, for example) as a sinecure, he presumably already assumes full profit responsi-bility for those brands which he manages. Moreover, since responsibility will be seen to be his, the rewards will be greater. The company which employs him will stand more chance of breaking new ground if it encourages him to express his own individuality and awards him appropriately for his success. It may indeed represent the only way that the independent entre-preneurial spirit can survive and possibly flourish within today's shrinking and conglomerating grey and featureless business land-scape.

But even this small hope will be dashed unless advertising agencies or rather, skilled and talented people employed in them, realise that their future lies not in aping the large organisations but in uniquely servicing them. Agency people are notoriously lax in taking their own advice. They will stress the importance of identity, tell the client to position its brand while, at the same time failing to identify themselves or define their own position. Very, very few agencies are big business. (How many for instance appear in *The Times* 1000?)

But if agency people define their own position, play their strength, capitalise upon their specialist skills, the chief of which is creativity, then their future is assured. Not, I hasten to add, as 'advertising agencies' in the accepted sense since traditional advertising will represent a decreasing proportion of their activities (and it may also decline in actual volume) and, given a fair wind and a points victory for commonsense over vested interest, the concept of 'agency' will disappear.

32

Summary

Meanwhile to draw this personal textbook to a close here in summary form are some observations of a bastard artist – some laws of an inexact scientist.

1. Advertising is the origination and/or communication of ideas about products or services which motivate consumers towards purchase.

2. Advertisements differ from each other not in size but in degree. All advertisements may be said to exist on the same continuum. What differentiates them is their degree of proximity to the action.

3. All advertisements are calls to action, i.e. actual purchase or action relevant to purchase.

4. Any advertisement may be made more effective by moving it along the continuum towards the action (i.e. by removing remoteness factors). 'The closer the ad to the action the better the chance of a sale.'

5. The definition (1) allows you to ask of any advertisement five basic questions.
   (a) What is the product?
   (b) What is the idea being communicated?
   (c) Who is the consumer?

   (*d*) What is he expected to do about it?

   (*e*) Why should he do it?

6. Advertising is a bastard art in the middle of an inexact science. There is no reason to try to make it an art, every reason to try to make it, if not a science, more scientific.

7. Advertising is part of a two-way communication process involving a manufacturer and a consumer. The loudest message from one to the other is performance, the loudest message from the other to the one is purchase.

8. Advertising communicates to a mass audience one at a time.

9. The essential creative job is to turn a proposition into an idea.

10. The proposition (or the product itself) may already be the idea: in which case the creative task is simply to communicate and not to originate the idea (to make sure that 'creativity' does not get in the way).

11. However, by and large, the proposition is arrived at through reason; the proposition becomes an idea by the application of imagination; the communication of that idea is largely a matter of craft.

12. An idea is the same as a proposition only different. Meaning is made more meaningful.

13. The idea is a relationship. Ideas happen when two thoughts come into collision.

14. Creative departments must be structured to encourage collision. The job of the creative leader is to maintain a state of disciplined anarchy.

15. The advertiser who seeks the involvement of the recipient and his participation in the message will realise that the best route between two minds is not always the shortest.

16. Concentration is the very essence of good advertising (one of many attributes the creation of advertising shares with poetry).

17. *Every* advertisement is a mixture of reason and tickle.

18. Humour is not irrelevant. Irrelevant humour is irrelevant.

19. Every advertisement must seek to achieve VIPS.

- *Visibility:* It must be seen by the target audience.
- *Identity:* The name of the brand must be identified inextricably with . . .
- *Promise:* 'The soul of an advertisement.'
- *Simplicity:* The advertisement must be single-minded. It may consist of several ingredients but will maintain a unity of purpose and mood.

20. Research can be the best thing that ever happened to the creative man. It puts him in touch with the consumer, tells him if he's communicating, reveals negatives. Above all it may allow him to attempt the untried.

21. Each medium has strengths. An advertiser should seek to utilise these different strengths rather than impose an artificial unity across all media.

22. Discipline is a creative necessity. A stimulus not a prison. The artist's job is to exploit his limitations.

23. The generic discipline of each medium must be re-examined in the light of specific disciplines of the communications task.

24. Whereas advertising uses the product to sell the product, sales promotion uses something *outside* the product. Below-the-line activity must reinforce above-the-line activity. Everything you do in the product's name affects the image of that product.

25. Advertising procedures (including the creation of advertisements) can benefit from the use of the reverse gear.

And, finally, as befits a business of ideas, advertising is fun.

INDEX

h. A trade press advertisement in The Grocer for Canada Dry.

i. A cinema commercial for seat belts prepared by the Central Office of Information.

j. A financial advertisement in the Daily Telegraph for Save and Prosper.

k. A tube card in the London Underground for Brook Street (secretarial employment) Bureau.

l. A Sandwich board for a furniture store.

m. A woman's magazine advertisement for Coty Emeraude.

a. A classified advertisement in the Evening Standard for a second hand car.

b. A poster for Double Diamond Beer.

Growing into Europe

c. A prestige advertisement in The Times on behalf of ICI.

d. A direct mail shot for Time Magazine.

e. A television commercial for Fairy Liquid.

f. A "bargain" space in the DailyExpress for a gardening implement.

g. A technical press advertisement in Construction Plant & Equipment for Atlas Excavators.